Men, Militarism,
and UN Peacekeeping

CRITICAL SECURITY STUDIES

Ken Booth, SERIES EDITOR
UNIVERSITY OF WALES, ABERYSTWYTH

Men, Militarism, and UN Peacekeeping

A GENDERED ANALYSIS

SANDRA WHITWORTH

LYNNE
RIENNER
PUBLISHERS

BOULDER
LONDON

Paperback edition published in the United States of America in 2007 by
Lynne Rienner Publishers, Inc.
1800 30th Street, Boulder, Colorado 80301
www.rienner.com

and in the United Kingdom by
Lynne Rienner Publishers, Inc.
3 Henrietta Street, Covent Garden, London WC2E 8LU

Published in hardcover in 2004.

ISBN 978-1-58826-552-4 (pbk. : alk. paper)

Printed and bound in the United States of America

⊗ The paper used in this publication meets the requirements
of the American National Standard for Permanence of
Paper for Printed Library Materials Z39.48-1992.

5 4 3 2 1

For Lynn and Aidan,
still

CONTENTS

PHOTOGRAPHS

PREFACE

There is probably nothing more annoying than a contradiction. This, at least, is how I felt when in January 1998 I watched (with tears in my eyes) as members of Canada's armed forces helped clear ice from my roof, chop wood, and otherwise contribute to my family's and community's safety through an ice storm that had cut our power, water, heat, and phone for two very cold wintry weeks. These men weren't wearing blue berets when they were deployed throughout eastern Ontario and western Québec on what was dubbed "operation ice rink," but they were some of the people who served on UN peacekeeping missions when deployed abroad. They were the people I had been studying already for a number of years, the people about whom I was writing a book, at that point entitled "Bullies in Blue Berets." They were jovial, decent, and dedicated, and all I wanted to do was hug them.

This wasn't the first, and wouldn't be the last, contradiction I would encounter in doing this project. In fact, the notion of a "contradiction" has come to form an important element of the argument I develop here. This particular one helped to illustrate, for me at least, one of the themes I would try to thread throughout this book. Much of what is written here concerns the struggle over meanings—of peace, security, national identity, masculinities, peacekeeping, and militaries. What I have uncovered during this research suggests that these contestations over meanings matter, and they matter not only to those who wage and sustain them, but they matter also to most of the rest of us who are left to live with the consequences.

One of the contradictions at the root of this discussion is that those consequences can be—but are not always—deeply negative ones. When I spoke with women in Cambodia about the peacekeeping mission that had been deployed there in the early 1990s, I heard firsthand a series of concerns that never made it into the UN's official "Blue Book" on that peacekeeping mission—charges of harassment and assault, cultural insensitivity,

1

reported rapes, and the rise of prostitution and HIV/AIDS. Almost every Cambodian woman I spoke with said she wished the UN had done it better, had been smarter and more thoughtful before they arrived, or had taken more seriously her concerns once they did arrive. At the same time, not a single woman with whom I spoke said she wished the UN had not come to Cambodia at all, and even the most critical among them prefaced their remarks with the observation that many aspects of their lives had improved since the mission.

Examining contestation and struggle does not mean that some of the things that are said or done in the name of peacekeeping are true while others are false. When I describe the ways in which soldiers deployed as peacekeepers are depicted as benign and altruistic (see Photographs 1 and 2), I am not suggesting that people who express feelings of security, friendship, and even joy upon the arrival of peacekeepers to their villages, cities, or towns are mistaken. Rather, I am suggesting that just as relevant is the experience of those people whose photographs do not end up forming part of the official account of what peacekeeping is: for example, women who ended up serving as prostitutes or who were assaulted by peacekeepers. Equally important is the experience of young men who were shot at, beaten, or as in the case of sixteen-year-old Somalian Shidane Abukar Arone, murdered by foreign soldiers. It does not mean that all soldiers and peacekeepers are involved in such acts, or that this is a final and more accurate

Photograph 1 Canadian operations officer greets a local Serbian woman with her sheep, March 14, 1994 *(CP Photo/Tom Hanson)*

account of what peacekeeping is; rather, it means that we will not understand the nature of the contradictions, indeed the very extent to which peacekeeping *is* a contradiction, unless these images remain as central in our minds as those that show peacekeeping's more positive record.

One of the main reasons peacekeeping *is* a contradiction is because of its almost exclusive reliance on soldiers. Soldiers are not born, they are made; and part of what goes into the making of a soldier is a celebration and reinforcement of some of the most aggressive, and most insecure, elements of masculinity: those that promote violence, misogyny, homophobia, and racism. This does not mean that all male military peacekeepers are beasts, that every individual soldier is violently homophobic, racist, or sexist. It does mean, however, that all soldiers have been subjected to the message that they have been given license to express these things, to act upon them, especially if that is what it takes to perform their duties as soldiers. Lying at the very core of peacekeeping is a contradiction: on the one hand, it depends on the individuals (mostly men) who have been constructed as soldiers, and on the other hand, it demands that they deny many of the traits they have come to understand being a soldier entails.

If militarized peacekeeping is contradictory, it is little wonder that the reactions to the arguments contained here have met with such fierce, but

Photograph 2 A UN peacekeeper is accompanied by local children while on security patrol in the Becora district of Dili, East Timor *(United Nations/ Department of Public Information photograph, Eskinder Debebe, February–March 2000)*

often very illuminating, responses. One of the first times I presented some of the questions that I raise in this book was in 1993 when I was asked to provide a commentary at the end of a three-day peacekeeping workshop organized in part through Canada's Department of National Defence (DND). Participation in the workshop was by invitation only, and the guests included academics, policymakers, representatives from the United Nations and the North Atlantic Treaty Organization (NATO), and military officers from a variety of countries. Those of us doing the summary comments were told that we would be kept strictly to our allotted three minutes, and I organized my remarks around the way in which much of our discussion over those three days had focused on a series of technical and policy-relevant questions; for example, about financing, command and control, storage, and communications. When questions are framed exclusively in technical terms, I argued, a number of things happen. First, political questions are left off the agenda—questions such as: Who benefits from peacekeeping operations? Who is excluded? What is the effect of peacekeeping missions on the people in those countries where the missions are deployed? This means that we did not explore whether the United Nations or certain member states benefited from the increasing interest in peacekeeping. Nor did we ever ask whether there were costs to local populations of particular peacekeeping missions.

When questions are posed in strictly technical terms, not only are a whole series of political questions silenced, but whole groups of interested people are excluded from the discussion, treated as if they were beside the point. Technical questions are answered by technical experts, and I pointed out to the conference participants that while some people around our table had experience in *delivering* different elements of peacekeeping missions, none of us had been *subjected* to one. In order to give voice to some of the people who were not invited to the workshop, I ended my comments by reading from a letter delivered to the UN Secretary-General's special representative in Cambodia just a few months before, which accused some peacekeeping personnel of the various things I would hear directly when I later traveled there myself: sexual assault, sexual violence, and the rise of prostitution and HIV/AIDS.

My fellow participants' reactions were threefold. First, in that cavernous room at the very bottom of Ottawa's Château Laurier Hotel, except for a few quiet chuckles, one almost certainly could have heard a pin drop. I don't think that silence was out of any sense of awe at the profundity of my remarks. Most people—and in particular the only other woman present at the table—shifted their bodies so that they were facing as far away from the head of the table as they could position themselves. The second reaction came from the Canadian brigadier-general who spoke after me. He devoted almost half of his precious three minutes to rebut my comments, and explained carefully that countries involved in peacekeeping—such as Canada—do not derive any benefit from doing so, that they do so at their own expense and for a common global good. The behavior of peacekeepers detailed in the letter I had read, he noted, amounted to an unusual and isolated event.

The final and most interesting reaction, though, came that evening at the dinner that closed the event. As soon as I arrived, a retired major-general walked over and asked, rather gruffly, "Just what were you saying this afternoon? Why did you read that letter?" I said something rather gruff back, but then he said, "No, no, I'm just a dumb soldier. I'm not sure I understood what you were saying." I summarized briefly what I had tried to convey at the workshop, and he reacted by slamming his hand on the table and exclaiming, "That's what I thought you said. And you're absolutely right! Why, I've been thinking about what you were talking about and it just opened up a Pandora's box for me. I've seen all sorts of things like what you were talking about." This self-described "dumb soldier" went on to regale me with stories that came out of his own peacekeeping experiences, some that illustrated what I was trying to argue, others that only complicated my arguments further. It was the first time I ever heard a person in the military describe himself as a "dumb soldier," and I have learned since that it often seems to be the most interesting and insightful soldiers who normally preface their remarks in this way.

Since that early talk, in addition to traveling to Cambodia to discuss with some women their views of the impact of the mission on their lives, I also attended Canadian hearings in what came to be called the Somalia Inquiry. At the same time that I was reading the letter from Phnom Penh to the Ottawa workshop, the Canadian media was beginning to report rumors that Canadian soldiers on duty in Somalia possibly had murdered a teenager. As information from both official and unofficial investigations trickled out, what Canadians learned was that Shidane Arone had been tortured and murdered by soldiers from Canada's elite Airborne regiment. Those soldiers had photographed the young man's ordeal, and other soldiers within the compound who had heard his cries throughout the night did nothing to stop what was happening. Videos from Somalia showed Canadian soldiers describing the mission as "Operation Snatch Niggers," and other videos captured some of the Airborne's initiation rituals: soldiers defecating, eating vomit, and forcing the only black member of that unit of the Airborne to walk around on all fours with "I love KKK" written on his back.

The Airborne regiment was eventually disbanded, a series of military investigations and court-martials were called, and some two years after Arone's murder, the Canadian government launched a commission of inquiry into the Airborne's mission to Somalia, an inquiry I attended as an observer. The Somalia Inquiry lasted almost two years, from 1995 to 1997, and though it was cut short and never actually heard evidence concerning

Shidane Arone's torture and murder, by its end it saw 116 witnesses and collected more than 150,000 documents. Although it likely never had the audience draw of, say, the O. J. Simpson trial in the United States, the portion of the inquiry devoted to testimony was open to the public and televised across Canada.

On the days I was able to attend the inquiry, I sometimes found the dynamic of the proceedings as revealing as the testimony itself. Much of the testimony was mundane, describing the minutiae of proper procedures, communications, and command and control. But there was never a day I attended that I did not find something fascinating in either what was said or how it was being said. In addition to the three commissioners, the room was filled with lawyers representing the commission, the government, the military, and a number of individuals and groups who had obtained official standing at the proceedings. There were also translators (Canada operates in two official languages), stenographers, and various assistants. As one might guess from even a passing acquaintance with feminist thought, the room was notable for its distinctive division of labor on the basis of sex—none of the commissioners, few of the lawyers, but almost all of the support staff, were women.

As serious as the proceedings were, I was struck one morning by the banter—recorded once the hearing had been opened and so noted for the record—between the various lawyers and the commissioners themselves. One of the commission's lawyers would be leaving at the end of the day, and lawyers from "the back of the room" (those representing either military personnel or interested groups that had been granted standing) suggested a number of possible replacements for the departing counsel: Pee Wee Herman, Danny DeVito, or possibly Tom Cruise. One of the commissioners suggested that Ms. Lovett, one of only two female lawyers present that day, would "probably go for Tom Cruise." When she suggested that she would likely ask for a female replacement, she was asked by the chair if she was trying to promote equality of rights.

The banter continued in this way—Ms. Lovett replied to the chair that she was operating on the assumption that the commission already had equality of rights—but eventually the assorted gentlemen and the very few ladies returned to the more serious matters at hand. The inquiry's banter was not unlike the kind of apparently innocent joking that takes place in any number of workplaces every day. It was "all in good fun," and it caused no direct physical or emotional harm, yet it delivered a clear message to everyone about who—and what—"counted" in that room. Coupled with the near absence of women in positions of authority, it was clear that the job of investigating the military was a predominantly masculinized affair. This was often confirmed by the defiant glare between witnesses and examiners—members of the military had long insisted their internal reviews and various court-martials had served as a more than sufficient investigation into the events in Somalia, and some came to the witness stand only because they were compelled to do so. It was also confirmed on occasion in the overheard discussions of strategy between lawyers. As one male lawyer eloquently said to his colleague just before cross-examining a very popular retired major-general: "I'm gonna take him on. I'm gonna bury him."

As interested as I became in the dynamics among the official participants at the inquiry, so too did I find myself taking mental notes about the other public observers to the commission's proceedings day after day. Sometimes I was seated alone, sometimes near family or friends of witnesses, and sometimes—much to my surprise—I found myself sitting beside Canadian tourists who were "taking in" the inquiry much as they might a trip to Canada's federal government on Parliament Hill or a boat trip down the Ottawa River or Rideau Canal. Whether among the tourists or the few "regulars" who rarely seemed to miss a day of the proceedings, I slowly realized that the chief audience to these proceedings seemed to be former members of Canada's armed forces, former soldiers who quietly served as "witnesses" to the investigations. What I had not anticipated, however, was that many were there not because they felt the legacy of which they had been a part had been tarnished by the Airborne's actions but rather that, as veterans, many of the inquiry's visitors held deeply critical views of the military themselves and waited to hear if some of those concerns would be given public voice through these proceedings.

There were numerous revealing moments at the inquiry, but one of the most difficult, and one that returned me to my musings about the core contradictions of peacekeeping, was when the young black soldier who had been made to walk on all fours with "I love KKK" written on his back gave his testimony. He was asked repeatedly whether in his view this and other acts depicted in the video were racist acts, and he consistently acknowledged that they were. When asked whether he had experienced racism in the Canadian forces or the Airborne regiment in particular, he was equally insistent that he had not. None of these things were said or done "from the bottom of their hearts," and moreover he remained proud of the regiment of which he had been a part and "would do everything he could to protect it."

Perhaps the most difficult task I have had in the writing of this book has been trying to "hear" the place from which contradictory positions such as this one—and the others I have encountered like it—were spoken with authenticity. The challenge has been, as it is for so many feminist analysts, to develop a way of thinking through these contradictions without simply suggesting that the young black corporal was suffering from "false consciousness," that he had been a victim of racism for so long that he just could not recognize it. Of course he could. But he also had other experiences and other commitments to which he was trying to give expression in that moment as well. A principal aim of this book is to name the many contradictions that are constitutive of peacekeeping and to think through their implications, both for the people who encounter peacekeepers and for peacekeepers themselves.

Whether or not I have been successful in this task, I have certainly benefited from the support and assistance of numerous people in trying to get there, some of whom include Juan Pablo Ordoñez, who could not have been a more caring or generous host, or a more insightful political analyst, during my visits to Phnom Penh; the many people who gave generously of their time in Cambodia, including in particular Kek Galabru, Kien Serey Phal, Eva Galabru, Oung Chanthol, Brigitte Sonnois, Genevieve H. Merceur, Koy Veth, Cathy Zimmerman, Pen Dareth, William Collins, Annuska Derks, and Andrew McNaughton; at Lynne Rienner Publishers, Richard Purslow, Sally Glover, Lisa Tulchin, and Lynne Rienner, all patient and thoughtful editors; Neil Blaney and Sheena Pennie at the Commission of Inquiry into the Deployment of Canadian Forces to Somalia, who were enormously helpful with documentation; and the many students and research assistants who have provided research support over the years, including Elaine Brown, Suzanne Baustad, Maya Eichler, Yumiko Iida, Samantha Majic, Nicole LaViolette, and Emily Saso.

A number of very kind people read the manuscript, some a couple of times: Lynn Andrews, Robert Cox, Elizabeth Dauphinee, Cynthia Enloe, Cristina Masters, Emily Saso, and two anonymous reviewers. Though of course any omissions and limitations remain my own, I know it is a better book because of the careful attention they gave to my work.

The early years of this project were funded by a Social Sciences and Humanities Research Council of Canada Standard Research Grant. Teaching release was provided by York University in the form of two sabbaticals and a Faculty of Arts Leave Fellowship. I am extremely fortunate to work in a department and university that affords me not only the time to conduct work such as this but allows me to surround myself with incredibly smart people—students and colleagues—whose enthusiasm, insights, directions to the perfect sources, and great humor have always kept me going whenever my own intellectual energy began to run dry. In particular I would like to thank Annanya Mukherjee-Reed, Marshall Beier, Shannon Bell, Ryerson Christie, Ann Crosby, Robert Cox, Elizabeth Dauphinee, David Dewitt, Maya Eichler, Wenona Giles, Deepika Grover, Krista Hunt, Cristina Masters, Stacey Mayhall, David Mutimer, Peter Nyers, and Jacqui True.

Support staff at York have helped with all the aspects of my working life, by keeping me organized, making sure the dissertation orals are scheduled, printing out the manuscript, and moving mountains to find course times to help me maintain the tricky balance that is my Toronto-Newington commute. I would especially like to thank Elma Anicic, Joan Broussard,

Barbara Budgell, Lissa Chiu, Celeta Irvin, Mike Kasaboski, Jlenya Sara, Sue Sbrizzi, Angie Swartz, Marlene Quesenberry, Germaine Quintas, and Sarah Whitaker.

In the summer of 2001, I was invited by Angela King, the UN's special adviser on gender issues, to work on a study with Dyan Mazurana, then of the University of Montana. The process of doing the study gave me great insight into how understandings become constructed within the UN—and about what can and cannot be said in official UN documents. I was inspired by a number of the women I met at the UN, in particular Angela King, Carolyn Hannan, and Sylvia Hordosch. Though I do not share their commitment to the United Nations, I greatly admire their indefatigable efforts in engaging with that institution. I also had the joy to work with Dyan and her research associate at Montana, Khris Carlson. I could not have asked for more faithful colleagues and companions in traversing and surviving our 1325 experience. Once their skating improves, they will be perfect.

I am privileged to be part of a larger intellectual community that is associated with the Feminist Theory and Gender Studies Section of the International Studies Association and with the *International Feminist Journal of Politics*. More than either a professional association or academic journal, these are the (unfixed) locations where I have found critical political engagement and enormous professional and personal support. In particular I would like to acknowledge Carol Cohn, Cynthia Enloe, Lily Ling, Marianne Marchand, Katharine Moon, Mark Neufeld, Steve Niva, Jane Parpart, V. Spike Peterson, Jindy Pettman, Anne Sisson Runyan, Simona Sharoni, J. Ann Tickner, Gillian Youngs, and Marysia Zalewski.

Sometimes it is the departures from work life that also contribute to completing projects such as this. Marc Muir and I never spoke about this book, and I'm not even sure he knows that I was writing it, but his virtuoso tours through landscapes like *Blues in A* certainly went a long way to helping me stay sane. So too did the gals at CWBHL, Long Sault, Minto, and WDLHL, where I not only had a bit of a break away, but also the (very) occasional, exhilarating, breakaway.

Friends and family have been engaged throughout this project as well, always knowing when to ask (or when not to ask), when to call, and when to issue lunch, dinner, or holiday invitations. Big hugs to Jan Andrews, Joyce Andrews, Gwen Gallagher, Colleen Glass, Sally Gose, Nicole LaViolette, Claire Sjolander, Rose Stanton, Barb Whitworth, and Neil Whitworth.

Finally, Lynn and Aidan make it all possible. Whether through the many small comforts of home, the joys and challenges of family, or the delights of long walks, punk music, farmland sunsets, and far too many dogs—none of it happens, or would be worth it, without them.

1

Introduction: The Costly Contradictions of UN Peacekeeping

When the Cold War began to unravel in the late 1980s, it may have caught theorists of international relations (IR) by surprise, but practitioners—not least among them the bureaucrats and policymakers of the United Nations—were quick to respond to the "new" emerging conflicts by turning to a popular UN invention that had seen only limited application to that point: United Nations peacekeeping. For a time, at least, it appeared that peacekeeping could serve as one of the cornerstones of a transformed, less bellicose, era. As Jarat Chopra observed:

> A new public image of the UN developed: national recruitment posters depicted troops in blue berets—in one case holding a baby with the slogan, "give life a chance, join the armed forces"—or transport planes in-flight supporting humanitarian assistance missions; news reports referred to "U.N. troops" or "U.N. vehicles" and did not distinguish national origins; and the Secretary-General claimed there is hope in "the first truly global era."[1]

Through peacekeeping, not just the UN but also various national militaries and possibly even global peace itself was to be given a new lease on life.

Peacekeeping had long been depicted as a welcome alternative to the traditional use of military force. Since its inception with the deployment of UN peacekeeping forces to the Suez in 1956, peacekeeping has been described as a creative use of national militaries, under the authority of the United Nations, for the purposes of forging a peace. One of the early architects of peacekeeping, Canada's Lester B. Pearson, would win the Nobel Peace Prize in 1957 for his involvement in the creation of that first mission, as would the UN's Blue Berets and Blue Helmets in 1988, some thirty years later.

This widespread faith in peacekeeping only increased with the collapse of Cold War tensions, as peacekeeping missions, and peace operations generally, moved center-stage within the UN's repertoire of diplomatic and military instruments.[2] Where previously there had been just a handful of peacekeeping missions, in the so-called new world order those missions proliferated and became more far-reaching in their scope and mandate. Early, or "first-generation" missions—of which there were only thirteen between 1956 and 1978—simply involved establishing an interposition force between belligerent groups that had given their consent to the establishment of a peacekeeping mission. The "second-generation" missions—of which there were some twenty-nine between 1988 and 1996—involved a whole host of tasks, including military and police functions, the monitoring of human rights, the conduct of elections, the delivery of humanitarian aid, the repatriation of refugees, the creation and conduct of state administrative structures, and so on.[3] Enthusiasm for peacekeeping was not limited to the hallways and corridors of the United Nations. Support has also come from more unexpected quarters: peace groups and women's groups, for example, have looked to peacekeeping as an important alternative to the more traditional "combat-capable" emphases of most militaries. Even critical IR theorists have included the support for peacekeeping as an important element of any "ethical engagement in the world."[4] On the terrain of a reordered global politics, it would appear, peacekeeping seems to be a hopeful place for many.

The near uniformity in support for peacekeeping served as one of the early motivations for writing this book. Even before launching this study, my own suspicion was that there might be more to the story than was generally reported in the media or by official sources. Part of the aim of this book is to disrupt the easy and often automatic association of peacekeeping with actual and substantive alternatives to military violence. The argument here is intended to challenge that association and demonstrate some of the ways in which the introduction of peacekeeping forces actually has served to *increase* some local people's insecurity rather than alleviate it.

What has remained neglected in the warm glow surrounding peacekeeping—and even in the occasional cautious acknowledgments that problems do exist—is any sustained analysis of the overwhelming reliance on soldiers to conduct peacekeeping operations. The vast majority of personnel deployed on peacekeeping missions have been soldiers, people skilled in the arts of violence and the protection of nation and territory. Yet as peacekeepers they are deployed on missions that apparently make a virtue out of otherwise unsoldierly skills. The blue-bereted peacekeeper is supposed to be benign, altruistic, neutral, and capable of conflict resolution in any cultural setting—a warrior-prince-of-peace. He is lightly armed and is directed to fire a weapon only in self-defense. As feminist scholar Cynthia Enloe describes it: "The form of military force that is inspiring perhaps the greatest hope is the United Nations peacekeeping force. It inspires optimism because it seems to perform military duties without being militaristic."[5]

Enloe cautions that "To date we in fact know amazingly little about what happens to a male soldier's sense of masculine license when he dons the blue helmet or armband of the United Nations peacekeeper."[6] Almost as soon as the "new" peacekeeping missions began, there were reasons to be concerned. The UN described its mission to Cambodia (United Nations Transitional Authority in Cambodia, or UNTAC) from 1991 to 1993, for example, as a success, but a small handful of observers insisted that some important information had been left out of the UN's official accounts. As Kien Serey Phal wrote: "Routine sexual abuse of women by UN soldiers and staff led several international development agencies to raise the issue with UNTAC head Yasushi Akashi, who caused shock and outrage by confirming the right of soldiers to act as they did by stating that 'boys will be boys.'"[7] "Bringing the peace to Cambodia," in other words, was accomplished in part through the deployment of soldiers who assumed that their prerogatives as militarized men included access to prostitutes, as well as a freedom to pursue, harass, and assault local women.

Since the mid-1990s, charges have begun to emerge of sexual and physical violence perpetrated by foreign peacekeepers against local citizens in numerous peacekeeping missions, so much so that even the United Nations has begun to acknowledge some of them. In Kosovo, the Democratic Republic of Congo, Cambodia, Mozambique, Eritrea, and Somalia, some male peacekeepers have been accused of harassing, exploiting, and physically and sexually assaulting women and girls.[8] In Mozambique and Bosnia, peacekeepers may have condoned the establishment of brothels and been involved themselves in the trafficking of women and children.[9] In Liberia and Sierra Leone, ECOMOG (Monitoring Group of the Economic Community of West African States) troops fathered thousands of children born to local women, many of whom were exposed to HIV and other sexually transmitted infections.[10] In Sierra Leone, after allegations of widespread sexual abuse and exploitation by humanitarian aid workers and peacekeepers in West Africa, a UN follow-up investigation concluded that of the few accusations that could be substantiated, one involved the rape of a fourteen-year-old boy by a male peacekeeper.[11]

This book provides detailed studies of Somalia, where two Somali men were shot and where sixteen-year-old Shidane Abukar Arone was tortured and murdered by Canadian soldiers, and of Cambodia, where women were widely harassed, assaulted, and prostituted to serve peacekeeping forces. However, it also explores the ways in which the contradictions of peacekeeping are sometimes borne by peacekeepers themselves. Soldiers who return from peacekeeping duty traumatized by their missions face not only the emotional and physical toll of post-traumatic stress disorder (PTSD) but are sometimes ostracized by the very militaries that deployed them on their tour of duty in the first place.[12] Depression, drug addiction, and alcoholism are not the only elements of PTSD; for many, so too is the discovery that they have failed to live up to the military ideal and are no longer welcome members of the military family.

* * *

It has become commonplace within the academic field of "security studies" to review with dissatisfaction the conceptual and practical limitations of traditional notions of "security." Once, not so long ago, there was some consensus that the chief object of security was the state, the primary sources of threat were military, and the reason that this took precedence over any other way of thinking about it was the anarchic nature of the international system; however, it is by now generally accepted that such a consensus no longer exists. In Barry Buzan's oft-repeated phrase, security is an essentially "contested concept."[13]

Problematizing the impact of peace operations on those most affected by them from a critical and feminist vantage point not only demands that we ask questions such as "security *for whom?* and security *from what?*"; it also points to the need to raise far broader political questions about the actual practices of peace operations, their contested meanings, and their internal contradictions. I am just as interested in the "representational practices" associated with peacekeeping as the peacekeeping missions themselves.[14] This is so because the representations and the actual behavior are integrally related.

My early sense that peacekeeping was too readily seen as a celebrated alternative to military force was only compounded by the fact that I live and work in Canada, a country in which peacekeeping serves as one of the "core myths"[15] of Canada's "imagined community."[16] That myth locates Canada as a selfless middle-power, acting with a kind of moral purity not normally exhibited by contemporary states.[17] Canadian representations of nation and military depend on the benign and altruistic image of Canada as peacekeeper, which comes to form the "background knowledge that is taken to be true"[18] about both the Canadian military and the Canadian state. My argument here is that the very "comfortable" sense of peacekeeping "we" have in Canada says more about what we think of "ourselves," about self-definition, than it says about what actually goes on when UN peacekeeping missions are deployed to various places around the world.[19]

Questions about national representation and imagined communities also raise important theoretical issues. As theorists of sovereignty and nationalism have noted, national identity is constructed through the use of images and ideas—through discourses—that give coherence and integrity to an otherwise disparate group of people.[20] Those discourses help set the boundaries of both the inside and outside of the state, delimiting not only who belongs but also how that state differs from "others." The example of peacekeeping provides an important illustration of these kinds of arguments. Peacekeeping tells us a great deal about the self-representations of states that deploy peacekeepers, but it also tells us much of the (re)presentations of those countries in which the missions are deployed: in the words of Anne Orford, as "disordered, chaotic, tribal, primitive, pre-capitalist, violent, exclusionary and child-like."[21] In this way, peacekeeping serves as part of the contemporary colonial encounter, establishing knowledge claims about both "us" and "them," knowledge claims that then serve to legitimize the missions themselves.

Discourses surrounding peacekeeping also serve as important organizing frameworks not only for particular nation-states but also for multilateral institutions, especially the United Nations. As suggested above, the post–Cold War period provided a unique opportunity for the UN to reassert itself as an active international political actor, and its involvement in, and representations of, peacekeeping missions served as an integral element of that assertion. So too are militaries constituted in part through these depictions. In countries where one of the chief activities of the national military is its involvement in peace operations, the images that pervade popular and political discourse concerning the military or soldiering are surprisingly different from those found in countries that privilege their military's combat-capable qualities. In Canada, male soldiers are rarely depicted as warriors; instead they appear donning the blue berets of the United Nations, normally assisting civilians in war-torn countries, and are seldom seen even carrying a weapon. Images of the average soldier as gentle peacekeeper are deployed even more frequently during election campaigns, and, in the Canadian case, during debates about Québec's separation from Canada. The representations of warrior princes tell a story about both the Canadian military and the Canadian nation.

While prevalent in Canada, this image of the benign soldier is not unique to there. The Netherlands, for example, also has a long association with contributing troops to peacekeeping missions and, as Stefan Dudink writes, is a country in which representations of the Dutch military emphasize its "gentle" qualities. According to Dudink, Dutch national identity is intimately linked to visions of a kinder, gentler military and to representations of a "moral" nation, one extraordinarily well suited to peacekeeping operations.[22] Peacekeeping serves as both an element of national identity for many states and as a way to legitimize militaries. Policymakers in countries such as Japan, Argentina, and Germany specifically pursued more active involvement in peacekeeping missions in the post–Cold War era both to resuscitate their respective national militaries and to revitalize national image and international standing.

Any analysis of depictions of the nation, and of the military, ought to include understandings of both "manhood" and "womanhood," masculinity and femininity.[23] One of the most important things about peacekeeping is the way in which the myths of manhood embedded within it are in many ways contradictory: "the more it asserts itself, the more it calls itself into question."[24] These contradictions exist because of the inherent tension between "proper" soldiering and peacekeeping. Feminists have long argued, as Cynthia Enloe notes, that militaries require a particular "ideology of manliness" in order to function properly.[25] Nobody knows better than militaries themselves what is involved in the creation of a soldier. As Major R. W. J. Wenek wrote in 1984: "The defining role of any military force is the management of violence by violence, so that individual aggressiveness is, or should be, a fundamental characteristic of occupational fitness in combat units."[26] These are the kinds of qualities feminist scholars point to when they note that the ideology of manliness required by militaries is one premised on violence and aggression, individual conformity to military discipline, and "aggressive heterosexism and homophobia," as well as misogyny and racism.[27]

Peacekeeping provides a unique case for examining militarized masculinity because on the one hand, peacekeeping resolved what had become a crisis of legitimation for many post–Cold War militaries—it was, for a time, one of the few military activities that remained in persistent, indeed growing, demand. On the other hand, peacekeeping resolved that crisis in a way that is not fully, or properly, militaristic. Restricting weapons use to self-defense and establishing a sometimes multilateral chain of command disrupt prevailing notions of military purpose and structure. In this way, often ridiculed and demeaned within traditional military culture, the resolution of the military's legitimation crisis becomes to some extent a crisis of masculinity. All the messages a soldier receives about appropriately masculine soldierly behavior are fundamentally at odds with what is expected in a peace operation.[28] The argument in this book is that this crisis has taken a number of forms and exists at a number of levels. At the level of peace operations themselves, the crisis has resulted in displays of hypermasculinity and violence.[29] At the level of national discourse, the image of the benign soldier (upon which a number of national militaries, and national identities, have been constituted) is no longer sustainable and has begun to unravel. This unraveling has shown the incongruity of deploying people trained to kill on missions dubbed "peace operations," but it has also precipitated a backlash from various centers of power, aimed at defending traditional images and understandings of both war-making and peacekeeping.

While crises of masculinity and confusions of soldierly and warrior purpose may help us understand why soldiers deployed on peace operations perpetrate acts of violence, they do not by themselves explain the reasons these issues remain almost entirely invisible within mainstream accounts of those operations. Part of the explanation lies with the general neglect accorded to *any* critical analysis of international relations or of security studies. As noted above, the long-held primacy of the state, power, and anarchy within traditional studies of global politics has left approaches that fall outside that triumvirate often invisible.[30] It is suggested throughout this book, however, that reasons quite specific to peacekeeping have contributed to the relative silence of critical readings. Invested as they are in the image of peacekeeping as benign and altruistic, certain nation-states, national militaries, and the United Nations itself tend to reproduce information that fits well into that view and to downplay information that contradicts it. When problems are acknowledged, they have too often been dismissed as "unusual, isolated events," "unsubstantiated," or the result of a "few bad apples."

However, it is necessary to interrogate the moments in which formal institutions *have* attempted to acknowledge the importance of gender and the kinds of issues that arise when soldiers are deployed on peacekeeping missions. These are the moments when the United Nations and national governments address the kinds of concerns that are raised throughout this book: prostitution, sexual exploitation, and physical violence directed at local citizens by peacekeeping forces. It is argued here, however, that while attention to gender has made some of these issues more visible within the UN and other formal venues, the manner in which it has done so has largely emptied gender concerns of their critical content. Gender critiques have been forced to fit into the UN's "way of doing business" without transforming how that business is done.[31] This kind of incorporation of gender is ultimately an effective way of silencing critique rather than straightforward dismissal because it ensures that deeper critical questions, those that look, for example, at militarized masculinity, do not end up on the formal agendas for addressing gender and peacekeeping.

It is worth returning, finally, to the question of widespread support for peacekeeping from actors and institutions one would have anticipated would apply a more critical lens. Women's and peace groups have not simply been duped into believing that peacekeeping is a panacea. They are faced with situations of conflict, humanitarian disaster, and human suffering in which there appear to be few viable alternatives with which to respond. Peacekeeping may not be the alternative it is presented to be, but in a world of few alternatives, it does seem sometimes to offer some prospect for a different way of approaching conflicts. While much of this book is critical of an inflated association of peacekeeping with real and substantive alternatives to military violence, it is not critical of the desire to seek such alternatives. Rather, we need to come up with viable alternatives, without closing our eyes to the limited nature of those that continue to rely on, and reassert the primacy of, militaries and militarism.

Outline of the Book

Chapter 2 situates the history of peacekeeping missions, asking how peacekeeping has been implicated in, and constitutive of, the production of certain meanings. It looks at the way in which early peacekeeping missions were concerned as much with addressing political crises *within* the UN as they were with threats to international peace and security. The chapter also examines how different national militaries and nation-states have used participation in peacekeeping to legitimize and resuscitate their respective domestic and international roles. Finally, it explores some of the ways in which countries that require peacekeeping missions have been constituted, and the manner in which peacekeeping has been one of the contemporary vehicles through which Western values, and in particular liberal democratic market ideology, is delivered to "backward conflict-prone" countries of the global South.

Chapters 3 and 4 provide detailed studies of the UN peacekeeping mission to Cambodia in the early 1990s and of the Canadian experience sending soldiers to Somalia at around the same time. The purpose of these two chapters is to make visible some of the impacts on local people's lives of deploying soldiers, especially the impacts that do not always make it into the official accounts of these missions, or which, when they are made public, are effectively silenced.

Chapter 5 surveys efforts made by the United Nations and some member states over the last decade to address gender and peace and security issues. The UN has produced apparently very good language and principles around which to organize its policies concerning gender and peacekeeping, but it has been less successful at living up to those principles. Rather than viewing the problem as one simply of the United Nations needing to make its "reality live up to its rhetoric" as some commentators have suggested, I argue that ignoring gender is entirely congruent with the understandings of women, peace, and security produced by the UN and by feminists who have engaged with the UN around these issues. The language the UN has adopted concerning gender is one that privileges UN priorities in addressing war, peace, security, and peacekeeping in such a way that gender becomes, at best, a tool for achieving problem-solving goals.

Chapter 6 elaborates on a set of arguments around militarized masculinity that do not appear on UN or other formal agendas but need to be explored in order to understand the many issues raised in Chapters 3 and 4. The treatment of militarized masculinity developed here, however, seeks to avoid replicating the standard essentialisms about militarized men. It explores cases of PTSD in soldiers who have returned from peacekeeping missions, arguing that it is not only *explosions* of militarized masculinity but also its *implosions* that make clear the ultimately contradictory base on which peacekeeping is built.

Finally, the conclusion returns to some of the "successes" reported by local people in the countries in which peace operations are deployed. It is often the nonwarrior qualities of soldiering that leave an impact on local people's security: building a park, reopening a hospital, or repairing a local school. Soldiers do not always make the best peacekeepers; sometimes it is carpenters, doctors, or lawyers who do, and sometimes it is soldiers who bring to bear a variety of skills that are not unique to soldiering. As complex as peacekeeping has become in the post–Cold War period, our approaches to what constitutes security and how it is to be achieved must become even more complicated as we sort through the various dimensions of what "keeping the peace" means.

Notes

1. Jarat Chopra, "United Nations Authority in Cambodia," occasional paper no. 15 (Providence: Thomas J. Watson Jr. Institute for International Studies, 1994), p. 8.

2. Robert A. Rubinstein, "Cultural Aspects of Peacekeeping: Notes on the Substance of Symbols," *Millennium* 22, no. 3 (1993): 548.

3. Janet E. Heininger, *Peacekeeping in Transition: The United Nations in Cambodia* (New York: Twentieth Century Fund Press, 1994), p. 5. See also Jocelyn Coulon, *Soldiers of Diplomacy: The United Nations, Peacekeeping, and the New World Order* (Toronto: University of Toronto Press, 1998), p. 26, and Allen Sens and Peter Stoett, *Global Politics: Origins, Currents, Directions* (Toronto: ITP Nelson, 1998), p. 277.

4. David Campbell includes meeting peacekeeping dues along with "providing adequate foreign aid even in times of economic recession" as one of his prescriptions for a U.S. foreign policy based on a "disposition of ethical engagement in the world and the responsibility to the Other" in *Politics Without Principle: Sovereignty, Ethics, and the Narratives of the Gulf War* (Boulder: Lynne Rienner, 1993), p. 99.

5. Cynthia Enloe, *The Morning After: Sexual Politics at the End of the Cold War* (Berkeley: University of California Press, 1993), p. 33.

6. Ibid.

7. Kien Serey Phal, "The Lessons of the UNTAC Experience and the Ongoing Responsibilities of the International Community for Peacebuilding and Development in Cambodia," *Pacifica Review* 7, no. 2 (1995): 132.

8. UN Secretary-General Study, *Women, Peace and Security* (New York: United Nations, 2002), available at http://www.un.org/womenwatch/daw/public/index.html #wps, p. 84, paragraph 268. See also Alex Last, "Porn Scandal Rocks Eritrean Peace Force," *BBC News World Edition,* December 20, 2002, available at http://news.bbc.co.uk/2/hi/africa/2595003.stm.

9. UN Economic and Social Council, "Integration of the Human Rights of Women and the Gender Perspective Violence Against Women," January 23, 2001, E/CN.4/2001/73, paragraphs 58–62; Graça Machel, "The Impact of Armed Conflict on Children: Report of the Expert of the Secretary-General," UN General Assembly, A/51/306, August 26, 1996, p. 31, paragraph 98; Magin McKenna, "Sins of the Peacekeepers," *Sunday Herald* (London), June 30, 2002, available at www.sundayherald.com/print25914.

10. Elisabeth Rehn and Ellen Johnson Sirleaf, *Women, War, Peace: The Independent Experts' Assessment on the Impact of Armed Conflict on Women and Women's Role in Peace-building* (New York: UN Development Fund for Women, 2002), p. 56.

11. UN Report of the Secretary General, "Investigation into Sexual Exploitation of Refugees by Aid Workers in West Africa," October 11, 2002, A/57/465, p. 10; see also Allan Thompson, "Peacekeepers Accused of Role in Child Sex Ring," *Toronto Star,* March 11, 2002, p. A8.

12. See André Marin, *Special Report: Systemic Treatment of CF Members with PTSD* (Ottawa: Government of Canada, February 5, 2002). On the experiences of Lieutenant-General Roméo Dallaire, who returned from serving as commander to the UN assistance mission in Rwanda with acute PTSD, see Samantha Power, *"A Problem from Hell" : America and the Age of Genocide* (New York: Basic Books, 2002), Chap. 10, and Roméo Dallaire, *Shake Hands with the Devil: The Failure of Humanity in Rwanda* (Toronto: Random House Canada, 2003).

13. For a fuller discussion of this, see Ken Booth (ed.), *Critical Security Studies and World Politics* (Boulder: Lynne Rienner, forthcoming 2005), and Keith Krause and Michael C. Williams (eds.), *Critical Security Studies* (Minneapolis: University of Minnesota Press, 1997).

14. The phrase comes from Roxanne Lynn Doty, *Imperial Encounters: The Politics of Representation in North-South Relations* (Minneapolis: University of Minnesota Press, 1997), pp. 10-11.

15. Daniel Francis, *National Dreams: Myth, Memory, and Canadian History* (Vancouver: Arsenal Pulp Press, 1997), p. 10.

16. Benedict Anderson, *Imagined Communities,* rev. ed. (London: Verso, 1991), p. 6.

17. See Mark Neufeld and Sandra Whitworth, "Image(in)ing Canadian Foreign Policy," in Wallace Clement (ed.), *Building on the New Canadian Political Economy* (Montreal: McGill-Queen's University Press, 1996); see also Mark Neufeld, "Hegemony and Foreign Policy Analysis: The Case of Canada as Middle Power," *Studies in Political Economy* 48 (autumn 1995): 7–29. It is not only critical theorists who have critiqued the notion of Canada as a "middle power"; realists have long been concerned that concentrating on the "selfless" qualities of foreign policy in Canada overlooks consideration of national interest. See, for example, Maureen Appel Molot, "Where Do We, Should We, or Can We Sit? A Review of Canadian Foreign Policy Literature," *International Journal of Canadian Studies* 1–2 (spring–fall 1990): 77–96.

18. Doty, *Imperial Encounters,* p. 10.

19. This formulation was inspired by Laura Macdonald, "Unequal Partnerships: The Politics of Canada's Relations with the Third World," *Studies in Political Economy* 47 (summer 1995): 111–141; she draws upon the work of postcolonial writers such as Edward Said in an analysis of Canadian foreign policy toward the "third world." See also Edward Said, *Orientalism* (New York: Vintage Books, 1978).

20. On theories of national identity and sovereignty, see Campbell, *Politics Without Principle,* p. 24; David Campbell, *Writing Security: United States Foreign Policy and the Politics of Identity* (Minneapolis: University of Minnesota Press, 1992); Roxanne Lynn Doty, "Sovereignty and the Nation: Constructing the Boundaries of National Identity," in Thomas J. Biersteker and Cynthia Weber (eds.), *State Sovereignty as Social Construct* (Cambridge: Cambridge University Press, 1996), pp. 121–147; and Cynthia Weber, *Simulating Sovereignty: Intervention, the State, and Symbolic Exchange* (Cambridge: Cambridge University Press, 1995). On myth and imagined communities, see Anderson, *Imagined Communities,* p. 6 and passim. See also Joanna Overing, "The Role of Myth: An Anthropological Perspective, or: 'The Reality of the Really Made-Up,'" in Geoffrey Hosking and George Schöpflin (eds.), *Myths and Nationhood* (New York: Routledge, 1997), p. 7, and George

Schöpflin, "The Functions of Myth and a Taxonomy of Myths," in Hosking and Schöpflin, *Myths and Nationhood,* p. 19.

21. Anne Orford, *Reading Humanitarian Intervention: Human Rights and the Use of Force in International Law* (Cambridge: Cambridge University Press, 2003), p. 47.

22. Stefan Dudink, "The Unheroic Men of a Moral Nation: Masculinity and Nation in Modern Dutch History," in Cynthia Cockburn and Drbravka Zarkov (eds.), *The Postwar Moment: Militaries, Masculinities, and International Peacekeeping* (London: Lawrence and Wishart, 2002), pp. 148–149 and passim. See also Marc de Leeuw, "A *Gentle*men's Agreement: Srebrenica in the Context of Dutch War History," in ibid., pp. 162–182, and Dubravka Zarkov, "*Srebrenica Trauma:* Masculinity, Military and National Self-Image in Dutch Daily Newspapers," in ibid., pp. 183–203. By contrast, in countries such as Fiji, which also has long been a troop-contributing country, involvement in peacekeeping is seen as an important element of a warrior tradition among traditional Fijians, one that privileges some of the features of militarized masculinity that will be discussed in Chapter 6: male bonding, loyalty, bravery, ethnic solidarity. See Karen A. Mingst, "Developing States as Peacekeepers: A Comparative Perspective," presented at the International Studies Association Annual Meetings, Toronto, March 18–22, 1997, p. 5.

23. For an analysis of gender and nationalism, see Nira Yuval-Davis, *Gender and Nation* (London: Sage, 1997), p. 1, and passim; for an analysis of gender and militarism, see references below.

24. Lynne Segal uses this phrase to describe masculinity, but I suggest here that the formulation applies to peacekeeping as well. See Lynne Segal, *Slow Motion: Changing Masculinities, Changing Men* (London: Virago, 1990), p. 123.

25. Cynthia Enloe, *Maneuvers: The International Politics of Militarizing Women's Lives* (Berkeley: University of California Press, 2000), p. xiii.

26. Major R. W. J. Wenek, "The Assessment of Psychological Fitness: Some Options for the Canadian Forces," Technical Note 1/84 (Ottawa: Directorate of Personnel Selection, Research on Second Careers, July 1984), p. 13; cited in Commission of Inquiry into the Deployment of Canadian Forces to Somalia, *Document Book no. 1: Hewson Report* (Ottawa, 1995), p. 46.

27. It is important to note that militarized masculinity, like all masculinities, is not one unitary set of qualities or characteristics that remain constant across time and place. See, for example, David H. J. Morgan, "Theater of War: Combat, the Military, and Masculinities," in Harry Brod and Michael Kaufman (eds.), *Theorizing Masculinities* (London: Sage, 1994), pp. 165–182; Enloe, *Maneuvers,* Chap. 4; Charlotte Hooper, "Masculinist Practices and Gender Politics: The Operation of Multiple Masculinities in International Relations," in Marysia Zalewski and Jane Parpart (eds.), *The "Man" Question in International Relations* (Boulder: Westview, 1998), pp. 28–53; and William Arkin and Lyne R. Dobrofsky, "Military Socialization and Masculinity," *Journal of Social Issues* 34, no. 1 (1978): 156.

28. See Donna Winslow, "The Canadian Airborne Regiment in Somalia: A Socio-Cultural Inquiry," prepared for the Commission of Inquiry into the Deployment of Canadian Forces to Somalia (Ottawa: Government Services Canada, 1997), pp. 267–270, and David R. Segal, Mady Wechsler Segal, and Dana P. Eyre, "The Social Construction of Peacekeeping in America," *Sociological Forum* 7, no. 1 (1992): 121–136. For first-hand accounts of the conflicts experienced by soldiers asked to perform what in their view are not appropriately soldierly duties, see Peter Worthington and Kyle Brown, *Scapegoat: How the Army Betrayed Kyle Brown* (Toronto: McClelland Bantam, 1997), and James R. Davis, *The Sharp End: A Canadian Soldier's Story* (Vancouver: Douglas and McIntyre, 1997).

29. I was first introduced to the idea of hypermasculinity through the work of Lily Ling; see her "Hypermasculinity," *Routledge International Encyclopedia of Women's Studies* (London: Routledge, 2001), pp. 1089–1091; "Cultural Chauvinism and the Liberal International Order: 'West Versus Rest' in Asia's Financial Crisis," in G. Chowdhry and S. Nair (eds.), *Power, Postcolonialism, and International Relations: Reading Race, Gender, Class* (London: Routledge, 2002), pp. 115–141; and "Hypermasculinity on the Rise, Again: A Response to Fukuyama on Women and World Politics," *International Feminist Journal of Politics* 2, no. 2 (2000): 278–286.

30. To list only a few of the many works that address this issue, see, for example, Cynthia Enloe, *Bananas, Beaches, and Bases: Making Feminist Sense of International Politics* (Berkeley: University of California Press, 1990), Chap. 1 and passim; Sandra Whitworth, *Feminism and International Relations: Towards a Political Economy of Gender in Interstate and Non-Governmental Institutions* (Basingstoke, UK: Macmillan, 1997), Introduction and Chap. 1; Mark Neufeld, *The Restructuring of International Relations Theory* (Cambridge: Cambridge University Press, 1995); and Fred Halliday, *Rethinking International Relations* (Vancouver: UBC Press, 1994).

31. This is paraphrased from Anne Orford, "Feminism, Imperialism and the Mission of International Law," *Nordic Journal of International Law* 71, no. 2 (2002): 281.

2

Narratives of Peacekeeping, Past and Present

We may . . . wake up one day lamenting the loss of the order that the Cold War gave to the anarchy of international relations.
—John J. Mearsheimer[1]

The United Nations can be proud of the speed with which peace-keeping has evolved in response to the new political environment resulting from the end of the cold war.
—Boutros Boutros-Ghali[2]

The post–Cold War period was dominated by two competing, and closely related, narratives. The first, exemplified by John Mearsheimer's concern that we will all soon miss the Cold War, depicted a "coming anarchy" of ethnic, religious, nationalist, and civilizational conflicts that would erupt once the order that had accompanied the Cold War system was lost.[3] By this view, as dangerous as the Cold War's nuclear balance of terror may have seemed, it had provided a degree of stability, certainty, and order that vanished along with the Soviet Union. As Mearsheimer warned, the "untamed anarchy" that had characterized European politics prior to the end of World War II might be about to make its return, and untamed anarchy is a "prime cause of armed conflict."[4]

The second vision was captured by former UN Secretary-General Boutros Boutros-Ghali. By this view, the United Nations could offer the world a way to tame anarchy, through "techniques" such as peacekeeping.[5] Observers write about operations that were a "force for peace"[6] and would "restore hope,"[7] "bring democracy"[8] to conflict-ravaged lands, and even "civilise" the "domestic affairs of less-developed states."[9] Where anarchy established the problem, the United Nations provided its solution.

Events during the 1990s and early 2000s seemed to confirm these narratives. As Fen Osler Hampson writes, from Rwanda to Bosnia, Kosovo, Sierra Leone, and East Timor, "neighbours have pillaged each other's

23

homes and murdered each other with a degree of vengeance and ferocity that is barely imaginable."[10] The "new wars" took place largely within state borders, rather than between them, and were brutally violent, a violence borne primarily by civilian populations.[11] At the same time, the United Nations was busier than it ever had been, with an explosion of peace missions, and an expansion of the size, scope, and budgets of those missions.[12] So busy did the UN become, however, that critics soon accused it of being overextended and unable to provide the material and logistical support necessary to properly conduct these increasingly complex, dangerous, and large-scale missions. As the commander with the UN Protection Force (UNPROFOR) in the former Yugoslavia famously complained, "If you are a commander of a UN mission, don't get in trouble after five P.M. or on the weekend. There is no one in the UN to answer the phone!"[13]

With the United Nations struggling under the burden of mission proliferation, coupled with the enormity of the atrocities inflicted on those who found themselves caught in the middle of the new wars, most studies of peacekeeping focused on "short-term, crisis-oriented, operational" analyses.[14] Numerous academic and policy reports appeared, which aimed to help the UN systemize its approach, build on its best practices, improve efficiency, and move away from ad hoc responses.[15] The United Nations set up a panel on UN peacekeeping in early 2000 to provide assistance on conducting its peace and security activities better in the future.[16] Within this context, it became easy to overlook larger critical questions that could be posed about peacekeeping. Indeed, even to suggest that there might be more to studying peacekeeping than simply figuring out better ways to do it can be met with moral outrage, as though raising such issues trivializes the horrors and violence of contemporary global politics.[17] As Elizabeth Dauphinee notes, "critique on any other dimension but the minor details of the implementation process is anathema."[18]

Despite the difficulties involved in doing so, raising larger critical questions is necessary because it draws our attention to some of the complexities associated with the horrors and violence of contemporary conflicts. All explanations may be partial, but some are decidedly more so than others. Peacekeeping, and the various narrative practices associated with it, has directed our attention to the appropriate bounds of inquiry and to the types of questions and analysis that are deemed legitimate. Typically, this focus has directed attention away from the manner in which peacekeeping is sometimes implicated in the very horrors and violence it seeks to address. Feminist analysis attempts to bring to light some of the questions that largely have gone unasked around peacekeeping.

The narratives associated with peacekeeping also point us to other practices that are part of the "unasked" questions feminists and other critical scholars seek to raise. The solution to anarchy that the United Nations presents entails a number of things, one of which is the UN itself. As François Debrix writes, "Thanks to peacekeeping, the UN was not left without meaning."[19] As much as the United Nations was challenged by the many new calls for peacekeeping, it was also "made possible" by those calls. This chapter will examine this issue, as well as the ways in which peacekeeping serves as a form of insurance for post–Cold War militarism. The mobilizing ideology that had characterized the rationale for military preparedness throughout the Cold War did not have to be abandoned with the demise of the Cold War, as many had hoped (and others feared); it only needed to be accommodated to the new forms of conflict and the new means of addressing those conflicts. Peacekeeping provides the rationale for a number of militaries that otherwise have no raison d'être. Finally, as something that gives meaning to both the United Nations and national militaries, peacekeeping also tells us a great deal about who conducts peacekeeping missions ("us") and who needs peacekeeping missions ("them"). Inherent in this view, the well-ordered, rational, liberal, free market global North brings peace in a variety of ways, not least by delivering through peacekeeping the very principles of rationality, liberalism, and free market economics so clearly absent in the anarchic global South.[20]

Understanding peacekeeping in terms of its role in the production of meanings, as opposed simply to a series of "missions" or "events," is necessary because it highlights some of the reasons why peacekeeping has been so narrowly construed, and why attempts to engage with it have been so actively resisted. That resistance is understandable once we see how peacekeeping is inextricably involved in the production of meanings associated with the UN, nations, militaries, and "us" versus "them." As Roxanne Lynn Doty writes, "Being democratic, freedom-loving, and humanitarian have been important constitutive elements in the construction of the Western 'self,'"[21] and one of the arguments of this chapter is that peacekeeping is a contemporary site through which the Western self is constituted, and inflicted on others. Engaging critically with peacekeeping, then, disrupts not only the silences accorded feminist questions around peacekeeping but also a series of taken-for-granted assumptions and meanings that are constituted through peacekeeping and its associated narratives.

A Note on Theory

A variety of theoretical insights inform this and subsequent chapters and are worth signaling briefly here. What should be clear already is that the commitment here is to contributing to critical, as opposed to problem-solving, theory. Robert W. Cox describes the difference in this way: problem-solving theory "takes the world as it finds it, with the prevailing social and power relationships and the institutions into which they are organized, as the given framework for action. The general aim of problem solving is to make these relationships and institutions work smoothly by dealing effectively with particular sources of trouble." Critical theory, by contrast, "stands apart from the prevailing order of the world and asks how that order came about. Critical theory . . . does not take institutions and social power relations for granted but calls them into question by concerning itself with their origins and how and whether they might be in the process of changing. It is directed toward an appraisal of the very framework for action, or problematic, which problem-solving theory accepts as its parameters."[22]

Critical theory thus rejects the positivist claim that research and theory-making are, or should be, value-neutral activities.[23] All activities, including the act of theorizing itself, are political, and have political implications. By this view, positivist-inspired theory also has associated normative commitments, even if those commitments remain largely unacknowledged and invisible. Those commitments include, among others, the importance of instrumental control, technical rationality, and efficiency.[24] Critical theorists do not share a consensus over what their normative commitments are or should be—some would claim a commitment to emancipation,[25] others to a feminist politics,[26] others still to an "ethical responsibility toward the Other."[27] What critical theorists do share, however, is a commitment to acknowledging the normative nature of their work and making explicit the normative implications of the positions they adopt.

Critical theorists also reject the positivist claim that knowledge can be read off a "world out there" in an unmediated fashion.[28] They reject, in other words, the idea of an objective reality that can be understood through simple observation. The material conditions of people's lives are important and must be documented, but knowledge about the world and all human activity also is produced through the discursive practices associated with particular phenomena, issues, or events. This means that ideas matter. Benedict Anderson has pointed to the role of ideas in the making of nations, and in particular the ways in which nations are "imagined communities." In his oft-quoted phrase, nations are "*imagined* because the members of even the smallest nation will never know most of their fellow-members, meet them, or even hear of them, yet in the minds of each lives the image of their imagined communion."[29]

The nation, in short, is constituted by a shared set of ideas and myths, through which an otherwise geographically separate and variously differentiated people come to "know" themselves as members of a territorially bounded, sovereign, political community.[30] The nation can only be understood *as* a nation through those shared myths and ideas—it does not exist otherwise and outside of those ideas. Importantly, for Anderson, any community larger than "primordial" villages of regular face-to-face contact are imagined communities.[31] Anderson's insights thus can be applied not only to nations but also to any large contemporary institutions, including national militaries and multilateral institutions. They are constituted in part through shared ideas that give them meaning.

Feminist theory contributes to these kinds of arguments by noting that the ideas that constitute nations and institutions are also inevitably gendered.[32] Often those ideas are associated with the exclusion of women and the presence of men, but they are associated also with the *particular* ways both men and women are "present" in nations, institutions, or events, and the particular expectations associated with both women and men, and masculinity and femininity. Those assumptions, feminists argue, affect how we understand different social phenomena and have an impact on the individual lives of men and women.

The ideas and assumptions that prevail about women and men in situations of armed conflict and political violence, for example, are a good way to illustrate this point. Women and men are *both* active "agents" and "victims" of conflict and political violence, but they are usually positioned quite differently: women have long been portrayed primarily as victims of conflict while men are portrayed as its actors and agents.[33] This has implications for both women and men. Women are seldom viewed as having held public power prior to the emergence of conflict, or as having served as combatants. As a result, they may experience greater freedom in organizing informal peace campaigns, but at the same time, they are usually ignored when formal peace processes begin and are normally excluded from disarmament, demobilization, and reintegration (DDR) programs, which give former combatants access to educational, training, and employment opportunities. Men, by contrast, are presumed to have held power and decision-making authority prior to the emergence of conflict and to have been combatants and instigators of the conflict itself. This sometimes makes their motivations suspect when they become involved in efforts to bring conflict to an end. At the same time, however, it is men who are invited to the formal "peace table" once it has been established, and they are the ones who primarily receive the benefits of DDR and other postconflict activities.[34]

Prevailing understandings about women and men can thus significantly shape their experiences in institutions, nations, or social processes like armed conflict. Equally important is an analysis of the ways in which assumptions about race and the colonial "other" not only interpolate with gender but also form part of the background knowledge that is taken to be true about peacekeeping and its legitimations. As Edward Said and other postcolonial theorists have argued, the political production of knowledge about racialized "others" both forms one of the bases of imperialist practices and produces the very idea of the "Orient" as that which is intellectually and morally backward and in need of salvation.[35] Peacekeeping forms one of the contemporary political sites through which these knowledge claims are produced.

The kinds of terms that will be used throughout this work, then, focus on not only ideas and imagined communities but also narratives, representation, and discursive practices. These terms signal that the ideas that constitute nations or institutions, or specifically racialized men and women or masculinities and femininities, are never closed or fixed; rather, they are constantly being produced and reproduced. We cannot understand what peacekeeping means, the impact that actual peacekeeping missions have, or the resistance to posing critical questions about peacekeeping missions without exploring also the ideas and discursive practices associated with them. A. B. Fetherston notes that "The power of discourse is to render 'right,' 'legitimate,' 'taken-for-granted,' 'natural' specific ways of knowing, acting and organizing social life. . . . Crucially, this rendering of 'right' silences other possibilities (they are unknowable since they are not possible)."[36] That silencing has rendered critical, feminist, and postcolonial questions as extraordinary and outside of the normal purview of peacekeeping analyses.

Examining ideas and discursive practices does not mean we will be inattentive to material conditions and empirical information. Much of the book is devoted to examining different empirical moments. As Doty writes, analysis that focuses on discursive practices

> does not deny the existence of the material world, but rather suggests that material objects and subjects are constituted as such within discourse. So, for example, when U.S. troops march into Grenada, this is certainly "real." . . . What the physical behavior itself is, though, is still far from certain until discursive practices constitute it as an "invasion," a "show of force," a "training exercise," a "rescue," and so on. What is "really" going on in such a situation is inextricably linked to the discourse within which it is located.[37]

How we have come to "know" what peacekeeping is, why it matters, or how one should study it, and what has been excluded in those knowledge claims, entails exploring how peacekeeping has been discursively represented, through the United Nations, member states and national militaries. It means exploring the presentations and representations of peacekeeping that go into the constitution of its meanings. The rest of this chapter explores some of these themes.

What Peacekeeping Makes Possible for the UN

In 1992, then Secretary-General Boutros Boutros-Ghali noted that peacekeeping "can rightly be called the invention of the United Nations."[38] He was reiterating the observation that the United Nations Charter does not explicitly name or describe peacekeeping. Chapter VI of the charter describes the role of the UN in the "Pacific Settlement of Disputes" and Chapter VII describes action that the United Nations can take "with Respect to Threats to the Peace, Breaches of the Peace and Acts of Aggression," but neither mentions peacekeeping. Instead, peacekeeping was created through the practices of the United Nations to respond to threats to international peace and security, in what former Secretary-General Dag Hammarskjöld said belonged to "Chapter Six-and-a-half" operations.[39]

Two early observer missions were established, one in Palestine in 1948 (the United Nations Truce Supervision Organization, UNTSO) and one in India and Pakistan in 1949 (the United Nations Military Observer Group in India and Pakistan, UNMOGIP). But it was not until 1956 that the United Nations deployed a "force-level" operation in response to the "Suez crisis"—the first peacekeeping mission ever mounted.[40] From its beginning, peacekeeping became a site of some of the largest early controversies faced by the United Nations and one through which the legitimate subjects (and objects) of UN peacekeeping missions were discursively constructed.

The Suez crisis erupted in 1956, when Israel, Britain, and France attacked Egypt after the Nasser government nationalized the Suez Canal Company. The attacks came as a surprise to much of the world and to the United Nations as well, which had been facilitating negotiations between the parties with some anticipation of success. Instead, in secret negotiations, France and Britain had arranged that Israel would invade Egypt as a ruse for an Anglo-French intervention. Two days after the Israeli invasion, France and Britain launched an aerial attack, followed by their own invasion, ostensibly to "protect" the canal and to "separate" Egyptian and Israeli combatants.[41]

In most accounts of the crisis, the fate of the people of Egypt, subject to invasion, manipulation, and shelling by various foreign governments, troops, and aircraft, is not widely discussed or described. Rather, the crisis that the invasion precipitated for the United Nations receives the most extensive attention. Even though the international community largely condemned the assault, both France and Britain were permanent, and therefore veto-wielding, members of the Security Council. As a result, the Security Council could not force either country to suspend its attack; every attempt to do so was blocked, in this way discrediting the only body within the UN system that was supposed to have enforcement powers. More importantly, the crisis threw countries that had previously been allies into confrontation. The Soviet Union threatened to retaliate against both Britain and France; the United States also strongly opposed the invasion and presented a motion to the General Assembly (where all UN members can vote and none hold a veto) calling for a cease-fire and the immediate withdrawal of all foreign troops from Egypt. Many UN diplomats, including Canada's Lester

B. Pearson, who eventually came up with the plan for a peacekeeping force, were concerned that the motion would cause an irreparable rift between important allies within the Security Council.[42]

The plan to deploy a UN force to the region was an attempt to allow Britain and France to withdraw from Egypt without being disgraced, bring an end to the hostilities, and confirm that the UN did have a role to play in preventing and resolving conflicts in the post–World War II era.[43] United Nations Emergency Force I (UNEF I) troops continued to act as a buffer between Egyptian and Israeli troops until 1967. By most accounts, UNEF I was a success.[44] It is credited also with establishing a series of principles that would serve as the basis of all peacekeeping missions that followed, including the importance of securing the consent of the parties to the dispute; the non-use of force, except for self-defense; and impartiality.[45]

But UNEF I also told a number of other important stories. First, as has already been suggested, the master narrative ignored the people of Egypt and placed the United Nations and the creation of this mission as the center of the story. UNEF I also constituted France and Britain, acting to retain control over their financial interests in the Suez Canal, as legitimately aggrieved actors. Rather than depict them as invaders, or violators of Egypt's sovereignty (as the United States' original resolution would have done), UNEF I recognized Britain, France, Israel, and Egypt as "parties to the dispute," whose consent was required before action could be taken by the UN. It was, moreover, British, French, and Israeli troops that UNEF I forces were sent to replace. Instead of constituting the presence of those troops as a "grotesquely disproportionate response"[46] to Nasser's nationalization, UNEF I also confirmed that the presence of foreign troops was a necessary condition for the peaceful resolution of the crisis.

UNEF I also told a story about the kinds of crises that did *not* warrant a United Nations peacekeeping mission. At the same time that the Suez held the United Nations in its grip, the government of Hungary was calling for UN support to protect it against a Soviet invasion. Increasingly open and public criticism of the Soviet Union had been growing within Hungary since the spring of 1956, and on November 1, the day after France and Britain started their bombing campaign in Egypt, the Hungarian government declared its neutrality, withdrew from the Warsaw Pact, and formally requested UN assistance.[47] *This* was the crisis that could seriously undermine international peace and security: unlike the Suez, on which the United States and the Soviet Union were in some broad agreement, Hungary was an issue that would bring the two superpowers into direct confrontation. Yet the Hungarian request did not provoke the same kind of diplomatic energy or creativity that was devoted to the Suez crisis. The General Assembly and Security Council issued several ineffectual calls for the withdrawal of Soviet troops, but the Soviet Union quickly crushed the rebellion, installed a new government, and arrested and executed thousands of people.[48]

The United Nations responded quite differently to each of these two "crises," but not because of their potential impact on global stability or international peace and security. Presumably the Hungarian crisis would have garnered the larger response had this been the case. The important differences between the two lay elsewhere. For one, there were important economic differences: the loss of the Suez Canal would have had a significant financial impact on its chief investors, Britain and France, and was also the primary shipping route between Britain and its markets and former colonies.[49] Hungary, by contrast, was already "lost" to the Soviet sphere of influence and posed no relative gain or loss for Western financial interests. More importantly, however, the Hungarian crisis likely did not attract the same kind of attention *by* the United Nations because it did not pose the same kind of crisis *for* the United Nations as did the Suez. Hungary was an instantiation of Cold War rivalries but nothing more than that. It reiterated an existing problem within the Security Council, but it did not create a new one. The breakdown of the United States/France/Britain alliance, by contrast, would have been devastating for the United Nations and for the Security Council. The Suez, in short, was not only a crisis of international peace and security, it was an even more serious crisis for the integrity of the UN. From its beginning, then, peacekeeping was created as much to salvage the UN from its internal political crises as it was to respond to threats to international peace and security.[50]

Whereas UNEF I was considered a success, a mission four years later in the Congo was viewed as something of a debacle. Like UNEF I, the United Nations Operation in the Congo (ONUC) tells us something of the UN's understandings of political crises. The mission was established when, after achieving independence from Belgium in January 1960, the Congo faced serious difficulties in establishing internal order and stability, including a mutinous military, the refusal of Belgium's forces and personnel to depart, and threats of secession from the mineral-rich Katanga province. As in the Suez crisis, what we learn from reading accounts of this mission is as much about its impact on the UN as on the people of the Congo. ONUC was the largest mission mounted by the United Nations until the large post–Cold War missions of more recent times; it involved 20,000 troops and approximately 6,000 civilian personnel. It lasted four years and suffered hundreds of peacekeeping casualties, including UN Secretary-General Dag Hammarskjöld, who was killed in a plane crash on his way to conduct negotiations.[51]

The mission was not only large, complex, and perilous, it precipitated yet another crisis for the United Nations itself. Some member states, notably the Soviet Union and France, protested the manner in which the mission had been established and the way in which it was conducted and so withheld their regular assessments to the United Nations. Once the Soviet Union fell two years behind in its UN dues, the United States (ironically, given the state of its own contributions in later years) presented a motion to rescind the Soviet vote within the General Assembly, in accordance with UN regulations. After active diplomatic intervention, the motion never came to a vote, but had it done so, as A. B. Fetherston notes, "the Soviet Union would probably have left the UN, along with its satellite states and other sympathetic states. This could well have dealt a blow from which the UN would not have been able to recover."[52]

The UN did recover, but ONUC established again that an important part of "what matters" about peacekeeping is the effect it has at the United Nations. One of the chief sources of conflict between members of the Security Council concerning ONUC focused on mission mandates, an issue that remains important to this day. A peacekeeping mandate is set through a Security Council resolution and establishes the scope of the activities to be undertaken in the mission.[53] From their beginning, mandates have been accused of being too ambiguous, leaving too much of the specifics of the mission open to interpretation. As Fetherston observes, mandates are the result of diplomatic negotiations both within the Security Council and between belligerents involved in a conflict. In order to reach a consensus, points of disagreement are usually left out and vague wording is used, reflecting "the lowest common denominator of agreement."[54]

Lowest common denominators are nonetheless revealing of the self-representations of the UN and of its missions. Most mandates begin with a statement that situates the mission in relation to "international peace and security." This is done either through noting that the dispute or conflict in question, if allowed to continue, will threaten or otherwise endanger international peace and security, and/or through a statement that "recalls" or "bears in mind" "the primary responsibility of the Security Council for the maintenance of international peace and security."[55]

Mandates also usually establish the mission goals. Some emphasize the "desire" or "conviction" that the measures outlined in the resolution will contribute to a "just and durable" solution to the conflict in question.[56] Others, such as the mandate for the ONUC mission, aim for "the complete restoration of law and order."[57] Others still, as in the case of the United Nations Peacekeeping Force in Cyprus (UNFICYP), aim for a "return to normal conditions."[58] Many post–Cold War peacekeeping mission mandates, as discussed at greater length below, have focused on establishing democratic institutions and autonomous self-government, holding free and fair elections, and promoting economic reconstruction.[59]

Some of the most controversial peacekeeping mandates of recent times were those concerned with the UN Assistance Mission for Rwanda (UNAMIR). Originally, it aimed at monitoring the Arusha peace agreement and contributing to the security of the capital city of Kigali, as well as monitoring the security situation in the period leading up to planned elections; as security tensions escalated, the mission was reduced through successive resolutions to a mere 270 troops.[60] This, despite warnings from its force commander, Lieutenant General Roméo Dallaire, of a coming genocide and his pleas for more troops and UN support. What shocked Dallaire most was not an expectation that he was to return Rwanda to "normal conditions"—as was called for in some mandates—but that he was expected to make evacuating his own troops, and foreign nationals, his priority: "Working on the withdrawal plan was anathema to my priorities. I thought, 'Who evacuates the Rwandans?' The answer was no one."[61] Evacuating foreigners meant that Rwandans were left without protection, in some cases left begging for their lives, as peacekeepers were redeployed to aid in the evacuation of expatriates. As Samantha Power notes, in the early few days of the genocide in Rwanda, some 4,000 foreigners were evacuated while 20,000 Rwandans were killed.[62]

Mandates thus are part of the constitutive practices that establish the authority of the United Nations to establish peacekeeping missions and maintain international peace and security. They also establish "order," "normalcy," "democracy," and "economic restructuring" as the goals of those missions and, in the case of Rwanda, identify who is to be saved and who is to be left to die. In the apparently indeterminate language of mission mandates, some very powerful messages are, in fact, being conveyed: that "order" and "normal conditions" are identifiable, that they existed at one point in time, and that some people's lives, as Roméo Dallaire continues to argue, are more important than others. Mandates that call for free and fair elections and economic reconstruction also signal the content that is given to order and normalcy: Western-style economic and political institutions.

In a variety of ways, then, mandates define the "subjects" of peacekeeping both in terms of *who* delivers it (the United Nations) and *what* is to be accomplished (order, Western political and economic institutions, and the protection of foreign nationals). Mandates also usually indicate, in the broadest of terms, *how* order and normalcy are to be accomplished. Throughout the history of UN peacekeeping missions, that has entailed the deployment of military troops under UN command. Though post–Cold War peacekeeping missions have become increasingly complex and include civilian police, de-miners, volunteers, electoral observers, human rights monitors, civil administrators, and a public information capacity, "military personnel and structure remain the backbone of most operations."[63]

States and Militaries, Militaries and States

During the Cold War, troop-contributing countries tended to come from "middle" and "small" powers such as Canada, Belgium, Ireland, Italy, India, Pakistan, the Netherlands, Austria, Bangladesh, and the Nordic countries.

Permanent members of the Security Council often provided logistical and other material support but only rarely contributed military personnel.[64] Even after the Cold War, permanent members did not participate widely, or in large number, in peacekeeping missions. Later chapters discuss in more detail some of the implications of relying on militaries for peacekeeping missions. This section examines what peacekeeping does *for* militaries: what it makes possible.

One common observation has been that national militaries can gain financially by contributing to peacekeeping missions. The United Nations compensates troop-contributing countries through a leasing agreement, and for militaries with lower relative operating costs (typically those from lesser developed countries), this can be very beneficial. For countries such as Pakistan, Bangladesh, Nepal, and India, compensation "helps them offset the large standing armies they wish to maintain for local strategic reasons."[65] Individual soldiers also often benefit financially: Nigerian troops, for example, earn their usual pay, a daily UN allowance, a Nigerian Special Overseas allowance, and a family allotment.[66] Officers too find the prospect of the extra financial rewards from peacekeeping duty attractive: the former Canadian chief of the UNPROFOR anticipated that "With any luck, I could save $40,000 during the year. That's U.S. dollars."[67]

Possibly even more tangible than direct financial gain, "small" and "middle" power militaries have long participated in peacekeeping missions because these are sometimes the only field missions available to them. This has been true, for example, of Canada, Scandinavia, Ireland, and Denmark. As Ray Murphy notes: "Since World War II, the Irish army [has] suffered from a lack of purpose and a certain ambiguity regarding its role."[68] In the absence of external threats, participation in peacekeeping has constituted the Irish Defence Forces as a legitimate military—it has little reason to exist otherwise. For P. Keatinge, it was only involvement in large-scale UN peacekeeping operations that lifted Irish "professional morale out of the routine rut of state ceremonials, guard duty, civilian emergencies and horse shows."[69] Peacekeeping, in short, makes some militaries possible *as* militaries.

This not only provides those militaries with opportunities for training and to prepare and approximate "combat readiness" in a context in which the likelihood of facing actual combat is practically nonexistent. It also establishes a link between militaries and the "imagined community" that is the nation. Modern nationalism has long been linked to militarism. The new kind of nation that emerged with the French Revolution of 1789 was a militarized nation associated with a new kind of war: national wars waged in the name of "the people."[70] A nation came to be defined, in part, by a citizenry willing and able to rush to its defense or to pursue its expansionary aims.[71] Countries without a legitimate military are not only vulnerable to invasion, they are suspect nations: immature and not fully formed. As failed

U.S. presidential candidate Pat Buchanan said of the United States's "middle power" neighbor to its north: Canada is a "whining, juvenile" nation that has been "freeloading" off the U.S. defense budget for decades.[72]

Though unlikely to satisfy the likes of a Pat Buchanan, peacekeeping does provide one resolution for nations faced with few opportunities for military exploits and the smaller military budgets that usually accompany such lack of "opportunity." Peacekeeping legitimizes these nations' militaries and at the same time legitimizes them as nations. As Karen Mingst reports, countries such as India and Nigeria found that involvement in peacekeeping was not just an acceptable activity "but one that helped to shape their national image."[73] Likewise, as the leader of Fiji said to Fijian soldiers serving in the 1978 UN mission in Lebanon: "You have helped us to keep our head high in the international scene."[74]

In addition to the long-serving peacekeeping countries, a number of new troop-contributing countries began to participate actively in peacekeeping missions at the end of the Cold War, many operating with a clear set of understandings about what peacekeeping would make possible for them.[75] Laura Hein and Mark Selden observe that the collapse of the Cold War did not simply have political, economic, and security implications, it also required a "reconceptualization of past and present."[76] Countries like Argentina, Japan, and Germany began to consider more active participation in UN peacekeeping missions as a means to reconstitute their militaries and to insert themselves into the global landscape as transformed, reconstituted actors.

The cases of Germany and Japan are particularly illustrative here. Both were defeated powers from World War II, and both adopted, through constitutional means, strict limitations on maintaining or deploying military forces. The two countries did have established armed forces throughout the Cold War (in the case of Japan, the SDF, or Self-Defense Forces, and in the case of West Germany, the Bundeswehr, or federal armed forces), but their focus was intended to be primarily self-defense and disaster relief.[77] During the Cold War and in particular after its demise, the governments of both countries began to reevaluate their respective militaries.

In Germany's case, with reunification there were increasing calls for the "normalization" of German foreign policy, which would require a "more responsible" membership in both NATO and the United Nations.[78] Part of that normalization entailed putting the stigma of World War II behind it, and one way to do this would be to deploy troops and personnel on peacekeeping missions. Germany's Constitutional Court decided in 1994 that German forces could be deployed on UN missions when supported by a majority vote in the federal parliament. Involvement in peacekeeping was a contentious political issue, with many arguing that Germany's role in World War II still demanded that it never deploy forces in foreign countries again. But those who supported German involvement in peacekeeping, as Albrecht Schnabel notes, argued that participation in UN peacekeeping missions not only provided a new purpose for the German armed forces but also contributed to enhancing Germany's international reputation and was a prerequisite for Germany's chances to secure a permanent seat on the Security Council.[79]

Similar motivations and debates were at play in Japan. As the country became an economic powerhouse after World War II, the incongruity between its global economic status and global military status became a source of concern, both for some Japanese intellectuals and elected officials and for international observers. Many conservatives within Japan argued that the country had unwisely given up its right to defend itself and had too easily abandoned some of the "fundamental obligations of a nation-state."[80] As in Germany, the assumption was that any chance for a permanent seat in the Security Council depended on more active participation in multilateral efforts to maintain international peace and security. Many within Japan were also stung by international—especially U.S.—criticism during the first Gulf War that Japan, though it had contributed U.S. $13 billion to the effort, was engaged in "checkbook diplomacy" and unable or unwilling to make the larger sacrifices expected from "responsible members of the international community."[81]

The debate in Japan, as in Germany, was not entirely one-sided, with many people, including feminist activists, committed to the pacifist principles that had been enshrined in the constitution. At the same time, government officials hoped to be spared in the future from what had been a humiliating situation in the Gulf War. The resolution came with the 1992 Peacekeeping Operations Bill; it permitted Japan to deploy troops in missions sanctioned by the United Nations and which abided by the principles that had been established on early peacekeeping missions (a cease-fire, consent of the parties, firing weapons only in self-defense, and so on). Japan confirmed, in short, that it was a committed international actor prepared to live up to its responsibilities by pledging to send SDF troops on peacekeeping missions, which it did for the first time in Cambodia in 1992. Those within Japan opposed to its deployment of military forces were somewhat placated by the restrictions placed on foreign deployments, and that they would be conducted entirely under the UN flag. As one observer commented: "now that our military personnel are working in Cambodia, constructing roads, building bridges and monitoring ceasefires, the Japanese people are getting a much more accurate image of actual peacekeeping operations."[82] Critics of militarism could be reassured, in part, by the promise that peacekeeping entailed only the benign use of military force.

A similar promise was made in Argentina, where postauthoritarian governments from 1990 onward sought to find new roles for the Argentine military, a force with a long history of active participation in domestic affairs, as well as in the internal repression of its own citizenry.[83] Argentina's military dictatorship had been replaced in 1983, and by the end of the Cold War, democratically elected governments were making concerted efforts to redefine the role of the Argentine military from one whose primary focus had long been to confront "enemies" within its own and its neighbors' borders (most especially leftist movements of any sort) to one involved in UN-sanctioned international missions.

After years of brutal repression against anyone even suspected of association with leftist movements, Argentina's military regime mounted its largest international foray in 1982 in an attempt to bolster popular support for its regime. Instead, its disastrous campaign to retake the Falklands/Malvinas Islands from the British gained neither the islands nor popularity; it not only increased public hostility toward the regime but also created what Deborah Norden calls an "image of military incompetence."[84] However, even after the military regime gave up power, democratic governments that followed faced serious obstacles in demilitarizing Argentine society. After years of direct involvement in national politics, the military was a formidable force and resisted efforts to weaken it. This was true despite the fact that even by 1983, as Norden notes, "it was already difficult to argue that the military faced a significant internal threat."[85] So effective had the military's efforts been to destroy leftist guerrilla groups, there was nothing left to fight.

There was also nothing that the Argentine government could offer as a replacement, and a series of rebellions plagued the military through the 1980s, until 1990 when the government shifted its energies from weakening Argentina's armed forces to redirecting them into international activities such as peacekeeping. Argentina first deployed troops in the Gulf War and was subsequently actively involved in peacekeeping missions. Norden writes: "Such new definitions undeniably could not entirely fill the military's dance card, but they could at least give them a reason to be out on the floor."[86] Individual members of the armed forces benefited from opportunities to gain "professional experience" and training, earn higher wages, and enjoy opportunities for travel. Among the most important benefit reported by members of Argentina's armed forces was "the opportunity to practice their profession in a publicly accepted, and even lauded manner."[87] The Argentine government also hoped that involvement in peacekeeping missions could be leveraged into more influence internationally and, in particular, would bolster its relationship with the United States, which had been a goal of each of Argentina's postauthoritarian governments. Through active participation in peacekeeping, the government hoped to resolve the crisis of the Argentine military, its alienation within Argentine society, and the crisis of the Argentine state and its own alienation from the international community.

Peacekeeping thus is not only the raison d'être of some national militaries, it is also an important part of the "reconceptualization of past and present" that many countries engaged in throughout the post–Cold War period as part of a reconstitution of the national and political "self." Participation in peacekeeping missions was seen as a means to resuscitate the role and image of local armed forces and to assert claims to nationhood and international standing.[88] If the discursive practices surrounding peacekeeping contributor countries established them as "normal" nation-states that could live up to their international obligations, it also inevitably told us something about the countries in which peacekeeping missions were deployed.

Conflict-Prone Third World Countries

Throughout its history, peacekeeping missions have been established primarily in countries of the Middle East, Africa, Asia, and Latin America. The comparatively fewer European peacekeeping missions have been concentrated in the Balkans and in Cyprus; none have been deployed to North America or Western Europe. During the Cold War, seven of the thirteen missions mounted were deployed to the Middle East, a region, as David Malone and Karin Wermester note, "of clear geostrategic importance to key permanent members of the Security Council."[89] With the proliferation of missions in the post–Cold War era, "geostrategic" interests no longer played as significant a role, but a clear set of understandings have emerged about the countries to which these missions were deployed. Scholars and other observers of international relations anticipated a coming anarchy in many parts of the world, especially the global South, where the collapse of Cold War stabilities had been replaced with the rise of ethnic, religious, social, cultural, and linguistic rivalries; failed states; corruption; warlordism; and violence.[90] Only adding to this deadly mix was that, as one observer noted ominously, "many conflict-prone third world countries now have their own arms industries."[91]

The common trait of these "conflict-prone third world countries" is illiberalism: an absence of centralized, democratically elected governments, market economies, and the institutions associated with Western forms of governance. They are, in short, not "normal" states. As Samuel Makinda wrote of Somalia: "At the time of this writing, Somalia has no army, no police force, no civil service, no banking system and no schools or hospitals that function."[92] Instead, societies are riven by "clan-based fiefs and their marauding gunmen,"[93] factionalism,[94] ethnic and religious hostilities, a "new barbarism,"[95] and elites who rule through fear and rumor without ever contemplating consultation with their populations at large.[96] As UN

Secretary-General Kofi Annan observed of Africa: "The nature of political power in many African States . . . is a key source of conflict across the continent."[97] That power, he said, was one based on patronage and a communal sense of advantage once political institutions had been seized, only made worse by "insufficient accountability of leaders, lack of transparency in regimes, inadequate checks and balances, non-adherence to the rule of law, absence of peaceful means to change or replace leadership, or lack of respect for human rights."[98]

Countries engaged in protracted conflict thus are understood by what they lack: the institutions and norms of Western liberal market democracies. "They" are understood insofar as they are different from "us" and "we" can be reassured that the kinds of irrational barbarism currently defining "their" lives will never come to define "ours."[99] Once illiberalism has been established as the problem, the solution, if not altogether easy to accomplish, is at least easy to comprehend: the establishment of liberal market democracies. As Roxanne Lynn Doty writes, many of the North's encounters with the South have involved a process of negation in which various regions of the "third world" are constructed as "blank spaces" waiting to be filled in by the West: "Within these blank spaces the West may write such things as civilization, progress, modernization, and democracy."[100]

Post–Cold War peacekeeping missions, though they may differ in many respects, have sought to fill in the blank spaces of conflict-prone third world countries with (paraphrasing Secretary-General Kofi Annan): sufficient accountability of leaders, transparency in regimes, adequate checks and balances, adherence to the rule of law, the presence of peaceful means to change or replace leadership, and respect for human rights. In some cases, the barbarism of the new conflicts is so profound that even liberalism cannot help. Mark Duffield observes that depictions of the Rwandan genocide as a "spontaneous blood frenzy born of old ethnic hatreds," as opposed to a politically organized campaign with, in part, economic origins, contributed to international plans to disengage from Rwanda: "Not only was the situation beyond rational comprehension and effective control, but, since the Rwandese had brought it on themselves, they should be left to sort things out on their own."[101]

Where the UN is prepared to deploy and stay, the missions, according to Roland Paris, "represent an updated version of the *mission civilisatrice,* or the colonial-era notion that the 'advanced' states of Europe had a moral responsibility to 'civilise' the indigenous societies that they were colonising."[102] As noted above, the vast majority of post–Cold War peacekeeping missions have "promoted free and fair elections, the construction of democratic political institutions, respect for civil liberties and market-oriented economic reforms."[103] This has been true in countries as disparate as Namibia, Cambodia, El Salvador, East Timor, Nicaragua, Somalia, Mozambique,

Angola, the Democratic Republic of Congo, and Bosnia. Disparate, yet at base similar insofar as each lacks the same essential institutions, forms of governance, and modes of economic organization that are found in the West.

Paris sees such missions as "in effect an enormous experiment in social engineering—an experiment that involves transplanting Western models of social, political, and economic organization into war-shattered states in order to control civil conflict: in other words, pacification through political and economic liberalization."[104] The problem is that these projects have often failed. For an observer such as Paris, the problem is not the goal but the manner in which it has been implemented. The practices of peace-building and peacekeeping, for him, have "been considerably more charitable and consensual than the behaviour of many colonial powers,"[105] but the process has been conducted far too quickly. The UN and other organizations involved in peacekeeping and peace-building, he argues, assumed that countries emerging from civil war could be transformed into democracies and market economies in just a few years, "a transformation that took several centuries in the oldest European states."[106] For Paris, what peace-keepers and peace-builders need to recognize is that "political and economic liberalization is inherently tumultuous and disruptive" and that its implementation requires "strategic liberalization," which retains the goals of liberalism but implements them in a more controlled and gradual form.

The problem, however, may be more complicated than simply moving too fast. In many, if not most, cases, the architecture of economic liberalism does not address the relations of inequality that prevail in countries experiencing conflict, which, moreover, are themselves already fully implicated within the global political economy. As Mark Duffield argues, it is not just that liberalism does not exist within countries experiencing conflict; rather, it is the particular way in which liberal power is present in situations of conflict that must be examined. For him, countries experiencing conflict are already involved in a series of "strategic complexes" that enmesh non-governmental organizations (NGOs), governments, international financial institutions (IFIs), military actors, the business sector, international governmental organizations (IGOs), private security companies, and others.[107] Likewise, as Anne Orford writes, the assumption that the international community has somehow been absent, or inactive, in countries prior to the emergence of conflict ignores the ways in which it has in fact been quite active, often contributing to the conflict itself, for example through aid programs and structural adjustment packages.[108]

Thus, it is not a "lack" of market liberalism that is the issue in "conflict-prone third world countries"; rather, it is the manner in which market liberalism has been made manifest that is being challenged through peace operations. The case of the Democratic Republic of Congo (DRC) is illustrative here. A defining element of the current conflict in the DRC has been a clash over natural resources and the emergence of transborder trade and the extralegal extraction of those resources by "illegitimate" actors. In one of its numerous resolutions on the DRC, the United Nations makes clear where it stands, reiterating that "the natural resources of the Democratic Republic of the Congo should be exploited transparently, legally and on a fair commercial basis." The point, the Security Council promises, is that such exploitation will be for the "benefit the country and its people." The Security Council also invites, "in the interests of transparency, individuals, companies and States . . . to send their reactions, with due regard to commercial confidentiality."[109]

What Security Council resolutions concerning the DRC fail to problematize is whether multinational mining or lumber companies have the best interests of the people of the DRC at heart any more than do so-called illegitimate actors, a view widely discredited by critics of large resource-extraction enterprises around the world. Likewise, what the resolutions fail to consider is the extent to which linkages already exist between "illegitimate" political actors and "legitimate" actors such as multinational corporations (MNCs). As Duffield has argued, transborder trade and the parallel war economies that have been established as part of the "new" wars do not exist separately or in isolation of legitimate commercial and trading networks; rather, they work with them.[110]

Other critics suggest that peacekeeping and its associated practices, so eager to turn "them" into "us," have failed to understand some of the fundamental ways that liberal transformation will be resisted by the peoples in conflict-prone third world countries. Imposing a set of Western institutions onto societies that are organized quite differently may not be as "charitable" as commentators such as Paris like to think. Moreover, attempting to do so may ensure the failure of any attempts to lessen widespread political violence in these countries. The case of Somalia is illustrative here. Organized as it is through a clan-based structure, Somalia was easily identified as "a 'primitive' society in the eyes of the West."[111] If any society needed democratic market liberalism, apparently Somalia did, and the peacekeeping mission there would serve as a bridge "between 'anarchy in Somalia' and 'a liberal democratic state in Somalia,' no matter how subtle and complex the Somali society actually may be."[112]

The United Nations, and then the United States, discovered how subtle and complex Somali society was, at great cost to themselves and to Somalis. In two UN missions (United Nations Operation in Somalia I and II, UNOSOM I and II) and the U.S.-led UNITAF (Unified Task Force) mission, some twenty-five Pakistani peacekeepers were killed and another fifty-four wounded, and eighteen U.S. Rangers were killed with another seventy-five wounded. In an incident that would trigger what many observers now describe as the "Somalia syndrome" (the reluctance of troop-contributing countries to put their soldiers at risk in conflicts far from home), a number of the killed Americans' bodies were dragged through the streets of Mogadishu, set on fire, and otherwise mutilated. Casualties to Somalis, of course, were enormous throughout the period of these missions also, but no record was kept of those figures.[113]

Tamara Duffey writes that: "To assume that because the Somali society was engaged in a protracted, internecine conflict, mechanisms to mitigate and resolve conflict were non-existent is erroneous. Somalis' rich history of traditional mechanisms for dealing with inter-clan disputes makes them 'as experienced at peacemaking and conflict resolution as they are at making war.'"[114] Instead, the UN mission there focused on establishing hierarchical political structures and holding formal, and as Duffey notes, highly publicized and costly, peace conferences. Efforts to establish a set of political institutions that paralleled those found in the West were based on a fundamental misunderstanding of the Somali clan system and the decentralized form of traditional Somali political institutions, she argues. Rather than promote the maintenance of clan equilibrium and power-sharing—something that would have been congruent with and "spoken to" existing forms of political organization within Somalia—the UN insisted that a clan should hold the presidency, and the mission became involved in reconciling the leadership within what it viewed as the most powerful clan. This not only disrupted the balance of the traditional Somali kinship system, it endowed some warlords with a level of power and authority they did not legitimately possess.[115] Add to this basic fumbles (such as distributing written leaflets explaining the mission to an overwhelmingly oral population),[116] and the mission was widely and soundly discredited. By the time UNOSOM II finally withdrew in 1995, it had achieved practically none of its objectives.

Pierre Lizée develops a similar argument about the peacekeeping mission in Cambodia. Existing political factions in Cambodia were understood by the international community to be incapable of arriving at any form of institutional governing arrangement that all would recognize as legitimate. Instead, the Paris Peace Plan that put Cambodia's peacekeeping mission into motion envisioned a "free and fair" election that would bring to power a government that, because of the support it had received from the international community, would be recognized as legitimate both within Cambodia and without.[117] After the elections were successfully conducted, the government was formed not by the party that had won the election but by a coalition of the two most powerful factions within the country, the one that had won (the Royalist Party, or FUNCINPEC), and the one that had, to that point, ruled Cambodia but had lost the election (the Cambodian People's Party, or CPP). Government departments were distributed between the two factions, and factional infighting and power struggles continued until 1997 when the CPP mounted a coup, followed by a (suspect) election in 1998 where it won a decisive victory.[118]

For many Western observers, the outcome was astounding: How could the party that had won the election be convinced to share power with its chief rival? A rival that would eventually, and successfully, oust it from government? Lizée argues that the problem lay with the assumptions embedded in the Paris Peace Plan itself. Its proponents assumed that Western-style elections and Western-style democratic structures would channel conflict in ways that would produce "legitimate" and "authoritative" forms of government. But politics within Cambodia had always had a logic, even if it was one not based on Western norms. That logic derived from "political traditions based on deep-rooted networks of personal relationships, and love or fear of forceful leaders."[119] The attempt to impose a Western-based system onto Cambodia, in short, confronted the political legacies already in place in that society, legacies that continued to exert influence, and inform and shape the political landscape.

The "blank pages" that peacekeeping was intended to fill in were thus not always as blank as the United Nations and other Western actors would have liked. Paraphrasing François Debrix, some of the actors, in this case Somalis and Cambodians, preferred to "improvise and follow their own scripts."[120] Once illiberalism had been established as the problem, however, a series of responses to "conflict-prone third world countries" presented themselves, regardless of whether those responses were embraced or resisted by local peoples, and regardless of whether they made sense within particular local contexts. UN-led peacekeeping missions, informed by the goal of establishing liberal market democracies where there were none and relying on understandings of countries engaged in conflict as substantially illiberal, became one of the primary responses in the post–Cold War era, confirming both the need for such missions and the appropriateness of peacekeeping as the response. It was, in short, the only way to make conflict-prone third world countries "normal."

Conclusion

Former UN Secretary-General Boutros-Ghali's post–Cold War statement, "An Agenda for Peace," was an ultimately optimistic document.[121] In it, he celebrated "our restored possibilities"; nations large and small recognized that "an opportunity had been regained to achieve the great objectives of the Charter."[122] One of the techniques through which those objectives would be achieved, he wrote, was United Nations peacekeeping.

In actuality, UN peacekeeping serves numerous goals, many of which have very little to do with the international community's cooperative pursuit of international peace and security. Even from its beginnings, peacekeeping has been as much concerned with responding to crises *within* the

UN as with crises on the global stage. Peacekeeping has "made possible" certain nations and national militaries, in some cases providing militaries with a raison d'être where there had been none, in other cases serving as the vehicle through which discredited or entirely inactive militaries could be resuscitated effectively. Peacekeeping has also told us a great deal about the countries that require peacekeeping missions, in particular that they lack the requisite institutions (Western liberal democratic market institutions) that would channel conflict in peaceful means, and which peacekeeping—it is promised—can deliver.

Peacekeeping thus has been about much more than the missions themselves; it has been about the constitution of identities: those of particular militaries, of particular states, of the United Nations, and of those countries in need of peacekeeping's various, if suspect, promises. This does not mean, however, that the missions themselves should be ignored; they tell us much about what happens to the people in countries to which missions have been deployed. The following chapter will examine in detail the case of the United Nations mission to Cambodia, or UNTAC.

Notes

1. John J. Mearsheimer, "Why We Will Soon Miss the Cold War," *Atlantic Monthly,* August 1990, p. 35.

2. UN Report of the Secretary-General, "Supplement to An Agenda for Peace: Position Paper of the Secretary-General on the Occasion of the Fiftieth Anniversary of the United Nations," January 3, 1995, A/50/60–S/1995/1, paragraph 33.

3. See also Samuel P. Huntington, "The Clash of Civilizations? The Next Pattern of Conflict," *Foreign Affairs* 72, no. 3 (1993): 22–28; Robert Kaplan, "The Coming Anarchy," *Atlantic Monthly,* February 1994, pp. 44–76; and Benjamin J. Barber, *Jihad vs. McWorld* (New York: Ballantine Books, 1996). For a discussion about the role of peacekeeping in the "coming anarchy," see Alex Morrison and Dale Anderson, "Peacekeeping and the Coming Anarchy," Pearson Roundtable Series: Report no. 1 (Cornwallis Park, NS: Canadian Peacekeeping Press, 1996).

4. Mearsheimer, "Why We Will Soon Miss the Cold War," p. 35 and passim.

5. François Debrix, *Re-envisioning Peacekeeping: The United Nations and the Mobilization of Ideology* (Minneapolis: University of Minnesota Press, 1999), p. 54; UN Report of the Secretary-General, "An Agenda for Peace: Preventive Diplomacy, Peacemaking and Peace-keeping," January 31, 1992, A/47/277–S24/11, p. 11, paragraph 20 and passim [hereafter, "An Agenda for Peace"].

6. Michael G. Renner, "A Force for Peace," *World Watch,* July–August 1992, pp. 26–33.

7. Thomas G. Weiss, "Overcoming the Somalia Syndrome—'Operation Rekindle Hope?'" *Global Governance* 1 (1995): 171–187.

8. Viberto Selochan and Carlyle A. Thayer, *Bringing Democracy to Cambodia* (Canberra: Australian Defence Studies Center, 1996).

9. Roland Paris, "International Peacebuilding and the '*Mission Civilatrice,*'" *Review of International Studies* 28 (2002): 637–656.

10. Fen Osler Hampson, *Madness in the Multitude: Human Security and World Disorder* (Don Mills: Oxford University Press, 2002), p. 1.

11. Whereas civilians constituted 5 percent of all casualties in World War I, and 50 percent in World War II, they constituted 90 percent of those killed in armed conflicts during the 1990s. Simon Chesterman, "Introduction: Global Norms, Local Contexts," in Simon Chesterman (ed.), *Civilians in War* (Boulder: Lynne Rienner, 2001), p. 2. The idea of "new wars" is drawn from Mark Duffield, *Global Governance and the New Wars: The Merging of Development and Security* (London: Zed Books, 2001).

12. A. B. Fetherston *Towards a Theory of United Nations Peacekeeping* (Basingstoke, UK: Macmillan, 1994), p. 23 and Chap. 2 passim.

13. Major-General Lewis MacKenzie, *Peacekeeper: The Road to Sarajevo* (Vancouver: Douglas and McIntyre, 1993), p. 330. As Ruth Wedgwood notes, the UN "was never set up to be a military command center. It has gained operational capacity very slowly." In the mid-1990s it established a twenty-four-hour situation room but still lacked real-time intelligence and even satellite telephones to communicate straight to the field. Ruth Wedgwood, "The Evolution of United Nations Peacekeeping," *Cornell International Law Journal* 28 (1995): 637.

14. This characterization is paraphrased directly from Peter Nyers's analyses of formal responses to refugees in "Emergency or Emerging Identities? Refugees and Transformations in World Order," *Millennium: Journal of International Studies* 29, no. 1 (1999): 15.

15. I make this argument in Sandra Whitworth, "Where is the Politics in Peacekeeping?" *International Journal* 50, no. 2 (spring 1995): 427–435. For a small sample of this literature, see Fetherston, *Towards a Theory of United Nations Peacekeeping* (in contrast to Fetherston's later, more critical, work); Mats R. Berdal, "Whither UN Peacekeeping?" Adelphi Paper no. 281, October 1993; Alan James, "Peacekeeping in the Post–Cold War Era," *International Journal* 50, no. 2 (spring 1995): 241–265; Michael Doyle, Ian Johnstone, and Robert C. Orr (eds.), *Keeping the Peace: Multidimensional UN Operations in Cambodia and El Salvador* (Cambridge: Cambridge University Press, 1997); John Roper, Masashi Nishihara, Olara A. Otunnu, and Enid C. B. Schoettle, *Keeping the Peace in the Post–Cold War Era: Strengthening Multilateral Peacekeeping,* report to the Trilateral Commission, no. 43 (New York, 1993); Paul F. Diehl, *International Peacekeeping* (Baltimore: Johns Hopkins University Press, 1994); Chetan Kumar, *Building Peace in Haiti* (Boulder: Lynne Rienner, 1998); and Jarat Chopra (ed.), *The Politics of Peace Maintenance* (Boulder: Lynne Rienner, 1998). Roland Paris also critiques the pragmatic and almost exclusively policy-relevant focus of peacekeeping literature in "Broadening the Study of Peace Operations," *International Studies Review* 2, no. 3 (December 2000): 27–44.

16. United Nations, "Report of the Panel on United Nations Peace Operations," August 21, 2000, A/55/305–S/2000/809. This report became more popularly known as "The Brahimi Report," after the panel's chair, Lakhdar Brahimi.

17. David Campbell speaks to this issue regarding the Gulf War in *Politics Without Principle: Sovereignty, Ethics and the Narratives of the Gulf War* (Boulder: Lynne Rienner, 1993), pp. 14–17. See also Paul Knox, "Peacebuilding Concept Imperilled, Conference Told," *Globe and Mail,* March 21, 1997, p. A12, which describes the reaction at an academic conference to a paper delivered by Laura Neack ("Peacekeeping's New Dark Age," presented at the International Studies Association Annual Meetings, Toronto, March 18–22, 1997). Neack pointed out that "local citizens generally see peacekeeping troops as useless or worse, with some

accusing them of fostering the spread of prostitution." She was criticized for overlooking the fact that "for all their flaws, UN peacekeepers have saved lives and kept some ceasefires intact." She was told, in short, that raising critical questions about peacekeeping potentially undermines peacekeeping's many positive accomplishments.

18. Elizabeth Allen Dauphinee, "You Can't Get There from Here: The Political Economy of Peace Operations," presented at the Canadian Political Science Association Annual Meetings, Toronto, May 29 2002, p. 6.

19. Debrix, *Re-envisioning Peacekeeping*, p. 17.

20. Ibid., pp. 29–30; see also Roland Paris, "Peacebuilding and the Limits of Liberal Internationalism," *International Security* 22, no. 2 (fall 1997): 54–89.

21. Roxanne Lynn Doty, *Imperial Encounters: The Politics of Representation in North-South Relations* (Minneapolis: University of Minnesota Press, 1996), p. 125. It is important to underline that neither Doty nor the application of her work here is intended to suggest an essentialized Western "self," but one that is constituted in a variety of ways through numerous discursive and other practices.

22. Robert W. Cox, "Social Forces, States and World Orders: Beyond International Relations Theory (1981)," in Robert W. Cox with Timothy J. Sinclair, *Approaches to World Order* (Cambridge: Cambridge University Press, 1996), pp. 88–89.

23. For a fuller elaboration of this argument, see Mark Neufeld, *The Restructuring of International Relations Theory* (Cambridge: Cambridge University Press, 1995), Chap. 5.

24. Ibid. See also Max Horkheimer, "Traditional and Critical Theory," in *Critical Theory: Selected Essays* (New York: Continuum, 1982); Michael Shapiro, *Language and Political Understanding: The Politics of Discursive Practices* (New Haven: Yale University Press, 1981), Chap. 1; and Jim George, *Discourses of Global Politics: A Critical (Re)introduction to International Relations* (Boulder: Lynne Rienner, 1994), Chap. 1.

25. See, for example, Neufeld, *The Restructuring of International Relations Theory.*

26. See, for example, Cynthia Enloe, *Bananas, Beaches, and Bases: Making Feminist Sense of International Politics* (Berkeley: University of California Press, 1990).

27. See, for example, Campbell, *Politics Without Principle.*

28. Friedrich Kratochwil, "The Monologue of 'Science,'" *International Studies Review* 5, no. 1 (March 2003): 124.

29. Benedict Anderson, *Imagined Communities: Reflections on the Origin and Spread of Nationalism,* rev. ed. (London: Verso, 1991), p. 6.

30. This is not to suggest that imagined communities are homogeneous. See, for example Partha Chatterjee, "Whose Imagined Community?" in Gopal Balakrishnan (ed.), *Mapping the Nation* (London: Verso, 1996), pp. 214–225.

31. Anderson, *Imagined Communities,* p. 6.

32. See, for example, Cynthia Enloe, *Maneuvers: The International Politics of Militarizing Women's Lives* (Berkeley: University of California Press, 2000), and Nira Yuval-Davis, *Gender and Nation* (London: Sage, 1997).

33. Caroline O. N. Moser and Fiona C. Clark, "Introduction," in *Victims, Perpetrators, or Actors? Gender, Armed Conflict, and Political Violence* (London: Zed Books, 2001), p. 4. See the rest of this collection, as well as Meredith Turshen and Clotilde Twagiramariya (eds.), *What Women Do in Wartime: Gender and Conflict in Africa* (London: Zed Books, 1998); Wenona Giles, Malathi de Alwis, Edith Klein,

and Neluka Silva (eds.), *Feminists Under Fire: Exchanges Across War Zones* (Toronto: Between the Lines, 2003); and Susie Jacobs, Ruth Jacobson, and Jennifer Marchbank (eds.), *States of Conflict: Gender, Violence, and Resistance* (London: Zed Books, 2000).

34. See also UN Secretary-General Study, *Women, Peace and Security* (New York: United Nations, 2002), esp. Chaps. 2, 4, and 7; Sanam Anderlini, *Women at the Peace Table: Making a Difference* (New York: UN Development Fund for Women, 2000); Kvinna till Kvinna, *Engendering the Peace Process: A Gender Approach to Dayton—and Beyond* (Stockholm: Kvinna till Kvinna Foundation, 2000); Dyan Mazurana, Susan McKay, Khristopher Carlson, and Janel Kasper, "Girls in Fighting Forces: Their Recruitment, Participation, Demobilization, and Reintegration," *Peace and Conflict* 8, no. 2 (2002): 97–123.

35. Edward Said, *Orientalism* (New York: Vintage Books, 1978), Introduction and passim; Geeta Chowdhry and Sheila Nair, "Introduction: Power in a Postcolonial World: Race, Gender, and Class in International Relations," in Geeta Chowdhry and Sheila Nair (eds.), *Power, Postcolonialism, and International Relations: Reading Race, Gender, and Class* (London: Routledge, 2002), p. 12 and passim; Anne Orford, *Reading Humanitarian Intervention: Human Rights and the Use of Force in International Law* (Cambridge: Cambridge University Press, 2003), pp. 47–51 and passim.

36. A. B. Fetherston, "Peacekeeping, Conflict Resolution, and Peacebuilding: A Reconsideration of Theoretical Frameworks," *International Peacekeeping* 7, no. 1 (spring 2000): 190.

37. Doty, *Imperial Encounters,* p. 5.

38. "An Agenda for Peace," p. 28, paragraph 46.

39. Thomas G. Weiss, *Military-Civilian Interactions: Intervening in Humanitarian Crises* (Lanham, MD: Rowman and Littlefield, 1999), p. 13.

40. Fetherston, *Towards a Theory of United Nations Peacekeeping,* p. 12.

41. Jocelyn Coulon, *Soldiers of Diplomacy: The United Nations, Peacekeeping, and the New World Order* (Toronto: University of Toronto Press, 1998), pp. 19–20; "Dag Hammarskjöld: The UN Years, 1956," available at www.un.org/Depts/dhl/dag/time1956.htm; "1956: Suez and the End of Empire," *Guardian Unlimited Politics: Special Reports,* March 14, 2001, available at http://politics.guardian.co.uk/politicspast/story/0,9061,451936,00.html; Robert Fisk, "New Crises, Old Lessons," *The Independent,* January 15, 2003, available at http://news.independent.co.uk/world/politics/story.jsp?story=368408.

42. Coulon, *Soldiers of Diplomacy,* pp. 20–25.

43. Fetherston, *Towards a Theory of United Nations Peacekeeping,* pp. 12–13; see also Coulon, *Soldiers of Diplomacy,* Chap. 2.

44. This, despite the fact that on the first evening of its deployment, UNEF I troops sprayed a minaret with machine-gun fire—UN soldiers having confused the call to prayer as a call to civil disorder. Brian Urquhart, *A Life in Peace and War* (New York: Harper and Row, 1987), p. 136, cited in Robert A. Rubinstein, "Cultural Aspects of Peacekeeping: Notes on the Substance of Symbols," *Millennium: Journal of International Studies* 22, no. 3 (1993): 547.

45. Fetherston, *Towards a Theory of United Nations Peacekeeping,* p. 13; Coulon, *Soldiers of Diplomacy,* p. 25. Other principles established through UNEF I, according to Fetherston, included the principle of voluntary contributions of contingents from small, neutral (not great power) countries to participate as peacekeepers and the principle of day-to-day control of the operations by the Secretary-General.

46. "1956: Suez and the End of Empire."

47. Coulon, *Soldiers of Diplomacy,* p. 18; Martin Gilbert, *A History of the Twentieth Century,* vol. 3: *1952–1999* (New York: William Morrow, 1999), p. 115.

48. Ibid.

49. Fisk, "New Crises, Old Lessons."

50. In a similar vein, Mark Neufeld argues that "from the beginning the principal function of peacekeeping has been to contribute to the maintenance of order and stability within the hegemonic sphere"; Mark Neufeld, "Hegemony and Foreign Policy Analysis: The Case of Canada as Middle Power," *Studies in Political Economy* 48 (autumn 1995): 27, n. 31.

51. Fetherston, *Towards a Theory of United Nations Peacekeeping,* pp. 13–14. See also Norrie MacQueen, *United Nations Peacekeeping in Africa Since 1960* (London: Pearson Education, 2002), Chap. 2.

52. Fetherston, *Towards a Theory of United Nations Peacekeeping,* p. 15.

53. Since 1962, all peacekeeping missions have been authorized through a Security Council resolution. Prior to 1962, missions were authorized in different ways, sometimes General Assembly resolutions, in other cases through UN committees established by a Security Council resolution, as well as through Security Council resolutions. See Claus Heje, "United Nations Peacekeeping—An Introduction," in Edward Moxon-Browne (ed.), *A Future for Peacekeeping?* (Basingstoke, UK: Macmillan, 1998), p. 5.

54. Fetherston, *Towards a Theory of United Nations Peacekeeping,* p. 37. Paul Diehl notes that although clear mandates are helpful, in some controversial situations, operations would never have received Security Council authorization without a vague mandate (Diehl, *International Peacekeeping,* p. 75).

55. See, for example, Security Council Resolution 47, April 21, 1948, which established the UN Commission for India and Pakistan (UNCIP), which in turn established the UN Military Observer Group in India and Pakistan (UNMOGIP); Security Council Resolution 145, July 22, 1960, part of a series of resolutions that established ONUC; Security Council Resolution 186, March 4, 1964, which established the UN Peacekeeping Force in Cyprus (UNFICYP); Security Council Resolution 743, February 21, 1992, which established the UN Protection Force (UNPROFOR) in the former Yugoslavia; Security Council Resolution 1279, November 30, 1999, which established the UN Organization Mission in the Democratic Republic of Congo (MONUC); and Security Council Resolution 1244, June 10, 1999, which established the UN Mission in Kosovo.

56. See, for example, Security Council Resolution 690, April 29, 1991, on the Western Sahara, and Security Council Resolution 717, October 16, 1991, on Cambodia.

57. Security Council Resolution 145, July 22, 1960.

58. Security Council Resolution 186, March 4, 1964.

59. See, for example, Security Council Resolution 1244, June 10, 1999, which established the UN Mission in Kosovo (UNMIK), paragraph 11; Security Council Resolution 1246, June 11, 1999, which established the UN Mission in East Timor (UNAMET), paragraph 4; and Security Council Resolution 717, October 16, 1991, on Cambodia.

60. See, for example, Security Council Resolution 912, April 21, 1994. See also Orford, *Reading Humanitarian Intervention,* p. 101.

61. Roméo Dallaire, *Shake Hands with the Devil: The Failure of Humanity in Rwanda* (Toronto: Random House Canada, 2003), p. 220.

62. Samantha Power, *"A Problem from Hell"*: *America and the Age of Genocide* (New York: Basic Books, 2002), p. 353. See also Orford, *Reading Humanitarian Intervention*, pp. 198–199.

63. Preface to *An Introduction to United Nations Peacekeeping*, from the United Nations Department of Peacekeeping Operations website, available at www. un.org/Depts/dpko/intro/index.htm.

64. David M. Malone and Karin Wermester, "Boom and Bust? The Changing Nature of UN Peacekeeping," *International Peacekeeping* 7, no. 3 (autumn 2000): 38.

65. Alan Bullion, "India and UN Peacekeeping," in Edward Moxon-Browne (ed.), *A Future for Peacekeeping?* (Basingstoke, UK: Macmillan, 1998), pp. 64–65. The direct financial benefits of peacekeeping suffer from the UN financial crisis, with some troop-contributing countries waiting years to be reimbursed by the United Nations. See Eric G. Berman and Katie E. Sams, *Peacekeeping in Africa: Capabilities and Culpabilities* (Geneva: UN Institute for Disarmament Research, 2000), p. 255.

66. Karen A. Mingst, "Developing States as Peacekeepers: A Comparative Perspective," presented at the International Studies Association Annual Meetings, Toronto, March 18–22, 1997, p. 7.

67. MacKenzie, *Peacekeeper*, p. 97.

68. Ray Murphy, "Contributors to Peacekeeping, Seasoned and Hesitant—The Case of Ireland," presented at the International Studies Association Annual Meetings, Washington, DC, March 28–April 1, 1994, p. 5.

69. P. Keatinge, *A Singular Stance—Irish Neutrality in the 1980s* (Dublin: Institute of Public Administration, 1984), p. 93, cited in ibid., p. 5.

70. Stefan Dudink, "The Unheroic Men of a Moral Nation: Masculinity and Nation in Modern Dutch History," in Cynthia Cockburn and Dubravka Zarkov (eds.), *The Postwar Moment: Militaries, Masculinities, and International Peacekeeping* (London: Lawrence and Wishart, 2002), p. 153.

71. See E. J. Hobsbawm, *Nations and Nationalism Since 1789: Programme, Myth, Reality* (Cambridge: Cambridge University Press, 1990), p. 89. As Benedict Anderson observes, the nation is "imagined as a *community*, because regardless of the actual inequality and exploitation that may prevail in each, the nation is always conceived as a deep, horizontal comradeship. Ultimately it is this fraternity that makes it possible, over the past two centuries, for so many millions of people, not so much to kill, as willingly to die for such limited imaginings" (Anderson, *Imagined Communities*, p. 7).

72. Maria Cook, "Bloomberg Blames Canada," *Ottawa Citizen*, August 15, 2003, p. A11.

73. Mingst, "Developing States as Peacekeepers," p. 4.

74. Ramesh Thakur, "Ministate and Macro-cooperation: Fiji's Peacekeeping Debut in Lebanon," *Review of International Studies* 19 (1984), cited in ibid., p. 5

75. Some of the "seasoned veterans" of peacekeeping, such as Canada and Ireland, in turn quickly moved to establish themselves as "trainers" of the new peacekeeping countries: Canada established the Pearson Peacekeeping Centre and Ireland established the United Nations Training School, both of which offered peacekeeping training courses to their own and foreign officers. See Alex Morrison and Suzanne M. Plain, "Canada: The Seasoned Veteran," presented at the International Studies Association Annual Meetings, Washington, DC, March 28–April 1, 1994, p. 1 and passim; and Oliver A. K. Macdonald, "Recent Developments in Peacekeeping— The Irish Military Experience," in Moxon-Browne, *A Future for Peacekeeping?* p. 47.

76. Laura Hein and Mark Selden, "Learning Citizenship from the Past: Textbook Nationalism, Global Context, and Social Change," *Bulletin of Concerned Asian Scholars* 30, no. 2 (1998): 5.

77. Takao Takahara, "Japan," in Trevor Findlay (ed.), *Challenges for the New Peacekeepers* (Oxford: Oxford University Press, 1996), pp. 53–55; Albrecht Schnabel, "An Agenda for Peace or An Agenda for Power? Russian and German Stakes in International Peacekeeping," presented at the Annual Meeting of the Northeastern Political Science Association, Providence, RI, November 10–12, 1994, p. 8.

78. Schnabel, "An Agenda for Peace or An Agenda for Power?" p. 11. See also Karen A. Mingst, "Why Co-operate? The New Peacekeepers—Japan and Germany," presented at the International Studies Association Annual Meetings, Minneapolis, March 1998, p. 4.

79. Ibid., pp. 11–12.

80. Kenneth B. Pyle, *The Japanese Question: Power and Purpose in a New Era* (Washington, DC: American Enterprise Institute Press, 1992), p. 128.

81. Hisashi Owada, "A Japanese Perspective on Peacekeeping," in Daniel Warner (ed.), *New Dimensions of Peacekeeping* (Dordrecht: Martinus Nijhoff, 1995), p. 107; Tsuneo Akaha, "Japan's Security Policy in the Posthegemonic World: Opportunities and Challenges," in Tsuneo Akaha and Frank Langdon (eds.), *Japan in the Posthegemonic World* (Boulder: Lynne Rienner, 1993), p. 102; Masaru Tamamoto, "The Ideology of Nothingness: A Meditation on Japanese National Identity," *World Policy Journal* 11, no. 1 (spring 1994): 89–90; Richard D. Leitch Jr., Akira Kato, and Martin E. Weinstein, *Japan's Role in the Post–Cold War World* (Westport, CT: Greenwood, 1995), p. 45. See also Mutsuyoshi Nishimura, "A Japanese Perspective on Peacekeeping—Japan's International Activities: The Road Behind; The Road Ahead," in Alex Morrison, Ken Eyre, and Roger Chiasson (eds.), *Facing the Future: Proceedings of the 1996 Canada-Japan Seminar on Modern Peacekeeping* (Cornwallis, NS: Canadian Peacekeeping Press, 1997), pp. 71–75; and Anthony McDermott, "Japan's Financial Contribution to the UN System: In Pursuit of Acceptance and Standing," *International Peacekeeping* 6, no. 2 (summer 1999): 64–88.

82. Jiro Hagi, "Japan and Peacekeeping: Starting from Zero," in Alex Morrison (ed.), *The Changing Face of Peacekeeping* (Toronto: Canadian Institute of Strategic Studies, 1993), p. 59.

83. This account is drawn primarily from Deborah L. Norden, "Keeping the Peace, Outside and In: Argentina's UN Missions," *International Peacekeeping* 2, no. 3 (autumn 1995): 330–349.

84. Ibid., p. 334.

85. Ibid., p. 335.

86. Ibid., p. 336.

87. Ibid., p. 341.

88. Laura Neack makes similar claims about peacekeeping but does so from a different perspective than is suggested here. In "UN Peace-keeping: In the Interest of Community or Self?" *Journal of Peace Research* 32, no. 2 (1995): 181–196, Neack explores, from a realist perspective, the ways in which states participate in peacekeeping to serve their own national self-interest.

89. Malone and Wermester, "Boom and Bust?," p. 38.

90. See also "An Agenda for Peace," p. 6, paragraph 11.

91. John Q. Blodgett, "The Future of UN Peacekeeping," *Washington Quarterly* 14, no. 1 (winter 1991): 210.

92. Samuel M. Makinda, *Seeking Peace from Chaos: Humanitarian Intervention in Somalia* (Boulder: Lynne Rienner, 1993), p. 11.

93. Ibid.

94. Pierre Lizée, *Peace, Power, and Resistance in Cambodia: Global Governance and the Failure of International Conflict Resolution* (Basingstoke, UK: Macmillan, 2000), p. 31 and Chap. 2 passim. Lizée's work is a critique of UN understandings that see factionalism as the only defining feature of Cambodian politics.

95. Duffield, *Global Governance and the New Wars,* pp. 109–113. Duffield too is using this term critically.

96. Kumar, *Building Peace in Haiti,* p. 35.

97. UN Report of the Secretary-General, "The Causes of Conflict and the Promotion of Durable Peace and Sustainable Development in Africa," April 13, 1998, A/52/871–S/1998/318, p. 5, paragraph 12.

98. Ibid. In some cases observers suggest that the people of these countries themselves are inherently violent, but it is primarily the absence of appropriate political structures that allows that violence to flourish. Andrew S. Natsios described the Somali people, for example, as "by instinct a remarkably ethnocentric culture" with deep-seated folklore and traditions that promote and perpetuate antagonism. Andrew S. Natsios, "Food Through Force: Humanitarian Intervention and U.S. Policy," *Washington Quarterly* 17 no. 1 (1993): 136, cited in Clement E. Adibe, "Learning from the Failure of Disarmament and Conflict Resolution in Somalia," in Moxon-Browne, *A Future for Peacekeeping?* p. 119.

99. The former commander of the UN mission to Yugoslavia, Major-General Lewis MacKenzie, captures this sentiment well, if in an indirect way, when he describes working together with Yugoslav soldiers in the latter years of the UNEF I mission and how surprising it was to imagine that in thirty years he would be deployed to a mission in Yugoslavia: "The Yugoslavians, incidentally, were tough soldiers and good athletes. If one of them had predicted that three decades later I would be serving in his country in the midst of a bloody civil war, I'd have thought he was joking." MacKenzie, *Peacekeeper: The Road to Sarajevo,* p. 23. As Anne Orford writes, humanitarian intervention narratives work "to reassure the 'international community' that there is a differentiated other, and to locate this other 'somewhere else, outside'" (Orford, *Reading Humanitarian Intervention,* p. 124 and Chap. 3 passim).

100. Doty, *Imperial Encounters,* p. 11.

101. Duffield, *Global Governance and the New Wars,* p. 111.

102. Paris, "International Peacebuilding," p. 650. For a more critical reading of the "heroic purpose" of humanitarian interventions than Paris offers, see Orford, *Reading Humanitarian Intervention.*

103. Paris, "Peacebuilding and the Limits of Liberal Internationalism," p. 63.

104. Ibid., p. 56.

105. Paris, "International Peacebuilding," p. 653.

106. Paris, "Peacebuilding and the Limits of Liberal Internationalism," p. 78.

107. Duffield, *Global Governance and the New Wars,* p. 12.

108. Orford, *Reading Humanitarian Intervention,* in particular, Chap. 3, which examines the impact of structural adjustment policies on conflict in the former Yugoslavia and aid programs as contributing factors to the Rwandan genocide.

109. Security Council Resolution 1457, January 24, 2003, paragraphs 4 and 11.

110. Mark Duffield, "Globalization, Transborder Trade, and War Economies," in Mats Berdal and David Malone (eds.), *Greed and Grievance: Economic Agendas in Civil Wars* (Boulder: Lynne Rienner, 2000), pp. 84–87.

111. Debrix, *Re-envisioning Peacekeeping,* p. 109.

112. Ibid., p. 110.

113. Anne Orford discusses the "erasure" of violence done in the name of humanitarian intervention through a refusal to track casualties inflicted on local populations (Orford, *Reading Humanitarian Intervention*, pp. 190–191).

114. Tamara Duffey, "Cultural Issues in Contemporary Peacekeeping," *International Peacekeeping* 7, no. 1 (spring 2000): 160; quote is from Mark Bradbury, *The Somali Conflict: Prospects for Peace* (Oxford: Oxfam, 1994), p. 6. For a more detailed account of the UN Mission to Somalia, see Chapter 4 of this volume.

115. Duffey, "Cultural Issues in Contemporary Peacekeeping," pp. 158, 160.

116. The first leaflets dropped on Somalia at the beginning of the mission read: "slave nations have come to help you." Apparently a translation error confused the United Nations with "slave nations" (ibid., p. 160).

117. Lizée, *Peace, Power, and Resistance in Cambodia*, p. 10.

118. Ibid., Chaps. 1 and 10, passim.

119. Jacques Bekaert, interview by Pierre Lizée, cited in ibid., p. 107.

120. Debrix, *Re-envisioning Peacekeeping*, p. 100.

121. Ibid., p. 54.

122. "An Agenda for Peace," p. 45, paragraphs 76–77; p. 1, paragraph 3.

3

When the UN "Succeeds":
The Case of Cambodia

Cambodia demonstrates what the international community can accomplish when the collective will of the major powers acts in concert for the larger good.

—Stephen J. Randall[1]

When the United Nations launched the UN Transitional Authority in Cambodia (UNTAC) in 1991, Chea Veth[2] returned to her home country after more than two decades away. Chea was a member of Cambodia's former elite and had left the country long before the U.S. bombings of the 1970s and the subsequent Khmer Rouge atrocities that would leave her homeland with the infamous moniker of "the killing fields." But when the UN went to Cambodia in the early 1990s to broker a peace agreement, Chea decided it was time to return in order to lend a hand. In her Phnom Penh neighborhood she not only carried the privilege of her background but was known to be well connected with the UN mission, and her facility with a variety of languages meant that she was sometimes called upon by neighbors who needed assistance in dealing with UNTAC officials and personnel. When a local woman whose daughter had been employed as a cook and cleaner by a number of men working as part of UNTAC asked for help in finding out why her daughter had suddenly quit her job and was not acting at all "like herself," Chea probably already had a good idea about what might be causing the unusual behavior. Likely, so too did the mother.

The neighbor's daughter eventually revealed to Chea that her employers had demanded she have sex with them and that when she resisted, they had raped her. The young woman was unable to tell anyone of her ordeal: the men who assaulted her ensured her silence—and compounded her sense of shame—by telling her repeatedly that she should have known from the beginning what was expected of her, that they had hired her to prostitute herself. A job she had felt fortunate to get, and through which she had proudly contributed to her family's income, had turned into a nightmare. As Chea described it: "I was not entirely surprised; we had all heard the stories by that point. I went with her to the UNTAC authorities, but the things that had happened to her had happened weeks before. UNTAC said there was no evidence, to go home, that we had waited too long to make our complaint. By the end of the mission, I knew directly of at least three other such complaints and heard of many more. We were so busy; we were trying to make the election happen. Maybe we should have tried to follow up on issues like this more than we did, but there were so many things happening and it was such a busy time."[3]

One of the first multilevel peacekeeping missions conducted by the United Nations in the post–Cold War period, the eighteen-month mission to Cambodia was considered something of a test case for the UN, insofar as its success or failure would have important implications for future large-scale missions.[4] Most observers cite a series of "lessons learned" that emerged from the mission, but by and large it is regarded as a success story for the UN.[5] Long-time Cambodia watcher William Shawcross, speaking at the general assembly of the International NGO Forum on Cambodia called it an "international triumph."[6] Lieutenant General J. M. Sanderson, the UNTAC force commander, said it "was unequivocally a success."[7] Then–UN Secretary General Boutros Boutros-Ghali wrote that UNTAC "set a new standard for peace-keeping operations."[8]

From a feminist or critical perspective, one of the tests of UNTAC would be to discover whether the thousands of young men deployed as soldiers on this mission would act any differently than soldiers deployed into more traditional forms of combat. Would wearing a blue helmet make a difference? The accounts of the mission given by the UN and mainstream observers seldom reported the enormous social dislocation that resulted from the deployment of 23,000 foreign personnel—some 17,000 of whom were soldiers—into a relatively fragile, conflict-weary society. That dislocation included skyrocketing inflation, the explosion of prostitution to service UNTAC personnel, and the exponential increase of HIV/AIDS in Cambodia, as well as charges of assault and harassment directed at UNTAC by both expatriate and local citizens.[9] Even as early supporters of the mission began to question UNTAC's effectiveness—especially after the 1997 coup mounted by Second Prime Minister Hun Sen—that questioning rarely included a consideration of the mission's impact on local people's sense of security, particularly on women's sense of security.[10]

This chapter explores the background to UNTAC and the mission itself. Far from "setting a new standard" for peacekeeping operations as Boutros-Ghali so enthusiastically proclaimed, soldiers deployed on this mission—along with their military and political leaders—were operating on the same assumptions about women, and "about the roles women must play if a male soldier is to be able to do his job,"[11] as soldiers deployed on more traditional military missions have operated on throughout history. Those assumptions include the expectation that prostitutes will be available to service male soldiers; that it is appropriate to pursue local women, whether prostitutes or not; and that a certain level of violence, both physical and sexual, directed toward the local population is part and parcel of any military operation. Those assumptions seriously undermine any real sense of security and lay bare the far too optimistic conclusions that the UN and its supporters drew about this mission. As Cynthia Enloe puts it, "Everyone who sends troops needs to rethink what kind of soldiering works to keep the peace. Because a peace that involves sexual exploitation and sexual violence is no peace at all."[12]

Background to the UNTAC Mission

The mission to Cambodia was unique not only because it was one of the first large-scale post–Cold War peacekeeping missions but also because it sought to address one of the first Cold War conflicts to unravel along with the Soviet Union itself.[13] As Grant Curtis observes, a configuration of events came together in the late 1980s that helped to facilitate the eventual October 1991 signing in Paris of the Agreements on a Comprehensive Political Settlement of the Cambodia Conflict, or the Paris peace agreements. These included the withdrawal of Soviet economic assistance from former client states, an increased international concern for human rights after the Chinese government massacre of student demonstrators in Tiananmen Square, and a growing economic interest in the region, by both Western and Asian investors.[14]

The previous twenty years had been difficult for Cambodians. In 1970 a military coup ousted from power the popular, but often erratic, Prince Norodom Sihanouk. His successor, General Lon Nol, was supported by the United States, and Lon Nol, in turn, aided his U.S. allies by engaging with Vietnamese troops both inside and outside Cambodian borders. According to David Chandler, "President Nixon, with no intended irony, announced that 'Cambodia is the Nixon doctrine in its purest form'—meaning that Cambodians, rather than Americans, were the ones who were being killed."[15] Along with the overwhelming and largely covert bombing of Cambodian targets by the United States, an estimated half million Cambodians, mostly noncombatants, lost their lives between 1970 and 1975, and many more were turned into internal refugees.[16]

The mayhem caused by the undeclared U.S. war in Cambodia set the stage for the Angkor Revolution—the overthrow of the Cambodian state, and indeed of all Cambodian society, by the Khmer Rouge beginning in 1975. The Khmer Rouge revolution, no doubt the most notorious period of Cambodia's recent past, was motivated out of an ideal to create an "egalitarian, communitarian society"[17] that would be "free from the injustice and influence of western, colonialist, imperialist outsiders."[18] Instead, the era of "Democratic Kampuchea" was quite simply catastrophic, by almost any measure. The Khmer Rouge left an estimated one and a half to two million Cambodians dead, out of a total population of only six or seven million.[19] People were executed, tortured, or died of disease, exhaustion, and malnutrition. Intellectuals, artists, professionals, and religious leaders were targeted in particular, but so too was anyone who resisted the Khmer Rouge's attempts to transform Cambodian society. People throughout Cambodia were displaced, the capital of Phnom Penh was emptied, and city-dwellers throughout the country were moved to the provinces to engage in agricultural labor. Rural people were shifted to different areas of the country to work in labor camps; families were separated; adolescents often worked in mobile work parties; and women and men were forced into arranged marriages.

When the Vietnamese government invaded Cambodia in 1978 to topple the Khmer Rouge, it may have brought an end to the genocide, but it did not bring an end to conflict in Cambodia. For the next decade, four factions engaged in a civil war within Cambodia: the Vietnamese-backed Heng Samrin–Hun Sen regime, or the Cambodian People's Party (CPP, which because it held power, would later also be called the State of Cambodia, or SOC); the royalist party, FUNCINPEC (the National United Front for an Independent, Neutral, Peaceful and Co-operative Cambodia, led by the former ruler Prince Norodom Sihanouk); the Khmer People's National Liberation Front (KPNLF); and the Khmer Rouge (the Party of Democratic Kampuchea, or PDK). The Hun Sen regime, which served as the government within Cambodia throughout the 1980s, was supported by both Vietnam and the Soviet Union. The other three factions waged a largely guerrilla war and received support from the West, China, and the Association of Southeast Asian Nations (ASEAN).[20] Civil war continued to displace Cambodians during the 1980s, and most suffered the extreme poverty that resulted at least in part from an international aid embargo mounted by the United Nations in an effort to force an end to Vietnam's occupation.[21]

There had been little immediate international reaction to the Khmer Rouge genocide (or auto-genocide as it is sometimes described), but the Vietnamese invasion drew a swift response. Though the Soviet Union vetoed a Security Council resolution, the General Assembly voted overwhelmingly to condemn the invasion. As Steven Ratner points out, Cambodia was isolated economically, politically, and diplomatically by China, ASEAN, and the West, motivated either out of an anti-Vietnam sentiment or out of concern that small states anywhere could be subject to such invasions. Even as details of the Khmer Rouge period received wider corroboration, it was the Khmer Rouge that would serve as Cambodia's representative to the United Nations until 1982, and until 1991 a representative of a coalition between the Khmer Rouge, FUNCINPEC, and the KPNLF served as Cambodia's UN delegate, but never a member of the Vietnamese-installed SOC.[22]

Throughout the Khmer Rouge period and subsequent civil war, a half million Cambodians fled the country to live in exile in Thailand and other parts of the world. Some 362,000 refugees were still in the refugee camps along the Thai border when the peace agreements were signed in 1991; many of them had lived in "the violent limbo [of] the border camps"[23] for as long as thirteen years. The camps were supervised by the United Nations High Commission for Refugees (UNHCR), the International Committee of the Red Cross (ICRC) and the United Nations Border Relief Operation (UNBRO), but they also were administered, separately, by each of the three ousted warring Cambodian factions.[24]

A study of one of the largest refugee camps on the Thai border described life there "as presenting every kind of human vice that can be imagined: from manslaughter, rape and robbery to gambling, trafficking of children and prostitution. Every evening, according to rules made by the Thai authorities, all UNBRO personnel had to leave the camp until the following morning and no legal authority was present in the dark hours, when guerilla soldiers came for recreation and new supplies."[25] It is little wonder, then, that many observers have noted that Cambodian society, almost in its entirety, exhibits what psychologists describe as post-traumatic stress disorder as a result of both the Khmer Rouge period and life in the camps. As a 1989 United Nations Children's Fund (UNICEF) report commented: "Every family has experienced loss of loved ones. The majority of adults have experienced or witnessed torture and have lived with the extreme deprivation of food and water. Many adults have witnessed brutal murder, including instances where their own children were the victims."[26]

Diplomatic efforts in the early 1980s failed to resolve the civil war, but by the end of the decade, the economic, military, and political price to Vietnam of directly maintaining its regime in Cambodia became increasingly costly at the same time that support from the Soviet Union began to diminish. Rising Western and ASEAN interests in the investment potential of Cambodia, diplomatic efforts on the part of Indonesia and France, and the withdrawal of China's support for the Khmer Rouge all pushed the various factions into a series of informal meetings and negotiations.[27] In October 1991, after several years of intense bargaining and international pressure, the four factions signed the peace agreements and committed themselves to a framework for achieving peace in Cambodia and an unprecedented role for the UN in implementing that peace.

The UNTAC Mission

The lengthy and detailed Paris peace agreements established both UNTAC and the Supreme National Council (SNC), a body composed of the four main Cambodian factions under the chairmanship of Prince Norodom Sihanouk.

The SNC was intended to serve as the sovereign authority of Cambodia during the transition to a democratically elected government.[28] Even before the agreements had been formally signed, it was decided that the UN should send observers to Cambodia as soon as possible, to help monitor the cease-fire and to prepare for the deployment of UNTAC. So almost immediately upon signing, in November 1991, the UN Advance Mission in Cambodia (UNAMIC) was deployed, involving initially only fifty military liaison officers and a twenty-person mine awareness unit. UNAMIC was viewed as being largely ineffective,[29] and by December 1991, the advance mission was expanded to involve an additional 1,100 personnel and to include a more extensive mine-clearance operation, road and bridge repair, and, in conjunction with the UNHCR, the preparation of repatriation routes, reception centers, and resettlement areas.[30]

UNTAC itself was not deployed until March 1992, formally absorbing UNAMIC.[31] It involved seven separate components: human rights, electoral, military, civil administration, police, repatriation, and rehabilitation.[32] The scale of the mission, and the authority invested in UNTAC, was unprecedented, as Michael Doyle and Nishkala Suntharalingam note:

> Aside from the precedent-setting responsibilities for controlling and supervising crucial aspects of the civil administration and organizing and monitoring the elections, UNTAC was also required to monitor the cease-fire and the withdrawal of all foreign forces, and to supervise the cantonment and demobilization of military forces. Additionally, part of the mandate required UNTAC to foster an environment in which respect for human rights and freedoms could be ensured, to coordinate with UNHCR the repatriation of 350,000 refugees living in camps on the Thai side of the border, and to encourage social and economic rehabilitation during the period up to the elections. Although the UN had experience in some of these areas through past peacekeeping operations, it was the combination of these tasks that made UNTAC the largest UN peacekeeping operation ever, requiring over 15,000 troops and 7,000 civilian personnel and costing over an estimated \$US2.8 billion during the span of 18 months.[33]

In addition to the UN personnel involved, the mission to Cambodia also recruited some 60,000 local Cambodian staff, most involved in election-related activities.[34] UNTAC, in short, was the first in a growing post–Cold War trend for the UN: enormously complex missions involving the vast expenditure of both resources and personnel.[35]

The scale of the mission may have been unprecedented, but its composition, worked out at UN headquarters in New York, reflected a fairly traditional, highly militarized, and male-dominated venture. Of the nearly 23,000 international military and civilian personnel, there were no women appointed to director-level posts within the mission, very few women in the military contingents, and little presence of women in high-level posts among international civil servants assigned from UN headquarters or UN specialized agencies. There were so few women appointed to UNTAC, in fact, that a UN Division for the Advancement of Women study on women's involvement in peacekeeping missions registers their presence, in statistical terms, as "zero."[36] As the UN study notes: one woman serving on the mission noted that more women in either the military or police components of the mission might have dispelled the local impression that the United Nations was "an army of occupation."[37]

Nonetheless, given the size and extent of the mission, it was little wonder that its success symbolized so much for the United Nations. As Janet Heininger writes: "UNTAC's success or failure is widely believed to have profound implications not only for Cambodia's future peace and stability, but for future UN peacekeeping efforts as well . . . by its very size, scope, and cost, UNTAC represented a turning point for the United Nations. The testing of a new model combining peace-building with peacekeeping held important lessons for the future."[38]

Luckily for the UN, most mainstream observers were happy to focus on UNTAC's various successes. Over eighteen months, the UNTAC mission contributed to some reduction in the violence that prevailed in Cambodia, it successfully repatriated the almost 370,000 Cambodian refugees who had been living along the Thai border, and perhaps most important, it conducted a relatively free and fair election in which some four million people, or 85 percent of Cambodia's registered voters, participated.[39] The UN claimed as well that the mission "boosted Cambodia's economy by raising funds internationally for economic rehabilitation and expansion throughout the country."[40]

The Official Criticisms of the Mission

Though UNTAC was considered a success, there are also some discussions within mainstream accounts of problems associated with the mission. For example, the UN failed to achieve a situation of political neutrality, as pledged in the 1991 Paris peace agreement, in part because the Khmer Rouge withdrew from the demobilization and cantonment process and threatened throughout the mission to disrupt the election campaign.[41] The Khmer Rouge claimed that the UN was not adequately monitoring the withdrawal of Vietnamese troops from Cambodian territory, and in its strongest accusations claimed that the UN mission would result in Vietnam's recolonization of Cambodia. That the Khmer Rouge could successfully withdraw from the peace process (and that some of their accusations about the UN's ineffectiveness were probably quite accurate) was widely attributed to poor planning and, in particular, the delayed deployment of UNTAC.[42] Mats

Berdal observes that the planning process in advance of the mission was ad hoc despite the fact that the UN had several years to prepare, and even after it was deployed, UNTAC lacked an effective intelligence capability to track the movement of troops (both Khmer Rouge and Vietnamese) across borders, locate arms caches, or even monitor its own performance.[43]

Likewise, UNTAC's presence may have diminished, but it did not stop, political violence, which was aimed at both political party members and ethnic Vietnamese.[44] The latter have long been the focus of ethnic hatred within Cambodia, partly because of perceived historical injustices, partly on account of the more recent period of Vietnamese occupation.[45] A number of commentators also noted the extent to which Western anticommunist (specifically, anti-Vietnamese) sentiment had already led to long-standing willful ignorance and obfuscation of Khmer Rouge atrocities within Cambodia, and that this continued right up to the signing of the peace agreements and even informed the implementation of the peace plan itself.[46] The massacres and exodus of ethnic Vietnamese, many of whom were second- and third-generation Cambodians, were not addressed by the UN. As Grant Curtis points out, "no party, including UNTAC, made efforts to protect the rights of Cambodia's ethnic Vietnamese population."[47]

The UN did not act in part because it was still intent on including the Khmer Rouge in the peace process, and it was the Khmer Rouge that was usually held responsible for the massacres (in March 1993 alone, forty-two people, mostly women and children, were killed). Most politicians remained silent about the murders and openly supported the departure of Vietnamese-Cambodians. Even Prince Sihanouk, who had condemned the killings, said that the only thing he could suggest was "to advise them to return to their own country—that is the Socialist Republic of Vietnam."[48] Indeed, the extent of the UNTAC response to the exodus of ethnic Vietnamese was mounted by a UN naval contingent, on its own initiative, and involved escorting fleeing people out of Cambodia in an operation dubbed "Safe Passage."[49] However, as Raoul Jennar writes, Operation Safe Passage effectively legitimized the forced departure of the Vietnamese.[50] The *Far Eastern Economic Review* evocatively described the operation in April of 1993:

> Sadako Ogata, head of the UN High Commission for Refugees (UNHCR) came to Phnom Penh [to celebrate the repatriation of more than 370,000 Cambodians from Thailand], to mark the end of the Indochina refugee crisis. As she spoke to reporters, her audience could clearly see through the windows of the conference room a large fleet in the Mekong River carrying ethnic Vietnamese fleeing persecution by Cambodians.[51]

In the end, over 150 Vietnamese-Cambodians were killed, or were missing and presumed dead, and an estimated twenty to thirty thousand fled Cambodia in the months leading up to the election.[52]

What Did Cambodians Say?

In addition to the criticisms revealed in official accounts of the mission, local Cambodian individuals and agencies and a few outside observers have raised a whole series of other concerns. One damning set of accusations focuses on the repatriation efforts, one of the mission elements usually touted as a success. While the UN did manage to repatriate the 362,000 refugees living along the Thai border in time for the election, it was widely reported that the speed of the operation resulted in many people remaining unsettled long after their return. Returnees were given freedom of choice in designating their destinations within Cambodia[53] and were offered three options through the United Nations High Commission for Refugees (UNHCR) to assist them upon their return: Option A, usually referred to as the land offer, included up to two hectares of agricultural land per family, $25, and food from the World Food Program for 400 days; Option B, usually referred to as the house offer, included a plot of land for a house, $25, and supplies to make a home, a household/agricultural kit, and food for 400 days; and, Option C, the cash offer, included $50 per adult and $25 per child under twelve, a household/agricultural kit, and food for 400 days.[54]

Option A was originally the most popular, but news soon filtered back to the camps from early returnees that the land which had been promised was often not available, either because it was filled with landmines or its ownership was contested, having already been claimed by other families.[55] In the end, some 87 percent of all returnees chose the cash option, which gave UNHCR some flexibility insofar as they did not need to find land for returning families. To some extent, the refugees also experienced the cash option as a more flexible one, as it allowed them to go wherever they wanted to look for land, work, family, or simply to escape the risk of continuing conflict.[56] However, other observers noted that the cash option also left many of the returnees in a particularly vulnerable situation, with only a relatively small amount of cash on which to subsist back home in Cambodia. As the outgoing spokesman for the UNHCR said at the time: "I wouldn't be surprised if we started to see some fairly unsettling statistics if people are using up their grant in three months and it's meant to last them a year."[57] Financial difficulties were compounded when some refugees lost their access to the promised food supply. Returnees were to return to their drop-off points to pick up food allotments every forty days, but if they left the immediate area in search of work they were not always able to return, either because of distance or the cost of travel. Some people lost their ration books and so could not prove that they were entitled to the food. As one woman noted two years after the completion of the mission: "UNHCR claims 100 percent success, but they were successful only in transferring people. Many of those people still have no place to live, and no food."[58]

Returnees' difficulties were compounded by the fact that many were coping with "real life" for the first time in thirteen years. They did not know how to operate in a money economy and had lived a completely dependent life in the camps, where most basic services, including schooling for children, had been provided free of charge. Some were robbed of their cash before even leaving the camps; others were robbed when they arrived at their repatriation destinations. Most faced discrimination once they were resettled, either because they were viewed as having taken the "wrong path" politically or because local Cambodians in their new communities viewed them as putting new pressures on overextended infrastructure and resources. Additionally, some 47 percent of the refugees were under the age of fifteen. Their adjustment was perhaps the most difficult. As Eva Arnvig notes: "Few have seen a rice field, a cow, a well or a forest. For them, rice is something brought to the camps in sacks, fuelwood and water on trucks, and vegetables and meat are something out of a plastic bag."[59] Yet they were expected to survive, usually with less than $200 in their pocket.

The Cambodia to which the refugees returned was also one that was experiencing the economic dislocation of the UNTAC mission. Court Robinson observes that "the signing of the Paris Agreements had unleashed what some observers called '*capitalism sauvage.*'"[60] In contrast to UN claims that UNTAC contributed to economic development in Cambodia, the mission was blamed instead for a dramatic escalation in the cost of basic goods and services. The average annual income in Cambodia in the early 1990s was roughly U.S.$130, but the volunteers, military personnel, and UN staff who arrived in Cambodia were paid considerably more. The least-paid among the international staff, for example, were the UN volunteers who ran the election, and they earned about $700 a month; civilian police received their regular salaries and a per diem of $130; and UN officials from New York received a daily cost-of-living allowance of $145 on top of their usual salary. As the *Phnom Penh Post* described it: "One Russian military liaison officer can't believe his good fortune. 'I earn 17 times what I earn in Russia, and three times more than the Russian ambassador here,' he exults."[61]

The influx of nearly 23,000 people into Cambodia, many of whom were making more in a single day than the average Cambodian made in an entire year, drove up the price of food, housing, and basic goods.[62] This was compounded by the government of Cambodia, which started to print more money to cover its own expenses, flooding Cambodian markets with increasingly worthless riels (the local Cambodian currency).[63] While UNTAC eventually tried to intervene to bring prices down,[64] the inflation's impact on local people was devastating. As Eva Arnvig reports, a consumer price index in 1992 showed a tenfold increase over five months, with the price of rice increasing by almost 250 percent and the price of fish increasing five and a half times.[65]

UN officials who negotiated rental prices within Phnom Penh did not bother to "haggle" over the price, as was common practice within Cambodian culture, but rather paid the first price landlords suggested; therefore, rental prices in the capital increased 400 percent within sixty days of the signing of the Paris agreements.[66] Having established the price of housing in the capital, the UN drove these inflationary pressures into the provinces by offering the same price for housing in rural regions as had been established in Phnom Penh. Local Cambodians not only faced rising prices in both food and housing, but many were evicted from homes they had lived in for more than a decade by landlords who quickly learned they could make considerably more money by renting to UNTAC than they could renting to Cambodians. So out of control did the economy become that the riel was eventually devalued by some 70 percent.[67]

Not only did UNTAC have an inflationary impact on the Cambodian economy, but many people reported that they were surprised at how little money the UN actually spent locally. Equipment came from abroad; UN personnel took vacations outside of Cambodia; and anything that was brought into the country, such as cars, building materials, and even the ballot boxes (reportedly supplied by Canada) left Cambodia as soon as the mission was over. As one Cambodian woman said: "They did not spend their money to buy things Cambodian; they did not trust anything from Cambodia. They didn't even buy their bottled water locally; they shipped it in from Thailand."[68] Perhaps more importantly, local Cambodians felt that the UN left little in the way of infrastructure, whether for education, health, or the judiciary; in many cases, other UN agencies and nongovernmental organizations (NGOs) had to fill in the gap in these areas after UNTAC left.[69]

One way UNTAC did contribute to the economy was by hiring local Cambodians to assist in the mission, but local staff were paid a fraction of the salary received by international staff, earning on average only $140 a month. Not only were local staff paid less, but sometimes the Cambodians were not paid at all. As William Shawcross reports, while the international staff received their salaries and their per diem on time, in many areas of the country the Cambodians went for months without being paid. In some cases, the international staff began to pay the Cambodian staff out of their own pockets, and in November 1992 threatened a sit-in at UNTAC headquarters if the Cambodians did not start getting paid.[70] In the end, salary payments to local staff comprised less than 1 percent of total local expenditure and had the added impact of drawing most of the trained or experienced Cambodians away from Cambodian administrative structures and into UNTAC.[71]

Much of the focus on establishing political and economic order in Cambodia has been to secure sufficient stability to encourage foreign investment. However, as with the investment that flowed into Cambodia during the

UNTAC mission, post-UNTAC investment focused in Phnom Penh on services and, now, tourism.[72] As the *Asian Recorder* noted prior to the end of the mission, the "UN has not yet brought peace and democracy to Kampuchea, but its presence has improved the quality of the country's restaurants."[73] While money flowed into the country to build hotels and casinos, de-mining operations could barely scrape together $100,000 to continue their efforts in removing the estimated eight million landmines in Cambodia.[74]

In addition to the mission's disruptive impact on the economy, the presence of 23,000 foreign civilian and military personnel also had a disruptive impact on Cambodian society. The specific impact on women will be discussed below, but there were other issues raised locally, and perhaps the most widespread concerned the poor and drunken driving habits of UN personnel, inflicting numerous injuries and fatalities on Cambodians as a result of traffic accidents. Many people sought compensation from UNTAC, in particular to be able to hold a funeral. Others only wanted their loss to be acknowledged. A report prepared for UNTAC on public perception of the mission described the efforts of one family after the death of their three-year-old child: "In this case, they had money for the service and really wanted someone to tell them officially that UNTAC was very sorry and to sit with them and listen to their sorrow. No one would take the time to make this expression of shared grief."[75]

The various critiques of the UNTAC mission, both official and unofficial, are usually described as a series of "lessons learned" that could improve future peacekeeping missions, not things that detracted from the overall success of this particular one.[76] In the end, the "numbers" that counted were not those that measured the economic impact of the mission, the number of people left homeless after repatriation or as a result of eviction, or the number of people killed as a result of careening white UN vehicles out of control in the streets of Phnom Penh. The numbers that counted were those that told us how many people were repatriated and how many people got out to vote. These latter are not inconsiderable, but neither are they the full story.

Cambodia, UNTAC, and Women

The picture of the UN peacekeeping mission to Cambodia becomes even more complicated if we ask the question, What was the impact on women? It is easy to "read" the peacekeeping mission in Cambodia without any consideration of gender: as the previous few sections illustrate, the history of the conflict is sufficiently complex, and the mission itself so enormous, that it is a daunting task just to convey the official accounts. So, it is perhaps not surprising that those accounts are silent not only about the mission's impact on local people generally but especially so about its effect on women.

Ironically, those accounts remain silent even when that impact is not entirely negative. Many women within Cambodia report that in addition to the formal proclamations of success, the UNTAC effort also achieved some notable successes with regard to women.

One of Cambodia's most striking demographic characteristics has long been its preponderance of women and children: at the time the Paris peace agreements were being negotiated, it was estimated that 65 percent of the population was female, 35 percent of households were headed by women, and more than half of the population was under the age of fifteen.[77] These characteristics were a direct result of Cambodia's violent past. As Judy Ledgerwood observes: "More women than men survived the traumas of [the Khmer Rouge] period. Women are better able to survive conditions of severe malnutrition, fewer women were targeted for execution because of connections to the old regime, and fewer women were killed in battles." Even after the Khmer Rouge fled to the northeastern part of the country, men continued to be "drained off" from society in order to serve as soldiers during Cambodia's long civil war.[78]

Despite that women significantly outnumbered men in Cambodia, women's position within Cambodian society was at best mixed, reflecting their revered status as wives and mothers coupled with a set of expectations about appropriate feminine behavior that was far more constraining than anything men faced. The revered status of women is described well by one Cambodian proverb: "One father is worth one thousand friends; one mother is worth one thousand fathers."[79] Women in Cambodia often managed the household economy, as well as the family itself, and women were legally entitled to inherit property from either spouses or parents.

At the same time, however, the virtuous Cambodian woman was expected to be shy, to act in a reserved manner, and to walk quietly, making as little noise as possible. Many young women in Cambodia do not continue in school after puberty, are expected instead to help their mother within the home, and, ideally, by the time they are eighteen years old will be married to a man chosen by their family. As in many societies in both Asia and the West, it is assumed that women will honor their vows of fidelity in marriage while men will not, and a woman who has dishonored her own reputation is dishonored forever. A common Khmer proverb holds that "women are like cloth and men are like gold," meaning men, like gold, can become covered with mud and yet be cleaned and shine bright once again, while women, like a piece of cloth, will never come clean should they ever be muddied through improper or shameful behavior.[80] As Chanthou Boua describes it, "the 'mud,' to a traditional Cambodian, could be simply the act of falling in love."[81]

Reflecting the assumption that Cambodian women are more properly involved within the household, work and political activity outside the home are not always available to Cambodian women. While of course many women have ended up participating in agricultural production and the paid labor force out of economic necessity (in some industries and in agricultural production generally, in fact, women outnumbered men[82]), they usually earned far less than their male counterparts.[83] Likewise, women in Cambodia were not well represented in positions of political decisionmaking authority. Grant Curtis wrote that in the Cambodian government of the 1980s, there was only one woman member of the Politburo and five women in the thirty-member Party Central Committee. The total number of women within the governing party membership as a whole was only some 5 percent.[84]

One of UNTAC's most notable successes with regard to women resulted from the freedom of association that prevailed during the peacekeeping mission and, in particular, the efforts of the United Nations Development Fund for Women (UNIFEM) to incorporate women's issues into the general election. UNIFEM engaged in public education and information campaigns in the printed media and on radio and television, as well as in a four-day National Women's Summit. The aim was to get women out to vote, to get them involved politically (whether within formal political structures of government, social movements, or nongovernmental organizations) and to get them talking with one another. UNTAC Radio, for example, offered a regular segment on some of the particular difficulties women faced in Cambodia, and in particular how these might affect their ability to vote in the upcoming general elections. Similarly, the Women's Summit brought together Cambodian women from all sectors of society in order to identify and prioritize women's issues for the purpose of lobbying political parties contesting the election and later the government itself.[85]

These efforts were not only successful in getting a large proportion of the female electorate to participate in the May 1993 elections, but they were also credited with encouraging the emergence of an indigenous women's movement within Cambodia. Specific material support was also directed to existing indigenous women's NGOs and to the creation of some new women's NGOs. These NGOs, in turn, mounted a very effective lobby of the Cambodian government, causing important equality rights provisions to be included in the new Cambodian constitution. Even more important, perhaps, they "set the tone" that women's participation in politics, broadly defined, was both legitimate and useful. Through the kinds of preliminary discussions that were made possible at the Women's Summit, Cambodian women's NGOs also have organized around some of the priorities identified in those meetings, such as literacy for women, economic independence, health, and so on.[86]

Another positive UNTAC contribution concerned domestic violence. The Project Against Domestic Violence in Phnom Penh reported that in a context where few cases of domestic violence are ever brought to the authorities and fewer still are prosecuted, one provincial judge described the only criminal case of domestic violence she had ever presided over as one in which UNTAC officers had brought in a man caught beating his wife in a marketplace.[87] Violence against women had also been politicized through the discussions at the Women's Summit, with a demand from participants that the new Cambodian state protect women against domestic violence, along with calls for measures to promote women's equality in the work-force, in politics, and to provide more equitable divorce laws.

UNTAC and Women: The Critique

Just as the positive consequences for women that resulted from the UNTAC mission did not merit much specific discussion within official sources, nei-ther did a whole series of more negative consequences. Adjusting to the UN's arrival in Cambodia was even more difficult for women than for local people in general. For those coming from the refugee camps, repatriation often meant being dropped into a situation of greater insecurity. Eight months into the repatriation effort, UNHCR designated female heads of household as an "at risk" group. Groups at risk were intended to receive extra support and extra counseling before the repatriation to help prepare them, but even after the designation, many female heads of households received no extra support and often only a few minutes of counseling to know what they might face upon their return.[88] Cambodian women's groups and human rights workers were concerned that many of the women who returned from the camps faced a life of homelessness in which their options were limited to becoming beggars or prostitutes.[89]

Indeed, with the arrival of UNTAC, prostitution became a booming business within Cambodia and certainly one to which many women turned in order to survive. The Cambodian Women's Development Association estimated that the number of prostitutes in Cambodia grew from about 6,000 in 1992 to more than 25,000 at the height of the mission.[90] While the presence of prostitutes was not new (according to numerous accounts, fre-quenting prostitutes is a regular feature of many Cambodian men's behav-ior), Cambodians were nonetheless alarmed by the dramatic increase in prostitution and its far more "open" nature. Prostitution spread to the provincial villages, whereas previously it had been concentrated in the cap-ital, and many observers reported also the rise of child prostitution.[91]

Early reports indicated that the vast majority, if not all, of the prosti-tutes were young Vietnamese women who had immigrated into Cambodia to take advantage of the growing prostitution business. These estimates resulted more from prevailing anti-Vietnamese sentiment than from any reflection of reality.[92] As the "ethnic other" in Cambodia, Vietnamese women represented all prostitutes, on the assumption that virtuous Cambodian women and girls would not partake of such an activity. The perception that prostitutes were all Vietnamese and the widespread use of prostitutes by UNTAC personnel played nicely into the hands of the Khmer Rouge in their efforts to undermine the peace process. They accused peacekeepers of being too busy with prostitutes to check on the presence of Vietnamese soldiers; as Judy Ledgerwood writes, "Some Cambodians were more inclined to believe Khmer Rouge propaganda that UNTAC was collaborating with the Vietnamese to colonize Cambodia when they saw UNTAC personnel taking Vietnamese 'wives.'"[93]

Of course, Cambodian women and girls did work as prostitutes, and as Cambodians began to realize that "even" good Cambodian women were being drawn into prostitution to service UNTAC personnel, their anger toward the UN flared.[94] As one man described it, "Everybody started to wonder what they had come here for, to implement a peace accord or to turn our women into prostitutes."[95] Other men reported their discomfort at some of the things they witnessed: while the use of prostitutes may be an acceptable feature of male Cambodian culture, watching women "strip" usually was not, and one man described rushing out of the barracks he shared with UNTAC personnel when they hired a prostitute and forced her to perform a strip-tease. A certain rivalry also emerged, with UNTAC personnel paying more for the prostitutes they hired than Cambodian men normally would pay—usually U.S.$10 a night, as compared to 10,000 riels or $4. Brothel owners preferred the higher fees coming in from UNTAC customers, but reaction from prostitutes themselves was reportedly mixed, with some complaining that "UNTAC customers could be more cruel."[96]

The influx of nearly 23,000 UN personnel and the dramatic rise in prostitution also appears to have resulted in a dramatic rise in cases of HIV and AIDS, with the World Health Organization (WHO) reporting that 75 percent of people giving blood in Phnom Penh were infected with HIV (though some observers consider this an inflated estimate) and another report indicating that 20 percent of soldiers in one French battalion tested positive when they finished their six-month tour of duty.[97] Most observers noted that while UNTAC was not responsible for bringing HIV and AIDS to Cambodia, it did contribute to its spread. Nonetheless, one of the pejoratives sometimes directed at UNTAC by citizens was to rename the acronym UNTAC to "the United Nations Transmission of AIDS to Cambodia." UNTAC's chief medical officer predicted that as many as seven times more UN personnel would eventually die of AIDS contracted in Cambodia than had died as a result of hostile action.[98] A United Nations training document published by the Department of Peacekeeping Operations and the Joint UN Programme on HIV/AIDS several years after the UNTAC mission confirmed that "over 100 peacekeeping troops were infected with HIV—and may have infected others—during the UNTAC Mission in Cambodia."[99]

As criticism toward UN personnel within Cambodia grew, a number of what Judy Ledgerwood describes as "telling" actions were announced. As the *Observer of Business and Politics* in Bombay noted, "Peacekeeping chiefs have warned their men to be more discreet, for example by not parking their distinctive white vehicles outside massage parlours and in red light areas."[100] Eva Arnvig also reports that in the same directive UN personnel were asked not to frequent brothels in uniform.[101] A second response was to ship an additional 800,000 condoms to Cambodia.[102]

In Cambodia, the association of peacekeeping with prostitution remains strong to this day. In the recently opened Cambodian Cultural Village in the city of Siem Reap, a wax museum displays different scenes from Cambodia's history and culture. Its representation of the UNTAC era depicts a male UN peacekeeper with arms draped around a prostitute (see Photograph 3). The display was not, apparently, intended as a criticism of the mission, simply as a presentation of typical scenes from different moments in Cambodia's past.

Photograph 3 Wax museum display of UN peacekeeper and prostitute, Cambodian Cultural Village, Siem Reap, Cambodia
(Photograph by Gordon Sharpless, December 2003)

In addition to prostitution, charges also emerged of sexual abuse and violence. Raoul Jennar reported that in 1993, "in the Preah Vihear hospital, there was for a time a majority of injured people who were young kids, the victims of sexual abuse by UN soldiers."[103] There were frequent claims of rape and sexual assault brought to women's NGOs but (as in the story with which this chapter opened) often days or weeks after the rapes were alleged to have taken place, so that the usual expectations surrounding evidence collection could not be carried out and claims could not be substantiated to the satisfaction of UN officials.[104] As one women's group organizer described, "I remember one nineteen-year-old girl who had bathed and didn't tell anyone about what had happened to her for two days. The UN said we had no evidence. We learned from that."[105]

It is also a widely shared view among many Cambodian women and men that the phenomenon of "fake marriages" was widespread during the UNTAC mission. Simply put, a UN soldier would marry a Cambodian woman, but only for the duration of his posting to Cambodia, at which point he would abandon her. Some women were reported to have been abandoned as far away as Bangkok and left to their own devices to make their way home. In addition to the emotional trauma of fake marriages, they were enormously shameful for women in a society with very strict norms about what is appropriate behavior in good women. For the same reason, they could also have deadly consequences for the men involved: some Cambodians and expatriates allege that at least one of the UN's casualties in Phnom Penh was a retribution killing in which family members murdered a soldier who had just informed his "wife" that he had no intention of bringing her with him once he was redeployed home.[106]

Women also reported being sexually harassed by UNTAC soldiers and personnel. As one expatriate woman described: "I thought, if this happens to me, think what Khmer[107] women have to face. . . . After 13 years of war, people feel afraid. There's no place for them to go, no support if they want to say no. And now they have another form of harassment: UNTAC."[108] A UN report confirmed the harassment and, rather belatedly, suggested some guidelines:

> Perhaps because many UNTAC personnel only have contact with Khmer (and Vietnamese) women through prostitution, there is a tendency on the part of some personnel to treat all women as though they were prostitutes. This includes grabbing at women on the street, making inappropriate gestures and remarks and physically following or chasing women travelling in public. UNTAC personnel should be briefed on the fact that gender conceptions in Khmer culture are different from their own. Physical contact between the sexes in public is never acceptable. If a woman laughs when she is touched, this laughter is probably a sign of embarrassment or fear and not encouragement. The problem is not exclusively one between Khmer women and male UNTAC staff, but is a generalized problem.

Female UNTAC staff have similarly expressed problems with sexual harassment. The problem is not a small problem.[109]

When concerns about the drunken behavior and sexual misconduct were brought to the attention of the UN Secretary-General's Special Representative to Cambodia at a meeting for NGOs, Mr. Yasushi Akashi stunned those in attendance by saying that it was natural for hot-blooded young soldiers who had endured the rigors of the field to want to have a few beers and to chase "young beautiful beings of the opposite sex."[110] Akashi's "boys will be boys" attitude galvanized those at the meeting, who then delivered an open letter of protest signed by 165 Cambodian and expatriate women and men accusing some UNTAC personnel of sexual harassment and assault, violence against women and against prostitutes, and of being responsible for the dramatic rise of prostitution and HIV/AIDS. The letter described how women felt restricted in their movements and powerless as a result of UNTAC's presence in Cambodia.[111] Having recovered from his earlier faux pas, Akashi pledged to assign a community relations officer to hear the complaints of the Cambodian community.[112]

One commonly held observation was that many of the problems associated with UNTAC were exacerbated by the fact that there were very few women involved in the mission. The UN may have had good ideas about women's participation in politics, but it did not practice what it preached. Many Cambodian women noted, for example, that although UNIFEM tried to highlight women's issues in the electoral process, because UNTAC itself had very few women involved at any level within the mission, and none at all in decisionmaking positions, it undermined UNIFEM's message about women's political participation. As one woman said: "We are trying to incorporate women at all levels of government, and we face opposition from men in Cambodia for trying to do that. We point to the UN to support our arguments about women's participation in politics. But there were no women in high positions in UNTAC. Why should men here give up positions of authority to women when the UN came here and didn't even do it themselves?"[113]

Too Few Women or Too Many Soldiers?

The problem, however, may not have been a lack of women but rather a preponderance of soldiers. UNTAC deployed 17,000 soldiers, and many contributing countries sent elite units on the mission. Yeshua Moser-Puangsuwan writes that Malaysia sent its Rangers because, as a Malaysian major reported, "they had the 'highest kill ratio' of any Malaysian military units against internal insurgents."[114] Other units, such as those from India and

Bangladesh, received commando training before their departure but little in the way of specific training for peacekeeping or Cambodia. The Indian unit had conducted counterinsurgency operations in Kashmir, Sri Lanka, and Assam, and the Bangladeshi unit was trained in counterinsurgency warfare and is regularly "sent on rotation to the Chittagong Hill Tracts in Bangladesh to wage war against non-Bengali indigenous groups."[115] Only the Indonesian military had provided extensive cultural and language training and information about the Paris peace accords, handling landmines, and the command structure of UNTAC, but it had put its training program together on its own initiative, having received no formal instructions from the UN about how to train troops for peacekeeping missions.[116]

As Moser-Puangsuwan notes, the International Peace Academy in its *Peacekeeper's Manual* describes the various ways in which combat units may need to "unlearn some doctrines and modify some standard operating procedures" in order to successfully conduct peacekeeping missions. Soldiers must unlearn, as is discussed in more detail in Chapter 6, some of the very traits that go into becoming a soldier: quick reaction, aggressive alertness, the disparagement of other country's militaries, and an "in there to win" attitude. Instead, "what is needed amongst populations who have been traumatised by warriors is people with good human relationship skills."[117]

Instead of human relationship skills, however, some members of the foreign militaries deployed to Cambodia were quick to dehumanize local citizens, seeing them and their country as hopelessly irrational and backward. The view of some soldiers was that the UN mission was to save Cambodia from itself.[118] As postcolonial theorists have long argued, those who "need to be saved" are often depicted as less than fully human. One Bangladeshi sergeant's comments are illustrative here: "[Cambodians] think nothing of laying mines. . . . They scatter them about like popped rice. Often they mine their own doorstep before going to bed. . . . They don't care who gets killed; life really has no value here."[119] As Amitav Ghosh observes, the Cambodian people—subject to massive bombing campaigns during the Vietnam War, a genocidal revolution, invasion and foreign rule, and international isolation—had managed remarkably well and were rebuilding steadfastly from scratch. Yet for some foreign soldiers, the dirt roads, broken buildings, and lack of infrastructure just proved how backward Cambodia was and "rendered meaningless those tiny, cumulative efforts by which individuals and families reclaim their lives—a shutter repaired, a class taught, a palm-tree tended."[120]

However, it was when they received assistance toward these tiny, cumulative efforts that local people report UNTAC contributed most to enhancing their real sense of security. For example, local citizens credited a Canadian unit for rebuilding a park in Phnom Penh where local children could play safely. An Indian unit received praise for building homes and schools. A German Field Hospital was applauded for accepting Cambodian citizens as patients as well as peacekeepers, and "treating all patients exactly alike." Similarly, the French Legionnaires contributed by repairing bridges and roads, providing medical assistance and building or repairing schools.[121] Though UNTAC had no specific mandate to undertake such "civic action programmes," it was often these very programs, when military units undertook them of their own accord, for which UNTAC is best remembered by local Cambodians.[122]

The tiny, cumulative ways in which people rebuild their lives do not provide the rationale for enormously complex multidimensional peacekeeping missions: the kinds of missions, in the words of Anne Orford, that depend on the "heroic narratives" of intervention—those that tell us who needs to be saved, and how (and by whom) they are to be saved.[123] They do not provide the legitimations for a militarized presence. Building schools and hospitals, parks and bridges, or providing medical services do not, in the end, depend on the specific skills associated with soldiering. They are skills that can be possessed by carpenters, engineers, or doctors.

In many ways, UNTAC made the biggest impression on Cambodians when it was involved in measures devoted not so much to "soldiering" but to "development." As Kien Serey Phal observes, there are important lessons to be learned from a mission whose military focus may not have been up to the task of the larger, and more long-term, concerns of community-building, peace-building, human security, and development:

> There is a need for the recognition of the success of the peace process in protecting the political rights of Cambodian people and facilitating the improved political participation of women but also of the relative failure of the process to promote social and economic equality, and in particular, to prevent and mitigate violence against women and ensure the protection of fundamental human rights.[124]

In deploying a highly militarized, and highly masculinized, peacekeeping mission to Cambodia, increasing, rather than alleviating, the insecurities of many local people was almost ensured.

Conclusion

Mainstream accounts of the kinds of issues raised here about the UNTAC mission are often attributed, as Janet Heininger writes, to the problems of establishing a "common standard of behavior" among contributing countries.[125] Or in Alan James's even more dismissive comments: "In Cambodia the libidinal proclivities of one contingent apparently led to a great deal of local embarrassment for the United Nations."[126] In other words, the problem is explained by the fact that some contributing countries, usually those with less experience in peacekeeping missions—or perhaps more libidinous proclivities—send troops not well suited to the expectations associated with peacekeeping. In the Cambodian case, the Bulgarians are cited as the chief offenders.

While not to deny that particular contributing countries' soldiers may have caused specific sets of problems, this kind of argument deflects attention away from critical concerns and turns soaring rates of prostitution and HIV/AIDS, sexual harassment, and exploitation into a set of "technical problems." Thus, rather than ask questions about the value of relying chiefly on soldiers as peacekeepers,[127] people deploy ethnic arguments so the primary concern becomes "problems of coordination." Rethinking how peacekeeping is conducted, or how soldiers are constituted, remain unasked questions.

One contributor country normally excluded from any concerns about "coordination," and which has been viewed in general as the peacekeeping country par excellence, is Canada.[128] If the Bulgarians are new to peacekeeping and so can be forgiven for failing to live up to UN standards, the Canadians are "seasoned veterans"[129] and are expected to know how to act when they don a blue helmet or blue beret. The following chapter examines both the representations of Canada as the peacekeeping country par excellence and the way in which that image began to unravel when Canadian soldiers were deployed to Somalia.

Notes

1. Stephen J. Randall, "Peacekeeping in the Post–Cold War Era: The United Nations and the 1993 Cambodian Elections," *Behind the Headlines* (spring 1994): 13.

2. All of the names of interviewees have been changed to protect their identity, except in cases where their interviews corresponded to material they have published or otherwise made public. Interviews, Phnom Penh, Cambodia, March–April, 1996.

3. Interviews, Phnom Penh, March–April, 1996.

4. Janet E. Heininger, *Peacekeeping in Transition: The United Nations in Cambodia* (New York: Twentieth Century Fund, 1994), p. 7; see also Yasushi Akashi, "To Build a New Country: The Task of the U.N. Transitional Authority in Cambodia," *Harvard International Review* 16, no. 1 (winter 1993): 34–37, and Jarat Chopra, "United Nations Authority in Cambodia," Thomas J. Watson Jr. Institute for International Studies Occasional Paper no. 15 (Providence, 1994), p. 8.

5. See, for example, Paul F. Diehl, *International Peacekeeping* (Baltimore: Johns Hopkins University Press, 1994), pp. 198–199, and sources below. For an engaging argument that examines the UNTAC mission as a failure, see Pierre Lizée, *Peace, Power, and Resistance in Cambodia: Global Governance and the Failure of International Conflict Resolution* (Basingstoke, UK: Macmillan, 2000).

6. Cited from R. M. Jennar, "UNTAC: 'International Triumph' in Cambodia?" *Security Dialogue* 25, no. 2 (1994): 145. See also Judy L. Ledgerwood, "UN Peace-keeping Missions: The Lessons from Cambodia," Analysis from the East-West Center no. 11 (Honolulu, March 1994), and Heininger, *Peacekeeping in Transition,* pp. 1–8. Peter Utting also notes the way in which "world opinion has been quick to label the United Nations operation in Cambodia 'a success,'" and he contrasts that view with the research presented in his volume on the social consequences of UNTAC. See Peter Utting, "Introduction: Linking Peace and Rehabilitation in Cambodia," in *Between Hope and Insecurity: The Social Consequences of the Cambodian Peace Process* (Geneva: UN Research for Social Development, 1994), p. 3 and passim.

7. Lieutenant General J. M. Sanderson, "UNTAC: Lessons Learnt. The Military Component View," *Pacifica Review* 7, no. 2 (1995): 69.

8. Boutros Boutros-Ghali, "Introduction," in *The United Nations Blue Book Series,* vol. 2: *The United Nations and Cambodia, 1991–1995* (New York: UN, 1995), p. 3; see also "What the United Nations Learnt in Cambodia," *The Economist,* June 19, 1993, p. 36.

9. An important exception here is the collection by Utting, *Between Hope and Insecurity.*

10. See, for example, an otherwise interesting collection by Frederick Z. Brown and David G. Timberman (eds.), *Cambodia and the International Community: The Quest for Peace, Development, and Democracy* (New York: Asia Society, 1998).

11. Cynthia Enloe, *The Morning After: Sexual Politics at the End of the Cold War* (Berkeley: University of California Press, 1993), p. 35.

12. Cited in Gayle Kirshenbaum, "Who's Watching the Peacekeepers?" *Ms.,* May–June 1994, p. 15.

13. Grant Curtis, *Cambodia Reborn? The Transition to Democracy and Development* (Geneva: UN Research Institute for Social Development, 1998), p. 6.

14. Ibid., p. 6.

15. See David P. Chandler, *The Tragedy of Cambodian History: Politics, War, and Revolution Since 1945* (New Haven: Yale University Press, 1991), p. 215.

16. Ibid. As Chandler notes, U.S. planes dropped half a million tons of bombs on Cambodia during this period, more than three times the amount dropped on Japan in the later stages of World War II (p. 225).

17. Ibid., p. 238.

18. Judy Ledgerwood, May M. Ebihara, and Carol A. Mortland, "Introduction," in May M. Ebihara, Carol A. Mortland, and Judy Ledgerwood (eds.), *Cambodian Culture Since 1975: Homeland and Exile* (Ithaca: Cornell University Press, 1994), p. 11.

19. Ibid., p. 14 and passim. Much of the information in this section draws on this work and Aihwa Ong, "Mother's Milk in War and Diaspora," *Cultural Survival Quarterly* (spring 1995): 61–64.

20. Michael W. Doyle, *UN Peacekeeping in Cambodia: UNTAC's Civil Mandate* (Boulder: Lynne Rienner, 1995), p. 16; see also "Introduction," in Michael W. Doyle, Ian Johnstone, and Robert C. Orr (eds.), *Keeping the Peace: Multidimensional UN Operations in Cambodia and El Salvador* (Cambridge: Cambridge University Press, 1997), p. 8 and passim, and Steven R. Ratner, *The New UN Peacekeeping: Building Peace in Lands of Conflict After the Cold War* (New York: St. Martin's, 1995), pp. 139–142.

21. See Eva Mysliwiec, *Punishing the Poor: The International Isolation of Kampuchea* (Oxford: Oxfam, 1988) and "Cambodia: NGOs in Transition," in Utting, *Between Hope and Insecurity,* p. 104.

22. The slow international response to the Khmer Rouge genocide was explained in part because Cambodia was almost entirely cut off from the outside world during this period, and the scattered reports that did emerge were not all corroborated. It was only in 1978 that a small group of countries raised the question of human rights violations in Cambodia at the UN Human Rights Commission. See Ratner, *The New UN Peacekeeping,* pp. 140–142.

23. Ledgerwood, Ebihara, and Mortland, "Introduction," p. 20, quoting Al Santoli, "Voices from the Refugee Camps," in R. A. Judkins (ed.), *First International Scholars Conference on Cambodia: Selected Papers* (Geneso, NY: SUNY Department of Anthropology and the Geneso Foundation, 1988), pp. 9–12.

24. Aungkana Kamonpetch, "The Progress of Preliminary Phase of Khmer Repatriation," Occasional Paper Series no. 6 (Bangkok: Indochinese Refugee Information Center, Institute of Asian Studies, Chulalongkorn University, May 1993), pp. 28–29.

25. Cited in Arnvig, "Women, Children and Returnees," p. 153.

26. Cited in ibid.

27. Doyle, *UN Peacekeeping in Cambodia,* pp. 21–24. The complexities of this series of negotiations cannot be covered in the detail that they deserve here. For a fuller account, see, among others, Doyle, *UN Peacekeeping in Cambodia,* Chaps. 2 and 3; Ratner, *The New UN Peacekeeping,* Chap. 6; Heininger, *Peacekeeping in Transition,* Chap. 2. For a detailed account of the background and Paris peace plan itself, see Amitav Acharya, Pierre Lizée, and Sorpong Peou (eds.), *Cambodia—The 1989 Paris Peace Conference: Background Analysis and Documents* (Millwood, NY: Kraus International, 1991).

28. Michael W. Doyle and Nishkala Suntharalignam, "The UN in Cambodia: Lessons for Complex Peacekeeping," *International Peacekeeping* 1, no. 2 (summer 1994): 120. As Doyle and Suntharalignam note, the status of the Supreme National Council was ambiguous, designated through the agreements as the legitimate sovereign authority of Cambodia—and in this capacity signed two international human rights conventions that would bind subsequent Cambodian governments. At the same time, the SNC could be overruled by UNTAC and the UN Secretary-General's Special Representative to Cambodia if it reached an impasse or if it made decisions that were seen to violate the intent and meaning of the Paris agreements. However, as Steven Ratner notes, the creation of the SNC allowed the UN to achieve something of a "contrived consent" for the mission: all UN peacekeeping missions require the consent of the host state, but in the case of Cambodia part of the conflict was reflected in the fact that two competing groups, the SOC and the coalition comprised of the Khmer Rouge, FUNCINPEC, and the KPNLF, each claimed to be Cambodia's government. The creation of the SNC allowed the UN to create, for a time, a body that would stand above the two governments but which represented all of the factions, and through which consent could be granted (Ratner, *The New UN Peacekeeping,* p. 147).

29. As noted in an article lamenting the powerlessness and vulnerability of UNAMIC, *The Economist* suggested that if a squad of UN soldiers encountered a serious cease-fire violation, they would have to "first contact their commanding officer in Phnom Penh, who will then contact the Security Council in New York for instructions on what to do next. In the meantime, the peacekeepers will twiddle their thumbs"; "UNclear," *The Economist,* February 29, 1992, p. 37.

30. Boutros-Ghali, *The United Nations and Cambodia,* pp. 10–11; Chopra, "United Nations Authority in Cambodia," p. 1.

31. Chopra, "United Nations Authority in Cambodia," p. 2; Curtis, *Cambodia Reborn?* p. 9.

32. Chopra, "United Nations Authority in Cambodia," pp. 2–4; Boutros-Ghali, *The United Nations and Cambodia,* pp. 12–14; see also Sonia K. Han, "Building a Peace That Lasts: The United Nations and Post–Civil War Peace-Building," *New York University Journal of International Law and Politics* 26 (1994): 846–851.

33. Doyle and Suntharalignam, "The UN in Cambodia," p. 121.

34. Grant Curtis notes that even though UNTAC's Cambodian staff received monthly salaries lower than that paid to the international staff, "thousands of Cambodian civil servants and teachers left their offices and classrooms to work for UNTAC, resulting in a serious curtailment of basic services" (Curtis, *Cambodia Reborn?* p. 9).

35. As A. B. Fetherston notes, "In 1992 alone there were three huge [UN] undertakings, in Cambodia (22,000 peacekeepers), former Yugoslavia (24,000 peacekeepers), and Somalia (30,800 peacekeepers)"; A. B. Fetherston, "Putting the Peace Back into Peacekeeping: Theory Must Inform Practice," *International Peacekeeping* 1, no. 1 (spring 1994): 7.

36. UN Division for the Advancement of Women, "Women 2000: The Role of Women in United Nations Peacekeeping," December 1995, no. 1/1995, p. 8. See also Cynthia Enloe, *Maneuvers: The International Politics of Militarizing Women's Lives* (Berkeley: University of California Press, 2000), p. 100.

37. Ibid.

38. Heininger, *Peacekeeping in Transition,* p. 6.

39. Ker Munthit, "Akashi: Election 'Free and Fair,'" *Phnom Penh Post,* June 6–12, 1993, p. 3; Nate Thayer and Rodney Tasker, "Voice of the People," *Far Eastern Economic Review,* June 3, 1993, p. 10. See also Doyle, *UN Peacekeeping in Cambodia,* Chap. 4 and passim, and Doyle and Suntharalingam, "The UN in Cambodia: Lessons for Complex Peacekeeping," pp. 117–147.

40. Boutros-Ghali, *The United Nations and Cambodia,* p. 54; see also Grant Curtis, "Transition to What? Cambodia, UNTAC and the Peace Process," in Utting, *Between Hope and Insecurity,* pp. 56–58.

41. Ramses Amer, "The United Nations' Peacekeeping Operation in Cambodia: Overview and Assessment," *Contemporary Southeast Asia* 15, no. 2 (September 1993): 211–231; Curtis, "Transition to What?" p. 59; Doyle, *UNTAC's Civil Mandate,* Chap. 4; Doyle and Suntharalingam, "Lessons for Complex Peacekeeping," pp. 124–127.

42. In addition to other sources cited above, see Nate Thayer, "Unsettled Land: UN's Delayed Arrival Starts to Undermine Peace Settlement," *Far Eastern Economic Review,* February 27, 1992, pp. 22–26; Jarat Chopra, John Mackinlay, and Larry Minear, *Report on the Cambodian Peace Process* (Oslo: Norwegian Institute of International Affairs, 1993), Chap. 3 and passim; and Jarat Chopra, "United Nations Authority in Cambodia," Part 2 and passim.

43. Mats R. Berdal, "Whither UN Peacekeeping?" Adelphi Paper no. 281 (London: IISS, 1993), p. 45. William Shawcross makes the same point in *Deliver Us from Evil: Peacekeepers, Warlords, and a World of Endless Conflict* (New York: Simon and Schuster, 2000), p. 53.

44. Nate Thayer, "Sihanouk Slams Political Violence," *Phnom Penh Post,* January 15–28, 1993, p. 1; Tom McCarthy, "Slaughter of Vietnamese in Phum Taches Was Cold and Calculated," *Phnom Penh Post,* January 15–28, 1993, p. 3; Nate Thayer, "UNTAC Fails to Stem Political Violence," *Phnom Penh Post,* February 12–25, 1993, p. 3; Andrea Hamilton, "Murders of Party Officials Continue," *Phnom Penh Post,* July 2–15, 1993, p. 1.

45. See Chou Meng Tarr, "The Vietnamese Minority in Cambodia," *Race and Class* 34, no. 2 (1992): 33–47; Jay Jordens, "The Ethnic Vietnamese Community in

Cambodia: Prospects Post-UNTAC," presented at Association for Asian Studies Annual Meeting, Boston, March 27, 1994; Sara Colm, "What's in a Name? A Not So Neighborly Debate," *Phnom Penh Post,* November 6–19, 1992, p. 9; Annuska Derks, "Vietnamese Prostitutes in Cambodia," *Cambodia Report* 2, no. 1 (1996): 4–6; Christine Leonard, "Becoming Cambodian: Ethnic Identity and the Vietnamese in Kampuchea," *Cambodia Report* 2, no. 1 (1996): 15–18.

46. John Pilger, "Return to Year Zero," *New Internationalist* 242 (April 1993): 4–7. Pilger describes an interview with UNTAC's force commander in Cambodia, Lieutenant General John Sanderson, in which, when asked about the wisdom of including the Khmer Rouge in the peace process, given the history of the Khmer Rouge genocide, Sanderson replied, "Genocide is your term!" (p. 6). See also Ben Kiernan, "Review Essay: William Shawcross, Declining Cambodia," *Bulletin of Concerned Asian Scholars* 18, no. 1 (1986): 56–63; Ben Kiernan, "The Cambodian Crisis, 1990–1992: The UN Plan, the Khmer Rouge, and the State of Cambodia," *Bulletin of Concerned Asian Scholars* 24, no. 2 (1992): 3–24; David Munro, "Cambodia: A Secret War Continues," *CovertAction* 40 (spring 1992): 52–57; and a series of commentaries by John Pilger, including "Peace in Our Time? The UN Is Normalising the Unthinkable in Cambodia," *New Statesman and Society,* November 27, 1992, pp. 10–11; "Black Farce in Cambodia: The Appeasement of the Khmer Rouge Continues," *New Statesman and Society,* December 11, 1992, pp. 10–11; "The West's War in Cambodia," *New Statesman and Society,* May 28, 1993, pp. 14–15; and "The West's Lethal Illusion in Cambodia," *New Statesman and Society,* July 9, 1993, pp. 14–15.

47. Curtis, "Transition to What?" p. 60; Peter Eng, "Little Sympathy for Vietnamese Victims," *Phnom Penh Post,* August 7, 1992, p. 4; Kevin Barrington, "Massacre Condemned But . . . " *Phnom Penh Post,* March 26–April 8, 1993, p. 1.

48. Nayan Chanda and Nate Thayer, "Rivers of Blood," *Far Eastern Economic Review,* April 8, 1993, p. 22. See also Sheila McNulty, "UN Investigation Concludes KR Slayed Vietnamese Families," *Phnom Penh Post,* August 27, 1992, p. 3; and Boutros-Ghali, *The United Nations and Cambodia,* p. 42.

49. Jordens, "The Ethnic Vietnamese Community in Cambodia," p. 8.

50. Jennar, "International Triumph in Cambodia?" p. 148.

51. Nate Thayer, "Wretched of the Earth," *Far Eastern Economic Review,* April 15, 1995, p. 21.

52. Jordens, "The Ethnic Vietnamese Community in Cambodia," p. 2.

53. The Khmer Rouge attempted to force residents in one of the camps that they administered to areas of the country under Khmer Rouge control but were successfully resisted. See Women's Commission for Refugee Women and Children, "Cambodia Can't Wait: Report and Recommendations of the Women's Commission for Refugee Women and Children" (New York, February 8–20, 1993), pp. 3–4.

54. Boutros-Ghali, *The United Nations and Cambodia,* pp. 32–33; Court Robinson, "Rupture and Return: Repatriation, Displacement and Reintegration in Battambang Province Cambodia," Occasional Paper Series no. 7 (Indochinese Refugee Information Center, Institute of Asian Studies, Chulalongkorn University, Bangkok November 1994), p. 10; Women's Commission for Refugee Women and Children, "Cambodia Can't Wait," p. 3; Arnvig, "Women, Children, and Returnees," pp. 156–162.

55. As Court Robinson notes, UNHCR identified available land initially through satellite imaging, which could not identify if it was mined, secure, or even, in many cases, occupied by others (Robinson, "Rupture and Return," p. 9).

56. Ibid., p. 10.

57. Sheila McNulty, "Returning Khmer Opting for Cash Grants, Mine-Free Land Scarcer Than First Thought," *Phnom Penh Post,* August 27, 1992, p. 3.

58. Interviews, Phnom Penh, March–April 1996.

59. Arnvig, "Women, Children, and Returnees," p. 158, 159; Paul Davenport Sr., Joan Healy, and Kevin Malone, "'Vulnerable in the Village': A Study of Returnees in Battambang Province, Cambodia, with a Focus on Strategies for the Landless" (Phnom Penh: Lutheran World Service, UNHCR, Japan Sotoshu Relief Committee, 1995), p. 13 and passim.

60. Robinson, "Rupture and Return," p. 10. For a fuller analysis of the economic impact of the mission on Cambodia, see Robin Davies, "UNTAC and the Cambodian Economy: What Impact?" *Phnom Penh Post,* January 29–February 11, 1993, p. 4, which is a response to the Economic Advisor's Office, "Impact of UNTAC on Cambodia's Economy," December 1992.

61. James Pringle, "Peacekeepers' Odd Ways Keep Khmers Guessing," *Phnom Penh Post,* July 10, 1992, p. 5.

62. Shawcross, *Deliver Us from Evil,* pp. 71–73. As Judy Ledgerwood points out, there was considerable disparity in the pay received by the international staff, which caused some tensions, in particular among soldiers from different contributing countries, some of whom received just their regular salaries and others who received both their regular salary and their UN per diem. See Ledgerwood, "UN Peacekeeping Missions, the Lessons from Cambodia," pp. 6–7, and Kevin Barrington, "Pay Dispute Undermines UNTAC Morale," *Phnom Penh Post,* March 12–25, 1993, p. 13.

63. See, for example, Sheila McNulty, "SOC Heeds U.N. Call to Stop Runaway Inflation," *Phnom Penh Post,* October 23, 1992, p. 13; Mang Channo and Sara Colm, "Glut of Small Banknotes Creates a Riel Problem," *Phnom Penh Post,* August 7, 1992, p. 1; Robin Davies, "Economic Warfare or a Riel Crisis of Confidence," *Phnom Penh Post,* March 26–April 8, 1993, p. 1; and Chris Burslem, "UNTAC Bubble Economy Set to Burst," *Phnom Penh Post,* May 7–20, 1993, p. 16.

64. Robin Davies, "Blue Berets, Green Backs: What Was the Impact?" *Phnom Penh Post,* October 22–November 4, 1993, p. 16.

65. Arnvig, "Women, Children, and Returnees," p. 147; see also Curtis, "Transition to What?" p. 62.

66. The reluctance to bargain or haggle over prices also affected the price of goods sold in markets. As one person described in a letter to the editor: "The merchants say they don't care whether you can afford to buy their things or not, because they can sell them to UNTAC. They say that selling things to UNTAC is very easy, because UNTAC does not bargain. For Khmers, until they decide to buy or not, they have to bargain and make a hot argument with the shop owners," "UNTAC Clears the Market," *Phnom Penh Post,* October 11, 1992, p. 9. Reports on housing prices come from interviews, Phnom Penh, March–April, 1996, and, Arnvig, "Women, Children, and Returnees," p. 147.

67. Interviews, Phnom Penh, March–April, 1996; Curtis, "Transition to What?" p. 62; Arnvig, "Women, Children, and Returnees," p. 163.

68. Interviews, Phnom Penh, Cambodia, March–April, 1996.

69. Ibid.

70. Shawcross, *Deliver Us from Evil,* p. 80.

71. Curtis, "Transition to What?" pp. 63–64.

72. Ibid., p. 61; Murray Hiebert, "Baht Imperialism: Thai Investors Pour into Cambodia," *Far Eastern Economic Review,* June 25, 1992, pp. 46–47. Outside the capital, investment focused on gems and logging, the pace of which is considered to

have had disastrous environmental consequences. Nayan Chanda and Rodney Tasker, "The Gem Stampede: Round-the-Clock Mining by Thai Companies," *Far Eastern Economic Review,* July 30, 1992, p. 20.

73. "Better Restaurants," *Asian Recorder,* February 19–25, 1993, p. 22934. Anne Orford makes a similar observation with regard to the 1999 UN Transitional Administration in East Timor (UNTAET), which encouraged foreign investment in the tourism and services sector despite the fact that the people of East Timor were still lacking in primary needs. Anne Orford, *Reading Humanitarian Intervention: Human Rights and the Use of Force in International Law* (Cambridge: Cambridge University Press, 2003), p. 136.

74. Amelia Casela, interview, Canadian Broadcast Corporation, June 1995. See also the report that the Cambodian government had found investors interested in producing a sound and light show at Angkor Wat; Susan Postlewaite, "Sound and Light for Angkor," *Phnom Penh Post,* November 17–30, 1995.

75. UNTAC, Information/Education Division, "Report on Public Perceptions of UNTAC in the City of Phnom Penh," September 18, 1992, Appendix 1 in Arnvig, "Women, Children, and Returnees," p. 177. See also "UNTAC Personnel Need to Learn How to Drive," in *Phnom Penh Post,* December 18–31, 1992, p. 2. Toward the end of the mission, numerous insurance claims were made against UNTAC, many of which UN staff felt were bogus. One claims officer argued that "People are literally throwing themselves in front of U.N. vehicles to get compensation. . . . Why should UNTAC pay?" At the same time, many local people argued that the UN was being "stingy" and that too often they were forced to bargain with disbelieving UN staff for compensation. Standard compensation for the death of a family bread-winner was $2,000. John Westhrop, "UNTAC Reels from Claims Rash," *Phnom Penh Post,* November 5–18, 1993, p. 7.

76. Heininger, *Peacekeeping in Transition,* p. 7. The extent to which the UN "learned" any lessons from Cambodia is questionable: almost a decade later Lesley Abdela reports that during the UNMIK mission to Kosovo, a Kosovar delegate at an NGO meeting said: "You 'internationals' are polluting our air and clogging up our roads with all your white vehicles. You refuse to employ us as professionals in your organisations. There are thousands of you. You all make promises but we neither see action from you 'internationals' nor do you provide us with funds to get on with things ourselves"; Lesley Abdela, Former Deputy-Director Democratisation, OSCE Mission, Kosovo, "Kosovo: Missed Opportunities, Lessons for the Future." Available at www.peacewomen.org/un/pkwatch/abdela.html

77. See Judy Ledgerwood, *Analysis of the Situation of Women in Cambodia* (Phnom Penh: UNICEF, February–June, 1992), p. 7; UNICEF, *Cambodia: The Situation of Children and Women* (Phnom Penh, 1990), p. 111; Ledgerwood, Ebihara, and Mortland, "Introduction," p. 15. As Ledgerwood notes, in some parts of the country, a figure of 25 percent of female-headed households might be more accurate, but in other areas some 41 percent of the households were headed by widows; other studies indicated it was not rare to find villages where the figure was 50 percent (*Analysis of the Situation of Women in Cambodia,* p. 7).

78. Ledgerwood, *Analysis of the Situation of Women in Cambodia,* p. 7.

79. The proverb was used by the UN Development Fund for Women as part of its efforts to advertise the National Women's Summit; see UNIFEM, "Report from the National Women's Summit" (Phnom Penh, March 5–8, 1993), n.p.

80. The proverb is also translated as "men are like a diamond and women are a piece of cotton wool." As numerous commentators have noted, the status of gender in Cambodia intersects with a variety of other social factors, including, for

example, age. See Ledgerwood, *Analysis of the Situation of Women in Cambodia,* pp. 3–6; Judy Ledgerwood, "Gender Symbolism and Culture Change: Viewing the Virtuous Woman in the Khmer Story 'Mea Yoeng,'" in Ebihara, Mortland, and Ledgerwood, *Cambodian Culture Since 1975,* pp. 122–123, 127–128; CARE International in Cambodia, "'Men Are Gold, Women Are Cloth': A Report on the Potential for HIV/AIDS Spread in Cambodia and Implications for HIV/AIDS Education," draft copy (Phnom Penh, 1993), p. 19 and passim; Arnvig, "Women, Children, and Returnees," pp. 145–146; Annuska Derks, "Perspectives on Gender in Cambodia: Myths and Realities," *Cambodia Report* 2, no. 3 (1996): 6–10; Chanthou Boua, "Cotton Wool and Diamonds," *New Internationalist* 242 (April 1993): 20–21.

81. Boua, "Cotton Wool and Diamonds," p. 20.

82. Secretariat of State for Women's Affairs, Kingdom of Cambodia, *Cambodia's Country Report: Women in Development* (Phnom Penh, July 1994), p. 10.

83. Arnvig, "Women, Children, and Returnees," p. 147.

84. Grant Curtis, *Cambodia: A Country Profile* (Stockholm: Swedish International Development Agency, 1980), p. 160.

85. "Report from the National Women's Summit" (Phnom Penh, March 5–8, 1993); interviews, Phnom Penh, March–April 1996. See also Mang Channo, "Women's Day Highlights Gender Inequalities," *Phnom Penh Post,* March 12–25, 1993, p. 1.

86. Interviews, Phnom Penh, March–April, 1996; "Report from the National Women's Summit." Kien Serey Phal of the Cambodian Women's Development Association described to me a series of projects in which they were involved; these focused on literacy training for women and girls who were illiterate, more advanced technological training or language training for those who had a high school education but could not yet find work, and loan programs for women who wanted to start small businesses. Perhaps the most innovative business program was the "loaning" of a cow to a woman for a full year during which the woman would use the milk from the cow and, at the end of the year, would inherit the calf produced by the cow. The original cow would then be loaned to another woman, and the cycle would start again. Other practices outlived UNTAC as well: though it was scaled back to once a week, a special radio broadcast continued that focused on women's issues, including literacy, health, and domestic violence against women.

87. Cathy Zimmerman, Sar Samen, and Men Savorn, "Plates in a Basket Will Rattle: Domestic Violence in Cambodia" (Phnom Penh: Asia Foundation, 1994), p. 141 n. 99 and pp. 137–142 passim.

88. Interviews, Phnom Penh, March–April, 1996; Women's Commission for Refugee Women and Children, "Cambodia Can't Wait," pp. 5–6.

89. Interviews, Phnom Penh, March–April, 1996.

90. Mang Channo, "Sex Trade Flourishing in Capital," *Phnom Penh Post,* February 12–25, 1993, p. 6; "The Problem of Prostitution," *Phnom Penh Post,* February 12–25, 1993, p. 6; Andrew Nettie, "Cambodia: UN Mission Cited as Sex Slavery Spreads," *Sunday Age* (Melbourne), June 25, 1995; Arnvig, "Women, Children and Returnees," pp. 166–169; Kien Serey Phal, "The Lessons of the UNTAC Experience and the Ongoing Responsibilities of the International Community for Peacebuilding and Development in Cambodia," *Pacifica Review* 7, no. 2 (1995): 129–133; Kirshenbaum, "Who's Watching the Peacekeepers?" p. 13. Interviews conducted in Phnom Penh in March–April 1996 as well as numerous reports by NGOs within Phnom Penh confirm these observations; see, for example, Mona Mehta, "Gender Dimensions of Poverty in Cambodia: A Survey Report" (Phnom Penh: Oxfam, 1993), p. 7.

91. Interviews, Phnom Penh, March–April 1996. The rise of child prostitution was linked to the arrival of UNTAC, but observers noted also that with the departure of UNTAC, while the overall number of prostitutes within Cambodia declined, so too did their average age, with a number of reports indicating that the average age of prostitutes working in some areas of Phnom Penh had dropped to fifteen years old. See, for example, UNICEF, "The Trafficking and Prostitution of Children in Cambodia: A Situation Report" (Phnom Penh, 1995), pp. 1–2 and passim, as well as the following reports in Appendix 2: Krousar Thmey, "Child Prostitution and Trafficking in Cambodia: A New Problem," March–October 1995; Keo Keang and Im Phallay, Human Rights Task Force on Cambodia, "Notes on the March–April 1995 Rapid Appraisal of the Human Rights Vigilance of Cambodia on Child Prostitution and Trafficking"; Human Rights Vigilance of Cambodia, "Combating Women Trafficking and Child Prostitution," March–April 1995. See also Cambodian Women's Development Association, "Prostitution Survey Results from Cambodian Women's Development Association" (Phnom Penh, 1994), and Human Rights Task Force on Cambodia, "Prostitution and Sex Trafficking: A Growing Threat to Women and Children in Cambodia" (Phnom Penh, n.d.).

92. Jon Swain, "UN Losing Battle for Cambodia in the Brothels of Phnom Penh," *Sunday Times,* December 27, 1992; Derks, "Vietnamese Prostitutes in Cambodia," p. 6; *Asian Recorder,* May 21–27, 1993, p. 23144.

93. Ledgerwood, "The Lessons from Cambodia," p. 7; Swain, "UN Losing Battle for Cambodia."

94. The Cambodian Women's Development Association indicated in 1994 that the majority of prostitutes working in the Toul Kork area of Phnom Penh were likely Cambodian, and others have indicated that the ethnic origin of prostitutes in Cambodia has always varied, depending on the location of the brothels; Cambodian Women's Development Association, "Prostitution Survey Results," 1994; interviews, Phnom Penh, March–April 1996.

95. Interviews, Phnom Penh, March–April 1996.

96. Ibid.

97. Swain, "UN Losing Battle for Cambodia"; *Asian Recorder,* February 5–11, 1993, p. 22903.

98. Twenty-one UNTAC personnel lost their lives as a result of hostile action, but UNTAC's chief medical officer, Col. Dr. Peter Fraps, estimated that as many as 150 would eventually die of AIDS. Katrina Peach, "HIV Threatens to Claim UNTAC's Highest Casualties," *Phnom Penh Post,* October 22–November 4, 1993, p. 4; "AIDS May Claim Highest UNTAC Toll," *Cambodia Daily,* October 25, 1993, p. 5; "Japanese UNTAC Troops Contracted AIDS Virus," *Cambodia Daily,* October 22–24, 1993, p. 1.

99. UN Department of Peacekeeping Operations and the Joint United Nations Programme on HIV/AIDS, "Protect Yourself, and Those You Care About, Against HIV/AIDS" (New York: United Nations, April 1998), p. 6.

100. Noted in *Asian Recorder,* April 16–22, 1993, p. 23060. Ledgerwood, "The Lessons from Cambodia," p. 8.

101. Arnvig, "Women, Children, and Returnees," p. 165.

102. Reuters Library Report, November 18, 1992.

103. Jennar, "International Triumph in Cambodia?" p. 154.

104. Interviews, Phnom Penh, March–April, 1996. See also Kirshenbaum, "Who's Watching the Peacekeepers?" p. 13.

105. Interviews, Phnom Penh, March–April 1996.

106. Ibid. This was not the only "gender retribution" killing; according to interviewees, a number of other soldiers were killed after they allegedly raped a brothel owner's wife. Those murders were attributed to the Khmer Rouge.

107. Though Khmer denotes a distinct ethnic group within Cambodia, some people use the term synonymously with Cambodian.

108. Sara Colm, "U.N. Agrees to Address Sexual Harassment Issue," *Phnom Penh Post,* October 11, 1992, p. 1.

109. UNTAC, "Report on Public Perceptions," in Arnvig, "Women, Children, and Returnees," p. 177.

110. Colm, "U.N. Agrees to Address Sexual Harassment Issue"; Swain, "UN Losing Battle for Cambodia."

111. "An Open Letter to Yasushi Akashi," *Phnom Penh Post,* October 11, 1992, p. 2; "Allegations of Sexual Harassment Hit U.N. Peacekeeping Forces in Cambodia," *Business Wire,* January 11, 1993.

112. Colm, "U.N. Agrees to Address Sexual Harassment Issue"; "Akashi Responds to Community Concerns," *Phnom Penh Post,* November 20–December 3, 1992, p. 2. The formal notice of the appointment of Ms. Hiroko Miyamura as UNTAC's community relations officer appeared on the back page of the *Phnom Penh Post* in a twelve-line notice: "UNTAC Community Relations Officer," *Phnom Penh Post,* October 23, 1992, p. 16.

113. Interviews, Phnom Penh, March–April, 1996; "An Open Letter to Yasushi Akashi."

114. Yeshua Moser-Puangsuwan, "U.N. Peacekeeping in Cambodia: Whose Needs Were Met?" *Pacifica Review* 7, no. 2 (1995): 106.

115. Ibid., pp. 106–107.

116. Ibid., p. 107.

117. Ibid., pp. 105–106.

118. Amitav Ghosh, "The Global Reservation: Notes Toward an Ethnography of International Peacekeeping," *Cultural Anthropology* 9, no. 3 (1994): 415.

119. Ibid.

120. Ibid.

121. Interviews, Phnom Penh, March–April 1996; Michael Hayes, "Indibatt Gets High Marks for Civic Work," *Phnom Penh Post,* September 24–October 7, 1993, p. 8; Moeun Chhean Nariddh, "German Doctors Prepare to Pack Up," *Phnom Penh Post,* September 24–October 7, 1993, p. 9; Michael Hayes, "With a Little Help from the Troops," *Phnom Penh Post,* April 23–May 6, 1993, p. 16.

122. Hayes, "With a Little Help from the Troops."

123. Orford, *Reading Humanitarian Intervention,* p. 160 and Chap. 5 passim.

124. Kien, "The Lessons of the UNTAC Experience," p. 132.

125. Heininger, *Peacekeeping in Transition: The United Nations in Cambodia,* pp. 75–76, 129.

126. Alan James, "Peacekeeping in the Post–Cold War Era," *International Journal* 50, no. 2 (spring 1995): 246.

127. A. B. Fetherston makes a similar argument in "UN Peacekeepers and Cultures of Violence," *Cultural Survival Quarterly* 19, no. 1 (1995): 19–23.

128. Joseph T. Jockel, *Canada and International Peacekeeping* (Washington, DC: Center for Strategic and International Studies, 1994), p. 1.

129. This term is used to describe Canada's role in peacekeeping in Alex Morrison and Suzanne M. Plain, "Canada: The Seasoned Veteran," presented at the International Studies Association Annual Meetings, Washington, DC, March 28–April 1, 1994.

4

Canada: Peacekeeping Country Par Excellence?

The image of a Canadian soldier wearing his blue beret, standing watch at some lonely outpost in a strife-torn foreign land, is part of the modern Canadian mosaic, and a proud tradition.

—General Paul Manson[1]

The fact is, peacekeeping is boring.

—Kyle Brown, former paratrooper[2]

Arone lapsed in and out of consciousness during the beating. When he was conscious, he was heard to scream "Canada, Canada," on several occasions.

—Commission of Inquiry into the
Deployment of Canadian Forces to Somalia[3]

The image of Canada as peacekeeper, so aptly described by former chief of the defense staff General Paul Manson, has long-served as one of the "core myths"[4] of Canada's "imagined community."[5] That myth locates Canada as an altruistic and benign middle power, acting with a kind of moral purity not normally exhibited by contemporary states and confirms Canada's premiere status as one of the most experienced peacekeeping countries in the world.[6] Thus, when two Canadian soldiers beat to death a Somali teenager, Shidane Abukar Arone, in March 1993—using their fists, their boots, a baton, a metal rod, and cigarettes—the myth was reasserted at the very moment it began to disintegrate. Arone's only words in English that night were to repeat the name "Canada, Canada" throughout his ordeal. The myth had been sold so well that even a sixteen-year-old Somali shepherd, murdered by those who were supposed to be its exemplars, apparently believed in it.

Arone's tragic death, and the shooting several weeks earlier of two Somali men by Canadian soldiers, sparked a series of court-martials and eventually prompted the Canadian government to launch a commission of inquiry to investigate the activities of its forces in Somalia. Intended to resuscitate the image of Canada's military and Canada's reputation internationally, many of those investigations focused on problems of a "few bad apples" or otherwise lamented a decline of traditional military values. More rarely were the events of Somalia associated with the problems of militarized masculinity and the use of soldiers—people trained to destroy other human beings by force—in peace operations.[7] The Canadian Airborne's mission to Somalia not only reveals some of the contradictions of one of Canada's "core myths" but also provides a unique case through which to study the complex and often contradictory configurations of racism, homophobia, and misogyny that sustain militarized masculinities. One thing that became clear through the inquiry, media coverage, and various exposés surrounding the events in Somalia was that soldiers trained for battle often feel cheated by their peacekeeping role. As military historian David Bercuson suggests, "Prolonged peace is a time of trial for any military."[8]

By the time the Airborne arrived in Somalia, their mission had been upgraded from a Chapter VI to a Chapter VII mission.[9] This was what Canada's celebrated Major General (retired) Lewis MacKenzie would later describe as a "non-blue-beret fight," a mission more prestigious than a traditional peacekeeping tour of duty.[10] Members of the Airborne, though they would not deploy by parachute as they had been trained to do,[11] *would* get to be real soldiers. Real soldiers are not limited to light arms or to firing only in self-defense. They might experience the adrenalin rush of coming under fire, or firing back in anger, something Peter Worthington notes no Canadian soldier had done since the Korean War.[12] As the only soldier charged in Arone's murder said after his release from prison (and apparently with no intended irony): "The fact is, peacekeeping is boring and we were much happier to be going to Somalia in a Chapter VII role. Personally, I was delighted."[13]

This chapter explores how Canadian representations of nation and military depend on the benign and altruistic image of Canada as peacekeeper—an image that is fundamentally at odds with the roles soldiers are expected, and indeed were *created,* to perform. As argued in Chapter 6, soldiers are not born; rather they are made, through training, institutional expectations, psychological conditioning, and a variety of material and ideological rewards. What has been particularly revealing in the Canadian case has been the dangerous behavior that erupts when soldiers trained "to engage in wanton destruction and to slip the bonds of civilized behaviour"[14] have historically been limited and constrained to mere peacekeeping duty. The Airborne, when it was chosen to go to Somalia by the Department of National Defence (DND), anticipated a traditional peacekeeping mission. By the time it arrived, its members had been given license, finally and without precedent for some forty years, to act like real soldiers. The events that resulted shocked people both in Canada and around the world. Canada's image as the liberal internationalist state and neutral arbiter of conflicts was built in part on the myth of a benign and altruistic military. What Somalia demonstrated was how precarious this image of Canada and how flimsy this myth of a wholesome military really were.

Canada and Peacekeeping

Peacekeeping is an extremely popular activity within Canada. Images of Canadian peacekeepers appear prominently on the Canadian currency, during election campaigns and national unity debates, and in Canadian politics and history texts. Peacekeeping was reviewed favorably in the most recent reviews of both foreign and defense policy and seen as central to Canadian foreign and security policies. As the 1994 DND statement noted:

> In virtually every one of these [successful peacekeeping] cases, Canada has played a constructive and often leading role. Canadians are rightly proud of what their country—their military—has done in this regard. Indeed, the demand for our services, and arguably the need, is growing. Since 1988, the United Nations has undertaken more peacekeeping missions than in the previous thirty-five years, and Canada has been a key participant in almost every one of them.[15]

The Standing Committee on National Defence and Veterans Affairs also affirmed Canada's commitment to peacekeeping, writing in 1993: "Canadians have always seen peacekeeping as an important element of their identity and of their country's position on the international stage, even when peacekeeping meant little to much of the international community."[16] Likewise, as Janice Stein reported to the special joint committee reviewing Canada's foreign policy in 1994, "the overwhelming sense [is] that this is an area of comparative advantage for Canadians."[17]

Canadian government documents reveal an assumption not only that Canadians are experienced and committed peacekeepers but also that peacekeeping is a clear extension of Canadian values on the international stage. According to the 1995 government statement, *Canada in the World:*

> Canadians are confident in their values and in the contribution these values make to the international community. . . . Our principles and values— our culture—are rooted in a commitment to tolerance; to democracy, equity and human rights; to the peaceful resolution of differences; to the opportunities and challenges of the marketplace; to social justice; to sustainable development; and to easing poverty.[18]

Or as Stéphane Dion, president of the Privy Council and Minister of Inter-governmental Affairs, enthusiastically commented: "Canada is a good global citizen, projecting beyond our borders our values of generosity, tolerance and an unswerving commitment to peace and democracy."[19]

Such widespread government support does not mean that there are no disagreements within the Canadian government about peacekeeping. The Department of National Defence's enthusiasm for peacekeeping is tempered somewhat by the fact that it does not require as much capital expenditure as the geostrategic defense of Canada and its allies. As the defense white paper stated repeatedly, there is more to defense than peacekeeping, or as Major General (retired) Glen Younghusband pointed out to the special joint committee reviewing Canada's defense policy in 1994, "To believe that Canada will never require a greater military capability than peacekeeping is wishful thinking, and a defence policy based on wishful thinking would be dangerous indeed."[20]

More recently, concerns have been raised about spreading the forces too thin and taking on too many peacekeeping roles. In general, however, the advantages of peacekeeping are widely accepted, and—DND anxieties notwithstanding—its popularity has been central in securing a certain amount of financial support for the Canadian military.[21]

Government support for peacekeeping is reflected within the general population. In a 1995 study, Pierre Martin and Michel Fortmann observe that peacekeeping has enjoyed a relatively high level of public support within Canada throughout its history, often receiving in public opinion polls higher support than any other role for the Canadian armed forces.[22] As Martin and Fortmann point out, the generally positive image of the military in Canadian society is in considerable measure due to its participation in UN peacekeeping forces. Also in 1995, a variety of women's groups appearing before a joint committee reviewing Canada's foreign policy made a number of important criticisms of peacekeeping, but the majority of the groups were quite supportive and encouraged expansion of peacekeeping.[23] Peace groups too have argued for a shift in emphasis of the Canadian military from "combat to peacekeeping."[24] Even the Citizens' Inquiry into Peace and Security (an "alternative" foreign and defense review organized by the Canadian Peace Alliance and funded by a number of largely peace, native, and labor NGOs) found that support for peacekeeping activities was "virtually unanimous."[25]

The image of Canada as peacekeeper serves the Canadian government's international interests as well. According to Joseph T. Jockel, "Canada's reputation as a good international 'citizen,' a reputation acquired partially through extensive peacekeeping, may have strengthened its position in the UN across a wide range of issues on the world agenda."[26] It certainly played a role in Canada's successful bid for a Security Council seat in 1998, and Jockel notes that in the post–Cold War period:

> Canada was the peacekeeping country *par excellence,* having contributed
> to virtually all UN peacekeeping operations . . . [its] peacekeeping expe-
> rience, coupled with its well-recognized commitment to the UN, appeared
> to have left it especially suited to play if not a leading role, then at least a
> significant one in the building of the new world order.[27]

Indeed, as numerous commentators have noted, it has been Canada's
involvement in peacekeeping and its "history of altruism, compassion, fair-
ness, and of doing things irrespective of our own national interest" that
gives it international influence far out of proportion to its military or economic power."[28] As Carol Off writes: "Canada is one of only a handful of
nations that include peacekeeping as a permanent part of their national
defence, and no other country gives peacekeeping such a defining role in its
international politics. It's in our genetic code as a nation."[29]

Assumptions about both peacekeeping and the Canadian nation are thus
inextricably linked and mutually reinforcing. The visual images associated
with Canada's proud tradition (see Photographs 1 and 4–5) (re)present the
blue-bereted soldier as benevolent, altruistic, and above all, peaceful. Peacekeepers are depicted serving food and drinks, talking with local citizens,
greeting elderly women, and playing with children. The Canadian soldier as
peacekeeper is not a warrior but a protector. These are (re)presentations that
fit very well with the more generalized notions of moral purity that pervade

Photograph 4 Canadian UN peacekeepers serve refreshments to Haitians,
November 1997 *(AP Photo/Daniel Morel)*

Photograph 5
A Canadian captain
swings one of 120
orphans at the Soeur
Donat Orphanage in
Kenscoff, Haiti
(CP Photo 1996/Jeff McIntosh)

Canadian foreign policies toward developing countries (in their presentation if not their substance)[30] and the much-touted view of Canada as a
"middle power," which has informed most government statements and
mainstream analyses of Canadian foreign policy since World War II. As a
middle power and peacekeeper, Canada quite literally stands as an interposition force between conflicting parties.[31]

    Canada's commitment to peacekeeping was also, in no small measure,
intended to contrast with the far more ambivalent position on peacekeeping
found in the United States, where peacekeeping does not receive the same
widespread public support and where peace operations generally are treated
with considerable caution, and sometimes outright hostility. It is difficult to
imagine the Canadian state falling into arrears to the UN for peacekeeping
contributions, a consistent problem with the United States, and equally
unthinkable that a Canadian soldier would be lauded by some political

elites for refusing to serve under UN command, as occurred in the United States with the 1995 case of Specialist Michael New.[32] As the Somalia commission wrote in 1997:

> Canada's foreign policy with respect to peacekeeping has been consistent since Canadians embraced peacekeeping in the late 1950s. Peacekeeping has become a characteristic Canadian metier, a function distinguishing us from Americans and reinforcing our sovereignty and independence. Americans were seen to fight wars, but Canadians pictured themselves as working for peace.[33]

Or, as Sherene Razack notes, "Peacekeeping as a national vocation, and as the dream of a middle power that exists next door to the United States, neatly enables Canada to tell a story of national goodness and to mark itself as distinct from the United States."[34] Through its policy decisions and the activities of its people sent abroad, Canada was depicted as the international community's "helpful fixer."[35]

The Reputation Tarnished: Canadian Forces in Somalia

The favorable image associated with both Canada and the Canadian military was shaken to its core when reports emerged from Somalia in 1993 of the shooting of two Somali men and then the subsequent torture and murder of Arone by members of Canada's elite Airborne Regiment stationed near the town of Belet Huen.[36] The two men who were shot, it was learned later, had been lured into the Canadian compound with food and water left out as bait by the Canadian soldiers.[37] Most of the soldiers involved reported that they did not see the Somali men carrying any weapons, and neither did they fear for their personal safety; but nonetheless, both men were shot in the back, and one, Ahmed Aruush, was killed. Those who overheard the shooting also reported that soldiers yelled "we got one" after the shots rang out.[38] The Canadians had been told that they were allowed to shoot infiltrators, though commander of the Airborne regiment in Belet Huen, Lieutenant Colonel Carol Mathieu, later changed the directive and indicated that soldiers should shoot trespassers in the legs, "between the skirt and the flip flops."[39] While an initial investigation concluded that the Airborne soldiers had acted properly, a Canadian military doctor later reported that the dead man had been shot once in the back and then "someone had finished him off with a . . . lethal shot to the head."[40] The doctor reported, moreover, that he had been pressured to destroy his medical records concerning the alleged murder.[41]

Two weeks later, Shidane Arone was caught by Canadian soldiers in a nearby abandoned U.S. compound. A "snatch patrol" had set out at nightfall on March 16 because the Americans had left various materials and garbage around their base, and not unlike the bait that had been left out the night Aruush was killed, it was expected that "infiltrators" would try to steal some of the leftover goods and garbage.[42] Arone's capture could not have come at a worse time: it was the first evening after platoon commanders received orders from Major Tony Seward that it was permissible to "abuse" infiltrators who resisted capture.[43] His intention, he said afterward, was to prevent shootings like those that had occurred earlier by convincing infiltrators that their lives would be at risk should they return.[44]

Arone was found hiding in a portable toilet, and he was taken to a bunker built into the sand, which the Canadians had been using to hold prisoners. Normally, anyone found within the Canadian or surrounding compounds would be held overnight and then turned over to local authorities in the morning. The Canadians were reportedly frustrated that prisoners usually were released immediately by the Belet Huen police. Arone was questioned through an interpreter, and he explained that he was looking for a lost child who had wandered away from his family's nearby huts. His feet and hands were tied, with a riot baton used to hold his arms behind him and limit his movements. The soldiers had already discussed Major Seward's abuse order, and after questioning Arone, the sergeant on duty left the bunker and said to the two soldiers who were to guard him, "I don't care what you do, just don't kill the guy."[45]

Master Corporal Clayton Matchee and Private Elvin Kyle Brown began by hitting and kicking Arone in the ribs, the legs, and the face. While Brown did not participate in the actual beating much beyond this, he did nothing to stop Matchee, who continued for over two hours to beat Arone with kicks, punches, and then with a riot baton and a metal rod. Matchee smashed a ration pack over Arone's head and burnt the soles of his feet with cigars or cigarettes. One of the doctors who examined Arone also said that he had burn marks on his genitals and had been anally raped with the baton.[46] Brown reported later that the more Matchee beat Arone, "the more berserk he got."[47] Matchee said repeatedly that he "wanted to kill this fucker."[48]

A number of soldiers came by the bunker throughout the evening—as many as seventeen—and saw Arone at various stages of the beating and some apparently delivered their own punches or kicks to the young man. One shoved the muzzle of a loaded rifle down Arone's throat, and another gave Matchee his loaded pistol, which he held repeatedly to Arone's head. Other soldiers could hear Arone's screams from their nearby tents, the sentry post, and even the command post. Sixteen-year-old Shidane Abukar Arone died shortly after midnight. In the sanitized language of the Somalia Inquiry's final report: "Death was preceded . . . by prolonged and severe pain and suffering."[49]

If the details of these atrocities were not enough, Canada's peacekeeping image was rocked even further when, at the court-martial proceedings, it was revealed not only that Shidane Arone had been horribly tortured before his death but that his torturers had also photographed his ordeal. The view of the Canadian forces suddenly, and very dramatically, changed, and the Canadian public started to see new and disturbing images of their beloved Canadian peacekeepers. The photographs—described as "trophy photos"—depicted Matchee and Brown striking various poses with the bloodied Arone, one of which showed Matchee holding the loaded pistol to Arone's head and another in which Matchee forced Arone's mouth open with the riot baton.[50]

Mainstream observers of peacekeeping in Canada initially dismissed the shootings and the Arone murder as the acts of a few "bad apples"[51]— and likely the result of years of defense underfunding. Joseph Jockel argued that the Somalia crisis was the result of a personnel shortage, caused in turn by economic downsizing. Under these circumstances, the army "felt compelled to send to Somalia a unit of the Canadian Airborne Regiment whose fitness for deployment was doubtful."[52] This was an unusual way to defend the Airborne, an elite unit within the Canadian forces, and one that in principle was prepared to deploy to any location in the world with little or no advance warning. The Airborne had been given some three months to prepare for Somalia.

The bad apple theory was undermined when, some months after an inquiry was called into the events in Somalia, a number of videos were released to the Canadian media. The first was a video from the Somalia mission, taken by Canadian soldiers on duty there as a personal record, portions of which portrayed Airborne soldiers describing the Somalia mission as "Operation Snatch Niggers" and others lamenting that "they had not shot enough niggers yet." The second video showed one of the Airborne commando unit's hazing (or initiation) rituals; they included Airborne soldiers vomiting or eating vomit, being smeared with feces, and simulating oral sex with a toy gun and anal sex with one another. In this video, the lone black soldier in the regiment was tied to a tree with white powder thrown on him and then forced to walk around on all fours with the phrase "I love KKK" written on his back (see Photographs 6–9).[53]

The problem was apparently far more pervasive than simply "a few bad apples," and it was not the shootings or the murder of Shidane Arone but the release of the hazing videos that led the minister of national defense to announce on January 23, 1995, that the elite Airborne regiment would be disbanded.[54] As Romeo St. Martin wrote:

> Allegations of racism, torture and murder weren't enough to bring down
> the Canadian Airborne unit. Even a videotape filled with racist comments

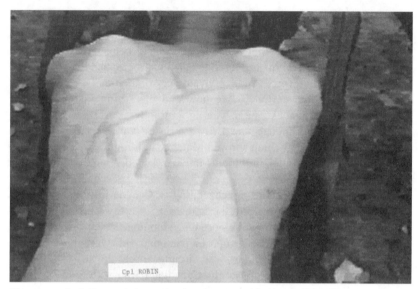

Photograph 6 From 1 Commando's hazing video: Corporal Chris Robin walking on all fours with "I love KKK" on his back *(Information Legacy: A Compendium of Source Material from the Commission of Inquiry into the Deployment of Canadian Forces to Somalia. Government of Canada, 1997)*

Photograph 7 From 1 Commando's hazing video: A member of the Airborne simulating oral sex on a toy gun *(Information Legacy: A Compendium of Source Material from the Commission of Inquiry into the Deployment of Canadian Forces to Somalia. Government of Canada, 1997)*

Photograph 8 From 1 Commando's hazing video: A member of the Airborne pretending to sodomize Corporal Robin *(Information Legacy: A Compendium of Source Material from the Commission of Inquiry into the Deployment of Canadian Forces to Somalia. Government of Canada, 1997)*

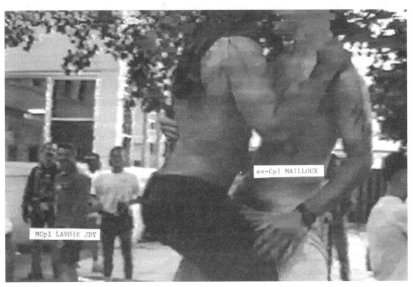

Photograph 9 From 1 Commando's hazing video: Two members of the Airborne involved in homoerotic play *(Information Legacy: A Compendium of Source Material from the Commission of Inquiry into the Deployment of Canadian Forces to Somalia. Government of Canada, 1997)*

was dismissed as "bravado" by the unit's supporters. However video of the Canadian troops frolicking in a sea of vomit, piss and shit outraged the public and was cause for swift action by Defence Minister David Collenette to disband the regiment.[55]

The court-martial eventually found Elvin Kyle Brown guilty of torture and manslaughter and convicted him to five years in prison and dismissed him in disgrace. Brown was released on full parole after serving one-third of his sentence, a little less than two years. Clayton Matchee apparently attempted suicide after his arrest in Somalia, suffered brain damage, and was found unfit to stand trial at his subsequent court-martial. A number of other soldiers were found guilty of lesser charges, including Major Seward, who had issued the abuse order, and Sergeant Boland, who had left the bunker in which Arone was being held with the words, "Just don't kill the guy." Boland served one year and Seward three months. Both were dismissed from the forces. Another officer, Captain Michael Sox, was found guilty of negligent performance of duty. Sox had planned the mission into the U.S. compound and had passed along to his men Major Seward's abuse order (though he did not know about or partake in the murder of Arone). He received a severe reprimand and a reduction in rank. Other soldiers, who had heard or seen what was going on in the bunker but had not stopped the beating and murder, were also charged with a variety of offenses, but all were acquitted.

The government inquiry that had been called to investigate the events in Somalia was halted before it could examine Arone's murder. The commissioners were accused of taking too long to conduct their investigation, though most of their requests for extra time resulted from a series of separate investigations that had to be launched into the delaying tactics of the Department of National Defence. The department refused to release some documents and claimed that others had been destroyed. Still other documents were found to be altered. Operational logs, for example, were missing pages, but only around the dates of the March 4 shooting and Arone's March 16 murder. The DND was not accustomed to this kind of scrutiny, and as then chief of the defense staff General Jean Boyle revealed in testimony at the inquiry, the department had regularly chosen not to provide documents to the commission if it could not see their relevance to the investigation. This despite the fact that a commission of inquiry is required, through Canadian federal law, to have access to all relevant information; information, in other words, not normally vetted by the very department under investigation.[56]

In the end, the Department of National Defence's slow pace so prolonged the inquiry's deliberations into what were considered "side issues" that the inquiry had exceeded its allotted time and was cut short. This was the first time in Canadian history that a commission of inquiry of this magnitude was brought to a halt before its completion. The commission was called on to deliver a report without ever hearing testimony or fully investigating the torture and murder of Shidane Arone, or allegations that the DND tried to cover up the details of the murder afterward. Arone, whose dying hours were partly responsible for calling the inquiry, remained largely unheard and invisible within the official investigation of his murder.

A Somali Teenager

The failure of the inquiry to investigate Arone's murder fits well with Daniel Francis's notion of forgetting: "As a community, we forget as much as we remember, and what we choose to forget tells as much about us as what we choose to remember."[57] The "forgetting" of Arone, in fact, had been happening long before the Canadian government halted the inquiry. Many newspaper reports quickly dropped any mention of Arone's name; for much of the coverage he was simply "a Somali teenager" and the murders themselves were regularly described as "unfortunate incidents." At the same time the inquiry was being conducted, the minister of defense ordered a series of parallel research reports into the Canadian forces from academics, most of whom operated out of university-affiliated research centers funded by the Department of National Defence. The minister was likely hoping for—and received—a series of academically sound investigations that would provide some helpful criticisms without seriously undermining the Canadian forces or DND. These reports, delivered to the public in the rarefied atmosphere of Canada's historic War Museum, made little mention of Shidane Arone or Ahmed Aruush.

At the inquiry, the focus of deliberations was limited strictly to an examination of the institutional shortcomings that had contributed to the events in Somalia.[58] Sherene Razack observes that "one of the earliest decisions made by the inquiry was to limit the participation of Somali and Somali Canadian voices." The inquiry would not go to Somalia to interview the peoples of Belet Huen; it would not consider videotaped testimonies; indeed it would not even hear from the Canadian forces' key Somali interpreter during the mission.[59] Similarly, at least some of the language of the inquiry reinforced the idea that its chief purpose was to inquire not into the loss of Shidane Arone but rather into the loss of Canada's elite Airborne unit. In an early comment, one of the commissioners pointed out that when the deputy minister of defense signed the final order to deploy the Airborne to Somalia, he was "unwittingly signing the death warrant of the regiment."[60] Commissioner Desbarats did not correct himself, or bother to remark even as an afterthought that this official had also unwittingly signed the death warrants of both Aruush and Arone. With little public outcry, the inquiry came to a close with the minister of defense noting that the military simply could not stand to be shaken by any further revelations.[61] The loss of the Airborne, it would seem, was quite enough.

Even in the absence of a full and complete investigation of Arone's death and the alleged cover-up, the commission issued a five-volume report, entitled *Dishonoured Legacy,* containing over 150 recommendations. While critical of the military in a number of important respects, the final report reproduced the theme that had already been emphasized by military apologists. The problem was not one of the military but rather one of a military gone wrong:

> It is the sharp contrast between [the events in Somalia] and the accustomed performance of our military that elicited reactions of alarm, outrage, and sadness among Canadians. In the end, we are hopeful that our Inquiry will yield corrective measures to help restore the Canadian Forces to the position of honour they have held for so long.[62]

The events in Somalia, the final report argued, were a result of poor training and even poorer leadership. Or, as David Bercuson argued, the Canadian military had become stifled by budget cuts, was over-bureaucratized and staffed by career-minded "cover your ass" officers who had replaced the disciplined and honorable leaders of the past: "Matchee and Brown killed Arone because Canada's people, government, military, and specifically its army have failed to keep real soldiers, combat effectiveness, and traditional military leadership at the centre of the Canadian army."[63] The problem, in short, was a failure of traditional military values. Somalia was a crisis for Canada not because of what happened to the Somali men brutalized by Canadian soldiers but because of what it said to Canadians about their beloved military.[64]

Feminist and Critical Questions

Feminist, postcolonial, and critical theorists might ask instead whether the "problem" was actually one of military values themselves. From their perspective, Somalia demonstrated not a departure from traditional military values but rather their brutal conclusion. In one of the first documents put on the agenda at the inquiry, a "Study of Psychological Fitness for Combat Duty," Major R. W. J. Wenek notes that militaries, by definition, must select for, and reinforce, aggressive behavior. Ominously, and in an observation that might have served as a prediction of the murders in Somalia some ten years later, he added that "it may be extremely difficult to make fine distinctions between those individuals who can be counted on to act in an appropriately aggressive way and those likely at some time to display inappropriate aggression. *To some extent, the risk of erring on the side of excess may be a necessary one in an organization whose existence is premised on the instrumental value of aggression and violence.*"[65] More chilling still, Wenek noted that while this is true in all combat units, it is particularly true in elite units such as paratroopers, commandos, and special service forces. Particularly true, in other words, of the kind of unit Canada deployed to Somalia.

It is imperative to ask, then, whether the selection for, training, hazing, and other measures that helped to turn Kyle Brown, Clayton Matchee, and their compatriots into soldiers "erred on the side of excess." What if Shidane Arone died a horrible death because that is a necessary if unfortunate feature of an organization whose existence is premised on the instrumental value of aggression and violence? The recipe for creating soldiers involves selecting for and reinforcing aggressive behavior; it also can entail an explosive mix of misogyny, racism, and homophobia, coupled with a siege mentality. A deeper analysis of the murders in Somalia and Canada's Somalia Inquiry reveals all of these ingredients to have been present in Canada's armed forces.

Rereading the Somalia Crisis

Soldiers in Canada's Airborne regiment were excited to be going to Somalia, especially as it became clear that it might become a Chapter VII mission. As was noted above, Elvin Kyle Brown, like many of his fellow soldiers, was "delighted."[66] The Airborne had been chosen to go while Somalia was still designated a "blue beret mission," but according to Major General MacKenzie, it was evident from the media coverage that this mission would be upgraded to a Chapter VII, and this would mean real soldiering. The mission indeed was changed in early December 1992, just before the Airborne deployed. As one soldier commented, "I think the men were glad when the mission changed from peacekeeping to peace making . . . this was more real. We're training for war all our lives, and the guys all want to know what it is like. That's why they join the army, to soldier."[67] Or, as Peter Worthington notes: "The change of mandate held promise of more challenge, more excitement, more responsibility, even action. They might even have to fight."[68]

Airborne soldiers also felt that they were members of an elite unit: "a cut above the ordinary infantry soldier. Members of the Airborne saw other combat troops and non-combat personnel as inferior."[69] Soldiers and officers joined the Airborne first by applying to, and passing, a "jump" course followed by the Airborne Indoctrination Course.[70] They were trained to deploy rapidly into almost any setting. The fact that Canada's elite combat-ready unit seldom had the opportunity to deploy on missions other than peacekeeping or internal security (such as Montreal's 1976 Olympic games) likely made the prospect of deploying to Somalia under a Chapter VII mission all the more appealing.

Apparently a number of Airborne soldiers were so excited by the prospect of real soldiering that they allegedly torched an officer's car and others went into a provincial park and fired off their weapons in a small shooting spree. Asked at the inquiry whether these acts might have signaled discipline problems within the Airborne, Major General MacKenzie replied that while it didn't excuse what the soldiers did, these incidents could be explained by the fact that there had been few Chapter VII missions in UN history to that point and the soldiers were all "psyched up." Somalia had become "a non-blue-beret fight," and although "some of this is macho stuff," there was "more prestige" for Airborne soldiers. The greater prestige resulted, he said, from the fact that soldiers on a Chapter VII mission can take "premeditated" action if they need to. They are no longer restricted, in short, to firing their weapons in self-defense.[71]

The change of mission would mean everything to the defenders of the Airborne who came later. The Canadian public, the inquiry commissioners, and the Canadian media were reminded regularly that the mission to Somalia was *not* peacekeeping. It was not going to be, as MacKenzie noted, "a nice, quaint little quiet, peacekeeping mission in Somalia."[72] A mission that was not, strictly speaking, peacekeeping, could not be judged by peacekeeping's standards. As Razack writes: "When the incidents of violence came to light, it became a fact of considerable importance that the mission was characterized as one not of peacekeeping, per se, but of peace enforcement. What this meant to those making the distinction was that the troops operated within a warlike and dangerous context."[73] And in war, ugly things happen. As one soldier commented, "The fact that it was peace making and not peacekeeping played a large role in what happened I think. The Airborne went in to expect the worst."[74]

But after their training, their preparation, and perhaps most important, their anticipation of real soldiering, the Airborne discovered that the war had moved on from Belet Huen. The country was hot, dusty, dry, and full of scorpions—which provided a certain amount of danger during otherwise boring daily routines, but little in the way of exciting military action. Life in Somalia was unpleasant, but Belet Huen was not a war zone. One soldier remarked, "When we got there, there was no war. The war had gone by. Probably for some guys that was a disappointment."[75] As Winslow notes, "Once the Canadians concluded that they were 'wasting their time' in Somalia, came the brutal conclusion that one could die 'for nothing.'"[76] Once Canadian soldiers came to that conclusion, their own brutal violence began.

The Canadians, indeed, had already decided that Somalis—in particular Somali men—could not be trusted. They were black; they were the enemy; they had no respect for their women; they were liars and thieves; they were not grateful for Canadian efforts; and they were even, in the opinion of many Airborne soldiers, homosexuals. Marked in this way, the violence perpetrated on them seems almost inevitable. As Razack argues, it "is a short step from cultural difference to naturalized violence,"[77] and this was certainly in evidence in Somalia.

While the release of the two videotapes was perhaps the most obvious indication of racism within the Airborne—and apparently shocked many Canadians—officials at the DND might not have been surprised at all. It was learned within the first week of the Somalia Inquiry's hearings that the department had been investigating the presence of racist skinhead organizations and neo-nazi activities within the Canadian Forces, and had identified the entire CFB Petawawa (home of the Airborne regiment) as "one of the several areas where right-wing activities are centred."[78] Senior military officials, in other words, had allowed members of the Airborne regiment who were either known members of racist skinhead organizations or who were under investigation for suspected skinhead and neo-nazi activity to be deployed to Somalia.[79]

The military's apologists were greatly relieved and quick to point out that none of the suspected skinheads in the Airborne regiment were actually charged in Arone's murder.[80] Whether or not the racism exhibited by Airborne soldiers was "organized" through neo-nazi or skinhead activity, much of the evidence from soldiers' testimonies, photographs, diaries, and letters home reveals the ways racism pervaded the Airborne. From posing in front of the Confederate rebel flag (a flag often used by white supremacist groups in the United States), through tattooing themselves with swastikas, to calling Somalis any number of racist pejoratives ("smufty," "smoofties," "moolie," "flip-flop," "nig nog," "nigger," and "gimmes"),[81] Canadian soldiers demonstrated repeatedly that they viewed the Somali people as "other" and inferior.

Many of the Canadians assumed that the desperate poverty they witnessed in Somalia was the result of a backward culture that fostered laziness among ordinary men and women. As paratrooper Robert Prouse recorded in his diary from the mission, fellow soldiers said that Somalia should be used "as a nuclear dump, it's worthless," and others asked: "F_____g [*sic*] tar monkeys, why should we help them? If they haven't improved in the last thousand years, they won't improve now. They're so backwards, why bother?" As Prouse commented, "The majority of our people hate the Somalis and the country."[82] Many also considered Somalis a people with little respect for human life, who had different standards, and different expectations about death and violence.[83] Kyle Brown reported that in Somalia, "[Violence is a] part of their culture, and a language they understand."[84] If nothing else, one soldier complained, it was hard to distinguish between the "good guys" and the "bad guys": "They're all Black, who's who? They all look alike."[85]

Airborne soldiers also saw Somalis as different from the Canadians in terms of their attitudes toward women. In interviews with Donna Winslow, soldiers reported how angered they were by the way Somali men treated both women and children. Soldiers found the practice of female circumcision disturbing, and so too the way in which Somali women and children seemed to do all of the work. As one soldier reported, "It's frustrating to see. Women do everything over there. They get the water, cook, do everything. . . . But the men, they sit around, don't do anything all day long. They visit their friends and that's about it." Another commented, "I didn't like the way they hit kids. I didn't like the fact that the children slept outside the huts. I didn't like what they did to their women which to me was mutilation . . . the women, and you would see little girls, with back breaking loads."[86]

The same soldier noted that, in the end, the contrast between Canadian and Somali attitudes toward women was a cultural one, part of what marked Somalis as different: "Certainly in your mind you say 'you lazy son of a you know. Why don't you get off of your [sic] and help that poor little girl.' But that's part of our culture. You don't treat women like that."[87] Other soldiers reported their efforts in forcing Somali men to do some work, or in ensuring that women and children had access to food supplies before the men: "When it came to distributing things, the men would all push to the front while the women and the children were at the back. The troops physically held the men aside so that the women and the children could go first. We know culturally that that's against the rules, but [it's] one thing that we couldn't deal with."[88]

Somali men not only seemed different in terms of how they treated women but also in terms of how they interacted with one another. Many of the Canadian men quickly concluded that "Everybody's gay here!"[89] Somali men wore sarongs, they held hands with one another as expressions of friendship and urinated by squatting. As one soldier described it: "Real men wear pants and stand to urinate and they certainly don't hold hands."[90] Soldiers reported to Winslow that the hand-holding was evidence that "there was quite a lot of homosexuality" in Somalia. Another commented, "The Somalis weren't as much of a man because they hold hands."[91]

The reviled and hated racialized and sexualized "other" all looked the same, treated "their" women badly, and were a bunch of homosexuals. But the last straw was that they also did not act nearly grateful enough to the soldiers who had arrived in "Operation Deliverance." Razack writes that "the Canadian military understood its role as 'putting that region of Somalia back on the path to a normal lifestyle.' Or, in the more direct language of the troops, their task was to 'look after' Somalis who, as it turns out, were neither properly grateful nor deserving, a source of considerable aggravation for the troops."[92] Winslow notes that "If the soldiers believed they would arrive and portray the soldier-hero-humanitarian, the reality of the field situation was a rude awakening."[93] That reality included having rocks thrown at them, being called insulting names, and confronting people who did not seem to appreciate the work that the Canadians were doing for them.[94] Canadian soldiers, in short, thought they had come to save a desperate people from themselves—or to paraphrase Gayatri Spivak, they came as white men to save brown women from brown men[95]—and discovered that neither the brown women nor the brown men were particularly interested in being saved.

As the soldiers became increasingly frustrated with the apparent lack of gratitude, the rock throwing, the begging, and the petty thefts, their own responses became correspondingly more violent. Soldiers started throwing rocks back at the Somalis, sometimes in order to disperse children begging for food and water.[96] Others taunted the children: "by putting water bottles on sticks and when the kids jumped for them the guy would pull them away."[97] One photograph showed a Canadian chaplain standing guard over a number of bound and blindfolded Somali children with a sign that read "I am a thief" hanging around their necks. In a letter home to his wife, Major Seward (who later issued the abuse order) described a "humourous" incident in which trespassing children were captured and threatened with having their hands cut off, "in accordance with Islamic law." Soldiers pretended to carry out the punishment, by crashing a machete down on a table just missing the outstretched hand of a blindfolded child, and then threw a bucket of ice cold water over him instead. The child "promptly fainted and defecated." Seward wrote: "It sounds awful, but if you were sitting here, you'd be laughing too. Soldiers' humour is infectious."[98] As one soldier described to Winslow, "Basically everybody beat up on the Somalis. Everybody did."[99]

Beating up Somalis was only part of the equation of violence, as became all too clear after the shooting and Arone's torture and murder. Robert Prouse wrote in his diary that after just a month in Somalia, "Everyone is itching to get a kill, even if it is an innocent."[100] Certainly this was compounded by the image Canadian military officials tried to establish in Somalia: the Airborne officer in charge of the Canadian deployment at Belet Huen, Lieutenant Colonel Carol Mathieu, let his men know that he wanted to establish a reputation as the "meanest warlord" in the area.[101] Reports also emerged in the military investigations, court-martials and the inquiry itself that it was widely known that Colonel Serge Labbé, commander of the joint force in Somalia, was rumored to have offered a case of champagne to the first soldier to kill a Somali.[102]

Warrior Princes?

The racism and violence witnessed in Somalia was largely attributed to the "frustration," "stress," and the profound "culture shock" Airborne members experienced on arrival in Somalia.[103] Arone's murder was linked also to the particular antimalaria drug Canadian soldiers used.[104] These types of explanation depoliticize the events in Somalia, and they excuse and explain away the racism and violence to preserve prevailing myths about both Canadian soldiers and Canada itself. As Razack puts it, "It enables the telling of a story of white innocence."[105] Canada's Somalia crisis was a crisis only insofar as it laid bare the fundamental contradiction of relying on soldiers in so-called peace operations and possibly threatened Canada's international reputation.[106] It was Somalis, in particular Somali men who were marked as racially and sexually "different," who bore the consequences of those contradictions.

If we were to examine instead the ways that race, gender, and sexuality are privileged sites in the creation of a soldier, we might be less surprised that these were the lines around which Canadian soldiers reacted. As Chapter 6 discusses further, race and racism often figure in military hazing and initiation rituals. Hazing normally involves tests of loyalty. As Joel Newman writes of the socialization in the Philippine military:

> The Honor System and the hazing process are essential . . . to the process of assimilation of a new identity. Enduring bonds of social solidarity are formed through the cadet's adherence to the strict precepts of the all-encompassing Honor Code and . . . the almost overwhelming hazing process.[107]

Race was apparently a factor in Kyle Brown and Clayton Matchee's hazing, especially on entering the Airborne. Matchee is full Cree and Brown part Cree, and reports indicate that in Matchee's case in particular, his "Cree heritage became a focus" of his hazing when he arrived at Petawawa to join the Airborne. Matchee, in turn, was one of Brown's "most feared hazers" when he joined.[108]

Alfred McCoy has argued that soldiers subjected to brutal hazing as cadets repeat that behavior later in their careers.[109] Thus, as Matchee beat Arone he told fellow soldiers that "The white man fears the Indian and so will the black man," and when asked the next day about the murder he boasted, "Indians: two, White man: nothing."[110] Brown claimed that his Airborne hazing was "a lot of fun." It did not involve the feces- and vomit-filled celebration of 1 Commando but was rather a "Zulu Warrior" ritual, in which new recruits tried to drink a bottle of beer before a strip of burning toilet paper stuck in the cheeks of the soldier's buttocks burned to the end. Brown commented that "No one was seriously hurt—a lot of soldier's bravado—but we all felt closer-knit and united after it."[111]

It is precisely that sense of unity that initiation or hazing rituals are intended to promote. As Alfred McCoy describes it, the hazing is often brutal and normally aims at "breaking down a cadet's civilian identity . . . creating what one study called a 'remarkable unity.'"[112] If Kyle Brown felt a greater comradeship with his compatriots after having his buttocks singed, so too—more surprisingly—did Corporal Christopher Robin. Robin was the only black soldier in the Airborne's 1 Commando Unit and was seen in the hazing video being forced to walk around on all fours and to bark like a dog with "I love KKK" written on his back. He was also shown on all fours while another soldier pretended to sodomize him, and he was tied to a tree as fellow soldiers poured white powder on him. When Robin was asked at the inquiry whether the acts depicted in the video were "racist," he said that they were. When asked if he had ever experienced "racism" in the Airborne, he said that he had not; rather, these incidents showed "what you can take under adverse conditions." He said also that no matter what people now thought, he was very proud of the regiment of which he was a part and said further that "I would do everything I could to protect its good name."[113]

Along with race, gender too is a locus of organizing a soldier's sense of self, and some indication of the Canadian military's attitudes toward women was conveyed quite clearly in one of the first documents presented at the inquiry. The Hewson report was a 1985 inquiry investigating whether there was a higher rate of criminal behavior within the Canadian forces than within Canadian society more generally.[114] It was introduced at the inquiry because Major-General Hewson reported that while there was no higher general incidence of crime, there were two "exceptions" to this observation: first, there did appear to be a higher frequency of sexual offenses within the Canadian forces than within the larger Canadian population; second, there was a higher incidence of violent crime within the Canadian Airborne regiment.[115] It was the latter observation that mattered most at the inquiry, but it was Hewson's explanations for both of these "exceptions" that unintentionally revealed some of the Canadian military's assumptions about women. Hewson explained the higher incidence of violent crime within the Airborne regiment in straightforwardly gendered terms: local "girls," he said, tended to be attracted to the "young single soldier with his new 'sporty' car, regular and higher pay and job security." The local male population was described as "robust and tough," and there simply were not enough girls to go around: "Disputes over girls," in other words, were almost unavoidable.[116]

But not worth investigating further. As it would be summarized later by David Bercuson, the earlier troubles in the Airborne resulted from the "social climate" in Petawawa: "There were too few ways for single soldiers to blow off steam; there was too much drinking; there were too few available women."[117] The strutting between males over "girls" was depicted as natural, so much so that former deputy minister of defense Robert Fowler, when asked at the inquiry about the number of offenses committed by Canadian Forces personnel and how they compared to the Canadian population more generally, could respond confidently: "we have done those sorts of studies . . . and it's about the same, bearing in mind the bias for a predominantly young male population."[118] Instead of problematizing the "bias" of a predominantly young male population, Fowler reproduced the same set of assumptions as the Hewson report had before him, as militaries all over the world have done throughout history: boys will be boys; they need to blow off steam; they need access to women. If they are denied this, higher than average rates of violence and crime will likely result. That's simply the price we pay, by this view, for having a military. Or more accurately, that's simply the way it is.

While the Hewson report addressed directly, and in an openly gendered way, the question of crime within the Airborne, it was more circumspect—but equally revealing—in its analysis of the higher incidence of sexual offenses within the Canadian forces. Hewson never stated *how much* higher the level of sexual offenses was, but he indicated that an appendix outlining "crime case synopses" "does not, statistically, reveal any significant or alarming trends."[119] This was far from the case. Hewson's crime case synopsis, in fact, indicates that the incidence of sexual crimes was dramatic. If one includes within the category of sexual assaults all assaults in which the victim was a woman, more than half of the 141 crimes listed were either sexual assaults or physical assaults against women: 76 out of 141 cases, or 54 percent[120]—hardly a figure that could be described as insignificant. What the Hewson report indicated to the Canadian military—but what was never followed up either after the Hewson report was issued or at the Somalia Inquiry over ten years later[121]—was something that feminists have long argued: that the level of violence against women is disproportionately high within militaries and that this is true also of the Canadian military.[122]

That level of violence toward women is quite at odds with the self-representations of Canadian soldiers as warrior princes, providers of humanitarian services, and helpers to the women and children of Somalia. It was but one of the ways Somali men were designated as inferior to the Canadian men, as described above, yet from Hewson's studies, the Canadian military's attitudes toward women may have been little different than that of the denigrated Somali "other." The evidence of violence toward women within the Canadian forces suggests that this is true, as does the Hewson report's cavalier attitude toward "disputes over girls." Even more dramatically, however, early questioning at the inquiry by the Canadian Jewish Congress alleged that members of the Airborne held a celebratory dinner to honor Marc Lepine, the man who massacred fourteen women at the Université de Montréal in 1989, shouting at them as he did so, "you're all a bunch of feminists." Lepine was angry at his own lack of success in gaining entrance to the university's engineering program and targeted female engineering students whom he assumed had taken his rightful place through affirmative action policies. A former member of the Airborne confirmed that the dinner honoring Lepine had taken place on the anniversary of the massacre and commented, "it would have been the same as having an Adolf Hitler party on his birthday. . . . It's just the shock value."[123] Airborne soldiers claimed they did not like the way Somali men treated "their" women and insisted that this was a cultural difference between the Somalis and Canadian soldiers; yet at the same time they participated in celebrations of a man who had massacred fourteen women in Canada.

Like their expressed attitudes toward women, the Airborne soldiers' attitudes toward homosexuality also seem inherently contradictory. While the interviews Winslow conducted portray stereotypical macho soldiers who are deeply homophobic, the hazing video and the torture of Arone suggest a more complicated story. One Commando's hazing video not only depicts Corporal Robin being sodomized (in jest, perhaps, but why are his pants pulled down to his knees, as are the pants of the soldier behind him?), but also shows two other soldiers in homoerotic play and other soldiers who appear to be performing oral sex on toy guns. For a group of macho homophobic soldiers, the ample use of homoerotic imagery—if not practice—is revealing and has an impact on actual behavior: as noted above, in Somalia, Arone himself may have been anally raped with a baton before he died.

Betrayal

A common theme throughout most of the soldiers' commentary about Somalia is that they were betrayed by their superiors, by their political leaders, by the media, and by the Canadian public.[124] At a minimum, as James Davis writes, soldiers must trust their political masters, and the Canadian government's betrayal in disbanding the Airborne regiment had undermined that trust: "In return for offering to give up their lives to achieve the government's goals at home and abroad, the government must undertake to protect their soldiers and not throw their lives away needlessly. Looking out for their welfare must be a fundamental of building a reliable national army. If the soldiers lose faith in their leadership at a political level, disaster will follow."[125] The Somalia Inquiry's final report confirmed this message and argued that "The soldiers, with some notable exceptions, did their best. But ill-prepared and rudderless, they fell invariably into the mire that became the Somalia debacle. As a result, a proud legacy was dishonoured."[126] Thus, Canadian soldiers, not the Somali men murdered by those soldiers, were depicted as experiencing the greatest betrayal.

Much was made too of the contributions Canadian soldiers did make to both Somalia and to the peoples of Belet Huen. The Canadians had helped to reopen the local school and had stocked it with pens, pencils, chalk, and paper sent by their families in Canada.[127] They also reopened the local hospital; rebuilt bridges, roads, and runways; tried to purify local water supplies; and were involved in mine awareness training and training of local constabulary and judiciary.[128] As Major General Lewis MacKenzie wrote (having forgotten the different ways "everybody beat up on the Somalis"): "Because of the tendency of the public to merely focus on a headline or a photo, the Airborne and its members never received a sliver of the credit they earned in Somalia. . . . These are places where our way of life is not threatened and where there are no clearly obvious national self interests, yet, we are prepared to accept death and injury to our own soldiers resulting from protecting someone else's human rights."[129] What few commentators who defended the Airborne noted was that Canadian soldiers were celebrated in Belet Huen for their otherwise *un*soldierly contributions: it was not as warriors that the Airborne regiment was well remembered, it was as carpenters, doctors, and engineers.

Conclusion

Canadians had never before seen their soldiers accused of atrocities against civilians. They did not have any public experiences that corresponded to the United States' Vietnam, to attacks like the My Lai disaster, or to the kind of cultural reflection as was witnessed in the post-Vietnam United States, through novels, documentaries, and even Hollywood-produced movies. Why would they? Canada's "imagined community" had long distinguished itself through different (re)presentations of the military: Americans fought wars, but Canadians made peace. The extent to which the notion of a soldier as altruistic and morally superior is, quite simply, a contradiction had never before been confronted. That this contradiction might also exist at the level of Canada as "nation" was unthinkable. As Razack writes: "Canadian naïveté and passivity as a nation constitute a narrative of innocence that blocks accountability for the violence in Somalia, just as it blocks accountability for racist violence within Canada. A nation so gentle could not possibly have participated in the acts of violence reported by the press."[130]

Once the contradiction was confronted, it had to be silenced, made invisible. It had to go away. Much of the media commentary about Somalia focused on the pain of disbanding the regiment and the loss of proud military traditions. Ahmed Aruush and Shidane Arone were forgotten quickly[131]—the former seldom mentioned at all and the latter seldom mentioned by name. The inquiry called to investigate their deaths was wrapped up without ever hearing testimony about the murder of Arone. Unquestioned "truths" about women and the military were reproduced without question; institutional racism in its various guises was quickly passed over; and the Canadian government returned to self-representations as peacemaker, liberal internationalist, and supporter of international organizations. The experience of soldiers in Somalia and the events at the Somalia Inquiry afterward reaffirmed, in very different ways, understandings about militarized manhood, agency, race, and civilization.[132]

This is why probing the gendered and raced dynamics of peacekeeping is so revealing. Peacekeeping as a practice confirmed not only visions of the Canadian state but also the qualities possessed by the men of the Canadian military—appropriately masculine, exercising choice, sent from a country that helps others, coming from a civilized world of superior race. They could hardly be held responsible for the consequences that befell ungrateful thieves, lazy, backward, even homosexual, Somali men. If the murders of Aruush and Arone did not unravel the cherished Canadian myths about the Canadian state and about the Canadian military as they should have, their violent deaths, as well as the experiences of women in Cambodia discussed in the previous chapter, demand that we ask deeper and more critical questions about the constitution of peacekeeping: for militaries, for international institutions, and for nation-states.

The following chapter examines the efforts made at the United Nations and by some national governments to address issues of gender, peace, and security. The kinds of questions posed above (questions explored at more length in Chapter 6) do not appear in the formal responses to these issues. "Gender" has increasingly appeared within the language of UN documents, but it has done so in a way that narrows dramatically the possibilities for gender to be a transformative analytical and political concept. The presence of women within the United Nations and its formal initiatives is gaining greater visibility, but critical issues of misogyny, militarized masculinity, and racism remain as invisible as ever.

Notes

1. General Paul D. Manson, "Peacekeeping in a Changing World," address to the Empire Club of Canada, Toronto, November 17, 1988, in *Canadian Speeches* 2, no. 8 (December 1988): 35–41.

2. Peter Worthington and Kyle Brown, *Scapegoat: How the Army Betrayed Kyle Brown* (Toronto: Seal Books, 1997), pp. 69–70.

3. From the general court-martial transcripts of Private Brocklebank, 1994, *Information Legacy: A Compendium of Source Material from the Commission of Inquiry into the Deployment of Canadian Forces to Somalia*, Vol. 3, entry 19.

4. Though he does not mention peacekeeping, Daniel Francis notes a number of the "core myths" that comprise Canadian national identity, including the Royal

Canadian Mounted Police and the Canadian Pacific Railroad, as well as other myths that demonize or vilify "anyone who seems to be frustrating the main cultural project," such as Indians, communists, or Québec separatists. See his *National Dreams: Myth, Memory, and Canadian History* (Vancouver: Arsenal Pulp Press, 1997), pp. 10–11 and passim.

5. Benedict Anderson, *Imagined Communities,* rev. ed. (London: Verso, 1991), p. 6.

6. Denis Stairs reviews the concept of middle power in "Of Medium Powers and Middling Roles," in Ken Booth (ed.), *Statecraft and Security: The Cold War and Beyond* (Cambridge: Cambridge University Press, 1998), pp. 270–286; for a critique of the notion of middle power in the Canadian context, see Mark Neufeld and Sandra Whitworth, "Imag(in)ing Canadian Foreign Policy," in Wallace Clement (ed.), *Building on the New Canadian Political Economy* (Montreal: McGill-Queen's University Press, 1996), pp. 197–214, and Mark Neufeld, "Hegemony and Foreign Policy Analysis: The Case of Canada as Middle Power," *Studies in Political Economy* 48 (autumn 1995): 7–29. Though not discussed in this chapter, Laura Macdonald explores Canada's development and aid policies with a similar concern in "Unequal Partnerships: The Politics of Canada's Relations with the Third World," *Studies in Political Economy* 47 (summer 1995): 111–141.

7. An important exception here is Donna Winslow's study produced for the Commission of Inquiry into the Deployment of Canadian Forces to Somalia. Although she does not discuss problems of militarized masculinity, she does address the problems of sending soldiers trained for combat on peacekeeping missions. See Donna Winslow, *The Canadian Airborne Regiment in Somalia: A Socio-cultural Inquiry* (Ottawa: Minister of Public Works and Government Services Canada, 1997). I make the same argument in Sandra Whitworth, "The Ugly Unasked Questions About Somalia," *Globe and Mail,* February 14, 1997, p. A27.

8. David Bercuson, *Significant Incident: Canada's Army, the Airborne, and the Murder in Somalia* (Toronto: McClelland and Stewart, 1996), p. 242. A study of Austrian peacekeepers indicated similar sentiments: "Soldiers who consider themselves warriors obviously need at least a touch of war or combat and some fighting among the conflicting parties from time to time. To cope with the 'status of peace' is probably the most difficult task for this type of soldier to imagine"; Franz Kernic, "The Soldier and the Task: Austria's Experience of Preparing Peacekeepers," *International Peacekeeping* 6, no. 3 (autumn 1999): 121.

9. Though peacekeeping is not defined within the UN Charter, peacekeeping missions are normally deemed to fall under Chapter VI, or "Pacific Settlement of Disputes." Chapter VII, "Action with Respect to Threats to the Peace," allows the Security Council to take what actions "as may be necessary to maintain or restore international peace and security" and is generally described as the peace enforcement mechanism of the UN Charter.

10. Major General (ret.) Lewis MacKenzie, testimony to the Commission of Inquiry into the Deployment of Canadian Forces to Somalia, Ottawa, February 1, 1996, author's notes.

11. Despite repeated claims by the minister of defense and current and former members of the Airborne, Canada's elite paratroopers had never been deployed by parachute, except in exercises. See "Airborne No More," *Ottawa Citizen,* January 30, 1995, p. A8.

12. Worthington and Brown, *Scapegoat,* p. 80.

13. Ibid., p. 70.

14. Bercuson, *Significant Incident,* p. 29.

15. Government of Canada, *Security in a Changing World, 1994: Report of the Special Joint Committee on Canada's Defence Policy* (Ottawa, 1994), p. 12. See also Government of Canada, *1994 Defence White Paper* (Ottawa, 1994), p. 12.

16. Government of Canada, Standing Committee on National Defence and Veterans Affairs, *The Dilemmas of a Committed Peacekeeper: Canada and the Renewal of Peacekeeping* (Ottawa, June 1993), p. 7.

17. Government of Canada, *Canada's Foreign Policy: Principles and Priorities for the Futures, Report of the Special Joint Committee Reviewing Canadian Foreign Policy* (Ottawa, 1994), p. 16.

18. Government of Canada, *Canada in the World, Government Statement* (Ottawa, 1995), p. 8.

19. Stéphane Dion, "Canada Is Going to Make It After All!," notes for an address by the Honourable Dion, President of the Privy Council and Minister of Intergovernmental Affairs at the biennial conference of the Association for Canadian Studies in the United States, Minneapolis, Minnesota, November 21, 1997, p. 1, cited in Wayne Cox and Claire Turenne Sjolander, "Damage Control: The Politics of National Defence," in Leslie Pal (ed.), *How Ottawa Spends, 1998–99: Balancing Act: The Post-Deficit Mandate* (Toronto: Oxford University Press, 1998), pp. 217–242.

20. *Security in a Changing World, 1994*, p. 14.

21. Stephen Dale, "Guns n' Poses: The Myths of Canadian Peacekeeping," *This Magazine* 26 (March–April 1993): 11–16.

22. Pierre Martin and Michel Fortmann, "Canadian Public Opinion and Peacekeeping in a Turbulent World," *International Journal* 50, no. 2 (spring 1995): 379.

23. See Sandra Whitworth, "Women, and Gender, in the Foreign Policy Review Process," in M. A. Cameron and Maureen Appel Molot, *Canada Among Nations 1995: Democracy and Foreign Policy* (Ottawa: Carleton University Press, 1995), pp. 83–98.

24. See, for example, Project Ploughshares' *Report to Donors* (Waterloo, ON, February 1996).

25. *Transformation Moment: A Canadian Vision of Common Security,* report of the Citizens' Inquiry into Peace and Security (Waterloo, ON, March 1992), p. 23.

26. Joseph T. Jockel, *Canada and International Peacekeeping* (Washington, DC: Center for Strategic and International Studies, 1994), p. 15.

27. Ibid., p. 1.

28. Cited in Andrew F. Cooper, *Canadian Foreign Policy: Old Habits and New Directions* (Scarborough, ON: Prentice-Hall/Allyn and Bacon, 1997), p. 20.

29. Carol Off, *The Lion, the Fox, and the Eagle: A Story of Generals and Justice in Yugoslavia and Rwanda* (Toronto: Random House Canada, 2000), p. 2.

30. Macdonald, "Unequal Partnerships," passim; see also David Black and Claire Turenne Sjolander, "Multilateralism Re-constituted and the Discourse of Canadian Foreign Policy," *Studies in Political Economy* 49 (spring 1996): 7–36.

31. See Neufeld and Whitworth, "Imag(in)ing Canadian Foreign Policy," pp. 197–214; see also Neufeld, "Hegemony and Foreign Policy Analysis," pp. 7–29.

32. See Joel J. Sokolsky, "Great Ideals and Uneasy Compromises: The United States Approach to Peacekeeping," *International Journal* 50, no. 2 (spring 1995): 266–293; "U.S. Soldier Discharged for Refusing to Serve UN," *Ottawa Citizen*, January 25, 1996, p. A8.

33. Commission of Inquiry into the Deployment of Canadian Forces to Somalia, in Government of Canada, *Dishonoured Legacy: The Lessons of the Somalia Affair*, vol. 1, p. 198, quoted in Sherene Razack, "From the 'Clean Snows of

Petawawa': The Violence of Canadian Peacekeepers in Somalia," *Cultural Anthropology* 15, no. 1 (2000): 156 n. 5.

34. Razack, "The Violence of Canadian Peacekeepers in Somalia," p. 134.

35. Neufeld, "Hegemony and Foreign Policy," p. 19.

36. Some of this material is drawn from Sandra Whitworth, "Gender, Race and the Politics of Peacekeeping," in Edward Moxon-Browne (ed.), *A Future for Peacekeeping?* (London: Macmillan, 1998), pp. 176–191.

37. Captain (ret.) Rainville, testimony to the Commission of Inquiry into the Deployment of Canadian Forces to Somalia, January 16, 1997, Hearing Transcripts, *Information Legacy,* vol. 146, p. 29777; see also testimony of Master Corporal Klick, November 12, 1996, Hearing Transcripts, *Information Legacy,* vol. 124, p. 24994, and testimony of Major Seward, January 15, 1996, Hearing Transcripts, *Information Legacy,* vol. 32, p. 6120.

38. Worthington and Brown, *Scapegoat,* p. 103. Kyle Brown said it made him think of "what it must have been like in the American South in the days of slaves, with a lot of good ol' boys whooping and hollering as they hunted down runaways." See also testimony of Captain (ret.) Rainville, January 16, 1997, Hearing Transcripts, *Information Legacy,* vol. 146, p. 29842, and statement by Mr. Noel, October 7, 1996, Hearing Transcripts, *Information Legacy,* vol. 112, p. 22297.

39. The language signaled that soldiers should shoot somewhere between the bottom of the sarongs normally worn by Somali men and their feet. Testimony of Lieutenant Colonel Mathieu, February 21, 1997, *Information Legacy,* vol. 170, p. 35041. As Sherene Razack writes, the language of this directive "both feminizes (in a typical Orientalist gesture toward Muslim men) and degrades, even while it advises to shoot to wound rather than to kill" (Razack, "The Violence of Canadian Peacekeepers," p. 142).

40. Testimony of Major Barry Armstrong, March 12, 1997, author's notes. In a letter home to his wife—which she later released to the media—Dr. Armstrong used even more evocative language, indicating that Mr. Aruush had been finished off "execution-style." Question by Mr. Vanveen to Captain (ret.) Rainville, January 16, 1997, Hearing Transcripts, *Information Legacy,* vol. 146, p. 29777.

41. David Pugliese, "Somalia: What Went So Wrong?" *Ottawa Citizen,* October 1, 1995, p. A6.

42. Worthington and Brown, *Scapegoat,* p. 112.

43. Ibid., pp. 112–113.

44. Ibid., pp. 113–114; Report of the Commission of Inquiry into the Deployment of Canadian Forces to Somalia, in Government of Canada, *Dishonoured Legacy,* vol. 1, p. 319.

45. General court-martial of Sergeant Boland, 1994, vol. 1, pp. 37–38.

46. Worthington and Brown, *Scapegoat,* p. 142.

47. Ibid., p. 127.

48. Ibid., pp. 127–128.

49. *Dishonoured Legacy,* vol. 1, p. 324. The description of Arone's beating is drawn from pp. 318–324; Worthington and Brown, *Scapegoat,* Chap. 6; Boland court-martial, vol. 1, pp. 36–38; general court-martial Private Brocklebank, 1994, vol. 3, pp. 546–547.

50. The phenomenon of "trophy photos" is not an uncommon practice on military missions. In the Somalia case alone, Belgian peacekeepers were photographed holding a Somali child over an open fire, also ostensibly to discourage him from stealing. Italian peacekeepers were photographed apparently applying electrodes to a Somali man, and another series of photographs depict Italian soldiers sexually

abusing a young woman. More recently in Iraq in 2004, photographs have emerged of British and U.S. soldiers abusing Iraqi prisoners by beating and urinating on them and posing with hooded Iraqis lying naked in a pile. John Tagliabue, "Photos of Troops Abusing Somalis in '93 Shock Italians," *New York Times,* June 14, 1997, p. 4; Matthew Fisher and Sean Rayment, "The Photographs That Shocked the World: Britain, U.S. Try to Quell Scandal," *Ottawa Citizen,* May 2, 2004, p. A1.

51. I raise this issue in Whitworth, "The Ugly Unasked Questions About Somalia." It is discussed also in *Dishonoured Legacy,* p. ES-1 and passim, and in Peter Desbarats, *Somalia Cover-Up: A Commissioner's Journal* (Toronto: McClelland and Stewart, 1997), p. 3 and passim. The phrase "a few bad apples" was used repeatedly, in particular by those hoping to defend the Airborne, and the Canadian military more generally. As the chair of the commission wryly put it one day, "I keep hearing the bad apple theory—sometimes I wonder if it's the whole barrel" (Commission of Inquiry, February 1, 1996, author's notes).

52. Jockel, *Canada and International Peacekeeping,* p. 33.

53. Christopher Dornan, "Scenes from a Scandal," *Globe and Mail,* January 21, 1995, p. D1. See also Commission of Inquiry into the Deployment of Canadian Forces to Somalia, *Document Book no. 6—Pictures Taken from Video no. 1, 1992—Initiation Party* (Ottawa, 1995), exhibit number P-53, 1995/10/02, passim.

54. Carol Burke in "Sex, G.I.'s, and Videotape," a work in progress, n.d., makes the same observation.

55. Romeo St. Martin, "Guilty of Conduct Unbecoming of an Officer on TV," *XPress: The Capital's Newspaper,* February 15, 1995.

56. General Jean Boyle, testimony to the Commission of Inquiry, August 13, 1996, author's notes. *Dishonoured Legacy,* pp. ES-35–ES-37; see also Desbarats, *Somalia Cover-Up.*

57. Francis, *National Dreams,* p. 11.

58. *Dishonoured Legacy,* p. 35, quoted in Razack, "The Violence of Canadian Peacekeepers," p. 49.

59. Razack, "The Violence of Canadian Peacekeepers," pp. 148–149.

60. Bob Fowler, testimony to the Commission of Inquiry, February 22, 1996, author's notes. The statement was made by Commissioner Peter Desbarats. Sherene Razack makes a similar point when she notes that through much of the inquiry's report, the "wronged party" is either the frustrated soldier who had faced a difficult mission with inept leadership or "Canada and its international reputation" (Razack, "The Violence of Canadian Peacekeepers in Somalia," p. 148). Not apparently either Aruush or Arone.

61. See Whitworth, "The Ugly, Unasked Questions about Somalia." The government tried other, more subtle ways to keep a lid on information emerging from the inquiry. Librarians and archivists at the inquiry, for example, were told that they would not be able to produce a CD-ROM of the proceedings, something that was becoming common practice with commissions of inquiry, and which would make searching the thousands of documents presented at the inquiry, along with the two years of recorded testimony, easier for researchers to access and analyze. The reason, they were told, was that the CD-ROM would have to wait until all of the relevant documents had been translated into both official languages, and as this was far too expensive, it would not happen anytime soon. As one of the librarians noted, this was a new and unprecedented requirement: in their most recent attempt to create a CD-ROM documenting a commission of inquiry, the government's librarians had reproduced the documents in whatever language a document had been submitted

(or, in the case of hearings, spoken). In the end, the Somalia Inquiry was reproduced in CD-ROM format.

62. *Dishonoured Legacy,* p. ES-5.

63. Bercuson, *Significant Incident,* pp. vi, 238.

64. Dubravka Zarkov makes a similar argument about the treatment of Dutch peacekeepers' involvement in the fall of Srebrenica. What came to be known in the Dutch media as "Srebrenica trauma" did not refer to the tens of thousands of Bosnian Muslim refugees expelled from the United Nations Safe Haven, or those who were killed, but rather to the trauma of the Dutch soldiers who served in Srebrenica and the national reaction to their failure to stop the events. See Dubravka Zarkov, "Srbrenica Trauma: Masculinity, Military, and National Self-Image in Dutch Daily Newspapers," in Cynthia Cockburn and Dubravka Zarkov (eds.), *The Postwar Moment: Militaries, Masculinities, and International Peacekeeping* (London: Lawrence and Wishart, 2002), pp. 183–203.

65. Major R. W. J. Wenek, *The Assessment of Psychological Fitness: Some Options for the Canadian Forces,* Technical Note 1/84 (Ottawa: Directorate of Personnel Selection, Research on Second Careers, July 1984), p. 13; cf. *The Hewson Report,* p. 46 (emphasis added).

66. Major General Lewis MacKenzie used the same word to describe his own soldiers' reactions in the former Yugoslavia: "I had soldiers under my command from 29 different nations that were delighted when they got some Chapter VII Rules of Engagement in Bosnia"; MacKenzie, testimony, February 1, 1996, *Information Legacy,* vol. 43, p. 8424.

67. Winslow, *The Canadian Airborne Regiment in Somalia,* p. 198.

68. Worthington and Brown, *Scapegoat,* p. 69.

69. Donna Winslow, "Misplaced Loyalties: The Role of Military Culture in the Breakdown of Discipline in Peace Operations," *Canadian Review of Sociology and Anthropology* 35, no. 3 (1998): 360.

70. This information is drawn from Donna Winslow, "Rites of Passage and Group Bonding in the Canadian Airborne," *Armed Forces and Society* 25, no. 3 (spring 1999): 431–436 and passim.

71. MacKenzie, testimony, February 1, 1996, *Information Legacy,* vol. 43, pp. 8420, 8424, 8518. Others have commented that the distinction between a Chapter VI and a Chapter VII mission is not as stark as the Canadians continuously purported. As Jean-Paul Brodeur notes, the mission in Somalia lay somewhere between a Chapter VI and a Chapter VII and was not viewed by the UN itself as a "peace enforcement" mission; Jean-Paul Brodeur, *Violence and Racial Prejudice in the Context of Peacekeeping,* prepared for the Commission of Inquiry into the Deployment of Canadian Forces to Somalia (Ottawa: Minister of Public Works and Government Services Canada, 1997), p. 12.

72. MacKenzie, testimony, February 1, 1996, *Information Legacy,* vol. 43, p. 8422. Other witnesses at the inquiry made similar claims, such as Master Warrant Officer Rui Amaral who testified that "Once we had the situation under control and everything was flowing . . . we should have come home, then the blue berets could have taken over"; testimony of Master Warrant Rui Amaral, September 18, 1996, *Information Legacy,* vol. 104, p. 20778. This argument is made also by Bercuson in *Significant Incident.*

73. Razack, "The Violence of Canadian Peacekeepers," p. 137.

74. Winslow, *The Canadian Airborne Regiment in Somalia,* p. 200.

75. Ibid., p. 231.

76. Ibid.

77. Razack, "The Violence of Canadian Peacekeepers," p. 146.

78. David Pugliese, "Military Brass Let Racist Skinheads Go to Somalia," *Ottawa Citizen*, October 13, 1995, p. A1; Commission of Inquiry into the Deployment of Canadian Forces to Somalia, *Document Book no. 8, Racism* (Ottawa, 1995), p. 13. The investigation had been prompted in part by the discovery of a photograph of Airborne private Matthew McKay in an Adolf Hitler t-shirt giving a Nazi salute. He apparently had been counseled by superior officers who were "satisfied" that he understood his actions were inappropriate, and he himself was quoted as having described his involvement in neo-nazi groups as "youthful folly." Though not linked to the murders, he appears in the video from the mission remarking that he had not yet killed enough "niggers."

79. *Document Book no. 8, Racism.*

80. Fowler, testimony and questions posed by Mr. Farber, representing the Canadian Jewish Congress, at the Commission of Inquiry, February 22, 1996, author's notes.

81. The latter was intended to refer to the constant begging by Somalis—and Winslow reports that the Canadians also purchased a "commemorative T-shirt with an outstretched Somali hand and the word 'gimme' on it" (Winslow, *The Canadian Airborne Regiment in Somalia*, p. 252). See also Hearing Transcripts, October 10, 1995, *Information Legacy*, vol. 3, p. 584; vol. 4, p. 595; vol. 32, p. 6086.

82. Robert Prouse, "The Dark Side That Emerged in Somalia Is Inside All Canadians," *Ottawa Citizen*, July 15, 2000, pp. A4–A6.

83. Winslow, *The Canadian Airborne Regiment in Somalia*, p. 235.

84. Worthington and Brown, *Scapegoat*, p. 123.

85. Winslow, *The Canadian Airborne Regiment in Somalia*, p. 249.

86. Ibid., pp. 233–234.

87. Ibid., p. 234.

88. Ibid., p. 235.

89. Ibid., p. 232.

90. Ibid.

91. Ibid., p. 233.

92. Razack, "The Violence of Canadian Peacekeepers," p. 137.

93. Winslow, *The Canadian Airborne Regiment in Somalia*, pp. 235–236.

94. Ibid., pp. 236–238; Razack, "The Violence of Canadian Peacekeepers," p. 138.

95. Gayatri Chakravorty Spivak, *A Critique of Postcolonial Reason: Toward a History of the Vanishing Present* (Cambridge, MA: Harvard University Press, 1999), pp. 284–311.

96. Winslow, *The Canadian Airborne Regiment in Somalia*, pp. 253, 256.

97. Ibid., p. 255.

98. Worthington and Brown, *Scapegoat*, pp. 110–111; quoted also in Winslow, *The Canadian Airborne Regiment in Somalia*, p. 244.

99. Winslow, *The Canadian Airborne Regiment in Somalia*, p. 255. For an account of Italian military violence in Somalia, see Natalia Lupi, "Report by the Enquiry Commission on the Behaviour of Italian Peacekeeping Troops in Somalia," *Yearbook of International Humanitarian Law* 1 (1998): 375–379.

100. Robert Prouse, "Everyone Is Itching to Get a Kill, Even If It Is an Innocent," *Ottawa Citizen*, July 16, 2000, pp. A4–A5.

101. Testimony of Major Barry Armstrong, March 13, 1997, Hearing Transcripts, *Information Legacy*, vol. 179, p. 37014.

102. Testimony of Corporal Richardson-Smith, September 26, 1996, Hearing Transcripts, *Information Legacy*, vol. 109, p. 21932.

103. Much of Winslow's analysis focuses on these.

104. See, for example, Worthington and Brown, *Scapegoat,* pp. 220–228.

105. Razack, "The Violence of Canadian Peacekeepers," p. 147.

106. Ibid., p. 148.

107. In Alfred W. McCoy, "'Same Banana': Hazing and Honor at the Philippine Military Academy," *Journal of Asian Studies* 54, no. 3 (August 1995): 695.

108. Peter Cheney, "Canada . . . Canada," *Toronto Star,* July 10, 1994, p. F1. As Razack points out, it was only the two Cree soldiers who faced the most serious military charges. Razack, "The Violence of Canadian Peacekeepers," p. 140.

109. Alfred McCoy, "Ram Boys: Changing Images of the Masculine in the Philippine Military," presented at the International Studies Association Annual Meetings, Toronto, March 18–22, 1997.

110. Corporal B. J. MacDonald, testimony of February 28, 1994, General Courts Martial Infobase, *Information Legacy,* vol. 7, pp. 1442 and 1434; Private D. J. Brockelbank, testimony of October 25, 1994, General Courts Martial Infobase, *Information Legacy,* vol. 4, p. 685. The final statement refers to the fact that it was a native soldier who shot and killed Ahmed Aruush in the March 4 incident.

111. Worthington and Brown, *Scapegoat,* p. 56.

112. McCoy, "Same Banana," p. 695.

113. Corporal Christopher Robin, testimony to the Commission of Inquiry, October 12, 1995, author's notes. Robin insisted that his experiences in the Airborne were no different than the kind of racism any black person experiences in Canadian society more generally and, indeed, that he had had worse things done to him than what took place during the initiation rituals. He was asked by lawyers for the Canadian Jewish Congress whether "In Canadian society, have you ever been tied to a tree, had KKK written on your back, been forced to simulate being sodomized and walking on your knees barking like a dog?" To which Corporal Robin replied, "Non."

114. David Pugliese, "Almost 20% of '85 Airborne Unit Had Police Record, Report Found," *Ottawa Citizen,* October 4, 1995, p. A4; Wenek, *The Assessment of Psychological Fitness,* p. 13; cf. *Document Book no. 1, Hewson Report,* p. 15.

115. *Document Book no. 1, Hewson Report,* p. 17.

116. Ibid., p. 19.

117. Bercuson, *Significant Incident,* p. 209.

118. Fowler, testimony, February 22, 1996; *Information Legacy,* vol. 51, p. 10223.

119. *Document Book no. 1, Hewson Report,* pp. 20–21.

120. Ibid., Annex G.

121. Hewson recommended that the higher level of sexual offenses be studied further, though he did not seem to think that this recommendation merited inclusion within his "Main Summary of Recommendations."

122. Much, though not all, of this violence is directed at the women (and children) within military families. This is examined in more detail in Chapter 6.

123. "Soldier Confirms Airborne Held Massacre Party," *Ottawa Citizen,* November 9, 1995, p. A3; "Army Commander Probes Report of Lepine Dinner," *Ottawa Citizen,* November 10, 1995, p. A3; "Racist Soldier with Criminal Past Allowed to Rejoin the Army, Inquiry Hears," *Ottawa Citizen,* November 3, 1995, p. A5. This issue is explored further in Chapter 6.

124. See, for example, James R. Davis, *The Sharp End: A Canadian Soldier's Story* (Vancouver: Douglas and McIntyre, 1997), pp. 260–270; Bercuson, *Significant Incident;* Worthington and Brown, *Scapegoat;* Lewis MacKenzie, "Airborne

Never Received a Sliver of the Credit It Earned," *Ottawa Citizen,* July 15, 2000, p. A6.

125. Davis, *The Sharp End,* p. 269.

126. *Dishonoured Legacy,* p. xxix; cf. Razack, "The Violence of Canadian Peacekeepers," p. 148.

127. MacKenzie, "Airborne Never Received a Sliver of the Credit," p. A6.

128. Allen G. Sens, *Somalia and the Changing Nature of Peacekeeping: The Implications for Canada,* prepared for the Commission of Inquiry into the Deployment of Canadian Forces to Somalia (Ottawa: Government Services Canada, 1997), p. 106.

129. MacKenzie, "Airborne Never Received a Sliver of the Credit," p. A6.

130. Razack, "The Violence of Canadian Peacekeepers," p. 135.

131. Razack's analysis focuses on the "forgetting" of violent racist acts in Somalia, as well as in Canadian colonial history and its own violent practices (ibid., passim).

132. These categories are drawn from Roxanne Lynn Doty, *Imperial Encounters: The Politics of Representation in North-South Relations* (Minneapolis: University of Minnesota Press, 1996), pp. 42–45.

5

When the UN Responds: A Critique of Gender Mainstreaming

During the same time that United Nations peace missions were becoming more numerous and more complex, the UN also began devoting more serious attention to women and to gender issues.[1] The UN had long been committed to the principle of "gender equality" and throughout the 1990s, the language of United Nations pronouncements began to include a commitment to promoting "gender balance" in all professional posts and the adoption of a strategy called "gender mainstreaming," which envisioned an assessment of the distinct implications for women and men of all planned UN actions, legislation, policies, and programs.[2] These commitments to gender equality, balance, and mainstreaming were intended to include the areas of armed conflict, security, and peace operations.[3]

By some measures, there have been real successes with "mainstreaming" gender around peace and security issues within the UN system, and in particular around peace operations. Some departments, including the Departments of Peacekeeping Operations (DPKO) and Disarmament Affairs (DDA), have issued research papers or briefing notes exploring the ways in which gender must be taken into account within their areas of operation[4]; there are efforts being made to develop a code of conduct that is informed by the gender dimensions of missions for peacekeepers and all personnel deployed on peace operations[5]; some training manuals for peacekeepers attempt to outline the issues associated with prostitution and HIV/AIDS[6]; the United Nations has established gender units or assigned gender advisers in six recent peacekeeping missions[7]; and, most important, the United Nations has adopted Security Council Resolution 1325 of October 2000, which calls for the incorporation of gender perspectives into peacekeeping operations.[8] Member states have also sought to implement gender mainstreaming around peace operations, in the case of Canada and the United Kingdom, for example, by developing gender training materials for peace support personnel.[9]

119

Whatever the advancements of gender mainstreaming in security issues and peace operations, however, these efforts also face serious obstacles. At one level, as many observers have noted, there is a real gap between policy pronouncements and research papers produced at UN headquarters in New York and the actual implementation of such policy measures "on the ground."[10] There has been little systematic assessment of whether the UN implements all of its policy commitments concerning gender at the departmental level or on actual missions, or if it does implement those policies, whether those measures have any impact on people's lives. The resources devoted to gender mainstreaming, in both staff and financial terms, are insufficient to meet the goals set by the UN itself.[11] Moreover, many people working with the UN—either at headquarters or in the field—admit they do not know what gender mainstreaming actually entails within their specific areas of responsibility.[12] They may be willing to mainstream gender, but they are uncertain how to do it.

As serious as these limitations seem to be, however, the larger question is not simply one of the difference between "rhetoric" and "practice" but rather whether the United Nations and its member states *ever could* provide anything more than technical fixes to the kinds of complex political problems that have been outlined in previous chapters. The UN context is one that privileges the idea of liberal internationalism as an always benign and humanitarian endeavor, while at the same time ascribing to the realpolitik principles of state sovereignty and power politics. The UN context is also one in which diplomatic protocol, departmental turf wars, and the protection of (some) member states' reputations take precedence over issues such as gender.

Feminists both within and outside the UN face a difficult and ultimately contradictory set of challenges. The UN is the chief global actor involved in peace operations, so it cannot be ignored, it must be engaged with. But in order to be "heard" within this context, arguments must be presented in a way that adopts the language of the UN, accommodates itself to UN-produced understandings of peace and security, and is alert to the hierarchies, protocols, and "stories" by which UN personnel define themselves.[13] A common strategy for feminists thus has been to try to convince UN bureaucrats or military personnel that "taking gender into account" will allow them to perform their jobs better. As one NGO brief argues, "gender mainstreaming is possible and can improve the effectiveness of operations."[14]

This approach has several consequences, the most important of which is that it turns a critical term ("gender") into an instrument for problem-solving goals. Trying to insert gender into the dominant discourse of peacekeeping being produced within a UN context significantly limits the possibilities of critique. Once the goal becomes helping UN bureaucrats or military personnel to become more effective in their work, a whole series of questions are ruled out of bounds; for example, whether peacekeeping is best conducted by militaries; whether peace and humanitarian operations are a form of imperialist practice; or whether the UN's embeddedness in liberal assumptions and its many peculiar organizational characteristics undermine arguments that require (nonessentialized) discussions of difference. It forces critics to abandon, paraphrasing Anne Orford, any alternatives for radical change that will be dismissed as impractical, idealistic, and irrelevant to the central concerns of the institution.[15]

These limitations empty "gender" of its radical political potential and shift our attention away from the people who are *affected* by peacekeeping missions and toward those who *conduct* those missions. Even in attempting to make the former visible, it is the latter whose priorities, limits, and concerns shape the questions that are posed and the boundaries of the responses. In an effort to be taken seriously within an institutional context such as the UN, many feminists have returned to the problem-solving and obfuscating moves that feminist challenges to peace operations had originally sought to critique.[16] This chapter outlines the efforts of the UN in mainstreaming gender around peace and security issues and develops these various arguments. A larger and more concerted effort must be made to challenge the role and limitations of the United Nations in framing contemporary debates on gender and security, to ensure that critical questions, not bureaucratic imperatives, inform feminist work on peace and security. Otherwise, rather than challenge the exclusions of UN practices, all that mainstreaming gender may accomplish is to further reinforce and facilitate militarism. As Trinh T. Minh-ha observes, "the more one depends on the master's house for support, the less one hears what he doesn't want to hear."[17]

Gender Culture at the UN—or, the Road to (and from) 1325

For feminists within and outside the UN, the unanimous adoption of Security Council Resolution 1325 on October 31, 2000, was a historic event. It was the culmination of a growing commitment to gender equality within the UN, joined by intensive lobbying of the Security Council by NGOs, supportive member states, and elements of the women's machinery within the UN, including the Office of the Special Adviser on Gender Issues, the United Nations Development Fund for Women (UNIFEM), and the Division for the Advancement of Women (DAW).

The resolution was the first time that the Security Council had formally recognized the differential impact of armed conflict on women and men, and observed that women and children represented the vast majority of those who are adversely affected by conflict, including the direct effects of being targeted in conflict but also their fate as refugees and internally displaced persons. The resolution also noted the distinct roles that women can play in conflict prevention, peace-building, and reconstruction processes and called for the increased representation of women at all levels and for more resources devoted to gender-sensitive training efforts.

Resolution 1325 acknowledged as well the importance of bringing a gender perspective to peacekeeping operations and peace negotiations, and it called for particular attention to be paid to women and girls as victims of all forms of violence, including gender-based and sexual violence. Resolution 1325 also emphasized addressing the different needs of female and male ex-combatants and requested that the Secretary-General's reports to the Security Council include reports on the progress of gender mainstreaming and all other aspects relating to women and girls on peacekeeping missions. For the independent experts appointed by UNIFEM to examine further questions of gender and conflict, the resolution

> is a watershed political framework that makes women—and a gender perspective—relevant to negotiating peace agreements, planning refugee camps and peacekeeping operations and reconstructing war-torn societies. It makes the pursuit of gender equality relevant to every single Council action, ranging from mine clearance to elections to security sector reform.[18]

Particularly important was the way the resolution placed responsibility for gender mainstreaming of peace and security operations with the United Nations and its member states. Now activists had "language" they could point to: after 1325, it should no longer be the case that they had to get the UN to take gender seriously around peace and conflict issues—the resolution confirmed that commitment.

As Carol Cohn has observed, 1325 was notable also because of the intensive involvement of outsiders with the UN. In a normally closed institution like the Security Council, NGOs were active and effective lobbyists in ensuring 1325's successful adoption. NGO efforts were important, and strategically interesting, according to Cohn, because the focus had been to achieve a Security Council resolution around these issues and not aim for a General Assembly resolution. NGOs, in short, went after the most difficult kind of resolution available at the United Nations—and one of the few instruments within the UN system that is actually binding—and they were successful.[19]

The resolution, and the various efforts that led to it, also reveal something of the "gender culture" at the UN. Observers of the United Nations have argued that the UN, like all large institutions, is distinguished by its own hierarchies, rules, norms, and even "moral universe." It is, in other words, an imagined community and is constituted in part through the shared ideas that give it meaning. Writing in another context, Michael Barnett notes that UN "bureaucratic culture situated and defined their knowledge, informed their goals and desires, shaped what constituted appropriate and inappropriate behavior, distinguished acceptable from unacceptable consequences and helped to determine right from wrong."[20] The same is true of the organizational culture within the UN concerning gender and women's issues. What 1325, and the efforts that both preceded and followed it, reveals is the inconsistent ways in which the UN bureaucracy treats gender—attentive when lobbied by women and women's organizations and often entirely silent when dealing with its "bread and butter" issues of war, peace, and security.

While there has been considerable activity within the UN around women and gender throughout its history, gender issues are not viewed as central within the larger UN system, and many people both within and outside the UN report a general hostility directed at gender issues. Women are highly underrepresented within positions of decisionmaking authority, and this has been true despite longstanding and repeated statements from the highest levels promising commitments to gender balance within all professional posts. The UN Secretariat is comprised of two main types of posts: general service and professional. The professional category contains five levels (P-1 through P-5), with two further levels of "Principal Officer" above it (D-1 and D-2) and then above this the highest levels of Assistant-Secretary-General and Under-Secretary-General.[21] In 1985 the Secretary-General proposed a goal of 30 percent of all professional posts filled by women by 1990, 35 percent by 1995, and 25 percent of positions at the D-1 level by 1995.[22] As of 2002, the United Nations had not yet reached its 1995 targets: women with appointments of one year or more to professional and higher level posts in 2002 in total constituted only 33.2 percent of all appointments, and comprised only 22.7 percent of appointments at the P-4 level, 12.1 percent at the P-5 level, 19.2 percent at the D-1 level, and 21.4 percent at the D-2 level. At the highest levels of the UN bureaucracy, women comprised only 10.5 percent (4 of 38) appointments at the Under-Secretary-General level and 12.5 percent (5 of 40) at the Assistant-Secretary-General level.[23]

In peacekeeping missions, women are also seriously underrepresented. As of 2002, women comprised only 24 percent of staff in peace operations. In twenty-eight peace operations in 2002, women accounted for 30 to 50 percent of staff in only six missions, while in another six, there were no women at all. There was only one woman out of fifty-one special representatives of the Secretary-General or special envoys on peace support operations in 2002, and throughout the history of UN peace operations, women have served as chief of mission on only four occasions.[24] Where women are present in peace operations, they are represented primarily in administration, legal and civil affairs, and human resources management.[25] Between 1957 and 1989, women represented only 0.1 percent of all military personnel on peace missions; by 2000, these figures had improved, but only to 2.6 percent of military personnel and 4 percent of civilian police peacekeepers.[26] From the perspective of officials within the UN, the problem of underrepresentation in peace missions is primarily a result of the failure of troop-contributing countries to send sufficient numbers of women. Nonetheless, UN policy pronouncements concerning women and peacekeeping continue to call for women's greater representation at all levels.[27]

More important than the issue of the representation of women within the UN system, in substantive terms, the UN approach to gender is also inconsistent. Over the past decade there has been more, and apparently better, language adopted in an attempt to pressure the UN to take gender issues seriously, including Resolution 1325, but that better language has not always corresponded to changed policies or practices. Some of the improved language around gender that led up to the resolution has been organized around a strategy called "gender mainstreaming," adopted in the Platform for Action from the Fourth United Nations World Conference on Women in Beijing in 1995. Though many find the term unwieldy, the reason for adopting a strategy called "mainstreaming" was to insist on the importance of incorporating attention to gender through all aspects of the UN's work and to move away from a simple count of the number of women within the UN.

As Jacqui True and Michael Mintrom describe it, mainstreaming is a potentially more radical strategy than simple liberal policies to include women; in principle, it subjects all policies to an analysis that takes into account the specific interests and values of both women and men.[28] Conceptually, the idea of gender mainstreaming is also relatively sophisticated. It accepts the idea that gender is a social construct, not a biological fact, and that the prevailing norms and assumptions concerning both women and men will differ across time and place. Mainstreaming views gender as shaped by cultural, class, religious, and ethnic differences and recognizes the power differentials between women and men, the fluid nature of those differences, and that these differences are made manifest in a variety of ways.[29]

At the same time that the UN established mainstreaming as the strategy for promoting gender equality at Beijing, the Platform for Action also designated "women and armed conflict" as a critical area of concern.[30] By doing so, the signatories to the Platform for Action intended to draw attention to the ways armed conflicts and occupations affect women and men differently, and the extent to which the social status of women and girls in societies contributes to how they experience conflict. Like the resolution that would come five years later, the Platform for Action insisted that the policies aimed at addressing the impact of armed conflict on affected peoples—whether that be peace missions, humanitarian efforts, electoral missions, or postconflict reconstruction—needed to take gender differences into account.

It is in its understanding of difference that the potentially more sophisticated elements of gender mainstreaming begin to unravel. Even prior to Beijing, the UN already had a history of acknowledging the differential impact of armed conflict on women. In 1969 the Commission on the Status of Women, for example, considered whether women and children should be accorded special protection during armed conflict and emergency situations, and the United Nations General Assembly adopted the Declaration on the Protection of Women and Children in Emergency and Armed Conflict in 1975.[31] In 1993 the United Nations World Conference on Human Rights recognized violence against women during armed conflict as a violation of human rights. Also in 1993 the United Nations General Assembly adopted the Declaration on the Elimination of Violence Against Women, which acknowledged that women are especially vulnerable to violence in situations of armed conflict.[32] The International Criminal Tribunals for the former Yugoslavia, established in 1993, and for Rwanda, established in 1994, as well as the Statutes of the International Criminal Court and the Special Court for Sierra Leone, all acknowledge the gender implications of armed conflict.[33]

By and large, these documents emphasize the ways that women are subject to sexual violence during armed conflict. Even documents that attempt to be more expansive tend to reproduce this theme. In 1998 the Division for the Advancement of Women published a study entitled "Women 2000: Sexual Violence and Armed Conflict: United Nations Response."[34] It outlined the ways in which understandings of sexual violence during armed conflict had changed within the UN: prior to the early 1990s and the armed conflict in the former Yugoslavia, understandings of sexual violence toward women saw rape and other forms of sexual violence as attacks against the honor or personal dignity of women, or they emphasized the importance of women in the family and as child-rearers. But this had changed, the study argued, to a recognition that crimes of sexual violence were violations of international human rights and humanitarian law that must be addressed through the UN system.[35] Whether a matter of personal honor or a human rights violation, "what it is about women that warrants protection"[36] in most of these documents focuses on women as victims of sexual violence.[37]

The idea of gender understood primarily as women's difference is raised also in UN discussions of the unique contributions that women can make to peace processes. One 1995 study produced by the Division for the Advancement of Women outlined the ways women can "make a difference" in peace operations.[38] The study argued that when a critical mass of women are present on peacekeeping missions they make a unique contribution, and that they are particularly successful in the diffusion of violence, are perceived to be compassionate, willing to listen, and sometimes employ unorthodox techniques, such as singing, to diffuse potentially violent situations. The study also noted that civilian women peacekeepers worked effectively with both military and police personnel and, contrary to some expectations, many women willingly accept the challenges of working in dangerous and isolated situations.[39]

In June 1999, the special adviser on gender issues called for further analysis and more detailed case studies of women and peacekeeping from both past and ongoing missions. Studies were prepared on peace operations in Namibia, Cambodia, El Salvador, Bosnia and Herzegovina, South Africa, and Kosovo.[40] The results of the general study and the case study materials were presented at a conference organized by the Department of Peacekeeping Operation's Lessons Learned Unit in Windhoek, Namibia, in May 2000. Although the case studies to date have never been released to the public by DPKO, the conference itself resulted in the "Windhoek Declaration" and the "Namibia Plan of Action on 'Mainstreaming a Gender Perspective in Multidimensional Peace Support Operations,'" as well as a more general report that goes by the latter title. The Windhoek Declaration and the Namibia Plan of Action were both presented to the Security Council as part of its deliberations leading up to 1325.[41] The declaration and plan of action, as well as the report, tended to emphasize issues of gender balance (get more women in, and get more women into senior positions), but they also raised some concerns about mainstreaming the mandates of missions, gender training, and the assessment of missions and postconflict efforts from a gender perspective. The case studies, according to Angela King, special adviser on gender issues, concluded that local women are more likely to confide in female peacekeepers; women negotiators understand the implications of peace processes for women better than men do; and, if at least 30 percent of mission personnel are female, local women will be more likely to join peace committees, which then are less hierarchical and tend to be more responsive to women's concerns.[42]

UN work on gender mainstreaming around peace and security issues thus has tended to focus not on gender relations or prevailing assumptions about masculinity and femininity, as is implied in the more conceptual accounts of what mainstreaming would entail. Instead the focus has emphasized women as different from men, both in terms of the particular vulnerabilities they face in situations of armed conflict and in terms of their potential contribution to peacekeeping efforts. In particular, as Judith Gardam and Michelle Jarvis argue, most of the formal recognition of women's vulnerabilities focus on women in terms of their relationship to others, as pregnant women, mothers, and victims of, or at risk of, sexual violence, and do not treat women as individuals, or as subjects, in their own right.[43] These same understandings about women and armed conflict were reflected in Resolution 1325. In Anne Orford's words, "As gentle handmaidens and victims of war, women have an important role to play in helping support peace-keeping and peace-making missions."[44]

Plus ça change, plus c'est la même chose

Despite these many limitations, the achievement of a Security Council resolution should have resulted in changed policies and practices within the UN, if only in the more narrow terms described by the resolution—to include women in existing peace practices and to ensure that women are protected from the risks that they face in armed conflict. Yet even by this less ambitious measure, attitudes toward gender and women within the UN do not reflect that commitment. When the UN turns to the "real business" of war, security, and peace operations—when it is not, in short, being pushed to explicitly address gender issues by women's machineries within and outside the UN—the silence accorded to gender (or women) is as deafening as it is revealing.

At the same time that the language and activism around mainstreaming was being refined, and the DPKO meetings and documents for Namibia were being planned, for example, the United Nations was also preparing a comprehensive report on future prospects for peacekeeping produced by the Expert Panel on United Nations Peace Operations, which became more popularly known as the Brahimi report, after the panel's chair, Lakhdar Brahimi.[45] The Brahimi report was intended to be an exhaustive and frank analysis of United Nations efforts in peace operations, which would provide concrete and practical advice on the improvement of those operations and become the framework for reforming how peacekeeping was to be conducted by the United Nations.

Although calls to take gender seriously within peace operations were circulating within official UN channels at the same time that the panel was deliberating, the Brahimi report nonetheless is largely silent on gender issues. It does note the importance of ensuring fair gender distribution in recruitment efforts (paragraph 132) and later acknowledges that UN personnel in the field need to respect local norms and practices, and in particular to be sensitive toward gender and cultural differences (paragraph 272). However, gender is otherwise entirely ignored, and though the report provides a sustained analysis of many aspects of UN peacekeeping operations—including calls for the integration of civilian, military, and political planning; more "robust" forces and mandates; strengthening the rule of law and protecting human rights; support for more preventive and postconflict peace-building activities; and ensuring demobilization and reintegration of former combatants—it does not acknowledge the barriers to, or contributions of, gender mainstreaming in peace operations.[46] The document that was created to serve as the framework for peacekeeping reform into the twenty-first century, in other words, was produced without any apparent awareness of the gender mainstreaming initiatives within peace operations that the special adviser, DAW, UNIFEM, and even DPKO had already initiated.

Feminist Lessons from Afghanistan

The United Nations revealed its indifference to women and gender yet again when it involved itself in negotiating a peace settlement in Afghanistan in November 2001. By that point, the commitments of Security Council Resolution 1325 were in place, so incorporating women into peace negotiations and conflict resolution should have been viewed as a requirement, yet only three of the thirty-three delegates at the UN talks on Afghanistan held in Bonn were women; no senior gender specialists from UN headquarters, including either the special adviser or the head of UNIFEM, were invited to the talks; and none of the organized women's groups in Afghanistan were contacted about participating.[47]

Prior to the rise of fundamentalist factions in Afghanistan in the 1980s, women made up more than 15 percent of the Loya Jirga, a greater percentage of women than in the U.S. Congress at the time; roughly 50 percent of university students in Kabul were women; and women accounted for some 70 percent of teachers, half of government workers, and many of the country's doctors, bankers, and small business owners.[48] With the rise of fundamentalism, women's opportunities, rights, and basic security were radically transformed: women were not allowed to work, or even to leave their homes unaccompanied by male relatives and without being fully covered with a *burqua;* education for those over the age of eight was banned; and women suspected of any form of sexual misconduct—charges that merely had to be uttered to be confirmed—were often stoned to death in public executions.

Indeed, part of the U.S. rhetoric in support of its assault on Al-Qaida, the Taliban, and Afghanistan after the attacks on the Pentagon and World Trade Center towers in September 2001 focused on the horrible injustices faced by women in Afghanistan under Taliban rule.[49] Yet, though the UN made every effort to ensure fair representation of the different tribal factions within Afghanistan at Bonn—political actors who had been important not only in contemporary Afghanistan but also during its recent past— women and organized women's groups were not viewed in the same light, despite that women had been specifically targeted for political persecution in Afghanistan. The document produced at the Bonn meetings did result in the creation of a Department of Women's Affairs and the appointment of two women to Afghanistan's interim government, but its minimal treatment of women and gender issues led the NGO Working Group on Women, Peace, and Security to issue a statement noting that "we are concerned that . . . this does not represent a gender integrated approach and the move towards gender mainstreaming agreed upon in Resolution 1325."[50]

Parallel meetings for Afghan women were organized by a number of European and U.S. women's organizations, including Equality Now, the European Women's Lobby, V-Day, the Center for Strategic Initiatives for Women, and the Feminist Majority, in collaboration with the UN's Office of the Special Adviser on Gender Issues and Advancement of Women and UNIFEM. These meetings, held in Brussels in early December 2001, involved forty Afghan women who presented a list of recommendations to the European Parliament outlining their demands with respect to the reconstruction of Afghanistan, including a call to reopen schools for both boys and girls; restart food programs, vaccination programs, and health centers; include Afghan women lawyers in the development of a new constitution; and require women's participation in the Loya Jirga and all peace processes.[51] UNIFEM and interested member states were involved in organizing other meetings for Afghani women, both outside and within Afghanistan.

However, it was only in organizing separately, outside of the formal peace talks that established the framework for Afghanistan's postconflict recovery—and after being pushed to do so by international women's groups—that Afghan women had opportunities to present their views on the peace process and reconstruction of Afghanistan to the United Nations. The first test case of the UN's resolve to abide by its commitments to Security Council Resolution 1325 thus demonstrated that very little had changed: as had been the case in the pre-1325 era, it was left to women's NGOs and women's machineries within the UN to remind bureaucrats focused on "bringing the peace to Afghanistan" that women's involvement in that process, and their views about the creation of a postwar society in Afghanistan, were as important as the views of the different political and tribal factions that had been active within Afghan politics for the past three decades.

Gender Advisers and Gender Units

Although the Brahimi report was silent on gender issues, and the UN's formal Afghan peace initiative was largely absent of women, a number of recent peace missions have included gender advisers and gender units. In

1999, prior to the adoption of Security Council Resolution 1325, gender units were established in two peacekeeping missions, the UN Mission in Kosovo (UNMIK) and the UN Transitional Administration in East Timor (UNTAET).[52] A gender unit was also established in the UN Mission in the Democratic Republic of Congo (MONUC) in March 2002.[53] The UN Mission to Bosnia Herzegovina (UNMBIH) and the UN Assistance Mission in Afghanistan (UNAMA) both have dedicated senior gender advisers and in the UN Assistance Mission in Sierra Leone (UNAMSIL), a gender specialist works with the Human Rights Section of the mission.[54]

Gender units and advisers are intended to acknowledge the importance of gender mainstreaming within a mission. They typically involve monitoring the gender balance of appointments to the mission but also focus on the provision of gender awareness training both to mission staff and local political, police, military, and civilian personnel, as well as liaison with local women's groups, dissemination of relevant and useful United Nations materials (such as translated copies of Security Council Resolution 1325) and other public information, and facilitation of meetings or events through which local women's organizations may become organized around particular campaigns, whether these be electoral campaigns, campaigns against impunity, or campaigns to address violence against women.

Though the mandate of the units is quite far-reaching and diverse, gender units thus far have faced a number of persistent problems, which also reflect the inconsistency of UN treatments of gender and peace operations. For one, many of the units are operating with minimal, and sometimes no, funding. In East Timor, for example, plans for the gender unit were initially shelved due to budget concerns, and it was only after pressure to reestablish the unit—from NGOs such as Oxfam, from some member states that had contributed to financing the mission, and from a number of senior UN women (the special adviser on gender issues and the advancement of women and the UN high commissioner for human rights)—that the Gender Affairs Unit was eventually reinstated in April 2000.[55] As Hilary Charlesworth and Mary Wood note, the initial cancellation of the gender unit had serious repercussions, not least of which was that the funding originally designated for the unit had been reallocated, and no program or operational budget was available even after the unit was reinstated.[56]

Without the appropriate resources, as Charlesworth and Wood suggest, gender mainstreaming on peace operations "can quickly become a token exercise."[57] Thus, on her arrival in East Timor, the new director of the Gender Affairs Unit spent the first several months fund-raising instead of performing preliminary and substantive tasks related to the unit's mandate, such as a needs assessment. Eventually, the unit grew to a part-time staff of several women, who were responsible for statistical analyses of the mission and all new appointments, legal advocacy and analysis, local networking and capacity building and promoting women's rights.[58]

In the UNMIK mission, the Office of Gender Affairs was originally expected to be a high-profile unit and a component of the Office of the Special Representative of the Secretary-General (who served as the chief of mission), but it was later moved to the Office of the Deputy Special Representative of the Secretary-General of Civil Administration. Observers were concerned that the downgrading of the office signaled a downgrading of gender as a priority issue, with less direct access to the chief of mission.[59] In the Democratic Republic of Congo, as of December 2002, the Office of Gender Affairs had a senior gender adviser who reports to MONUC's deputy special representative of the Secretary-General, one gender affairs officer, two UN volunteers, and one local administrative assistant. At the same time, however, the office functions without a budget for developing its activities.[60]

Problems of underresourcing units, in both staff and budgetary terms, are compounded when the units have little direct access to UN headquarters in New York. A follow-up to the Brahimi report by the Secretary-General, which outlined the resources required to implement its recommendations, called for the establishment of a gender unit at UN headquarters within DPKO.[61] However, the budget allocation for such a unit, as of 2004, has never been provided. Critics note that without such a unit, there is no individual within DPKO designated to focus full-time on gender and provide support for gender advisers in the field. Such a position, moreover, could also coordinate and advise within DPKO on gender initiatives and prepare reports for the General Assembly and Security Council on the progress of gender mainstreaming within peace missions and within DPKO more generally, among other things.[62]

Another concern is one that has plagued separate women's "offices" or "parties" throughout history: a separate gender unit tends to result in local women's NGOs liaising with the unit, while other local political actors—the majority of whom will likely be men—deal with UN officials in mainline departments and offices, the majority of whom are also men and who often enjoy more direct access to the chief of mission.[63] A special but separate unit that ends up dealing with women's organizations, in short, effectively marginalizes those organizations at the same time that it attempts to ensure they have some access to the mission they might otherwise not have had.

In addition to problems of resources, communications, and priority, serious questions have also been raised about the effectiveness of the gender units once they are in place. In Kosovo, critics noted that the gender office failed to make strong links with local women's organizations, resulting in little follow-up on general recommendations, such that "local women have become very wary of this arm of UNMIK administration."[64] In Sierra Leone, which operated with a gender focal point, "none of the women's NGOs in Freetown had even heard of the focal point person, who had not asked any of them to document human rights violations."[65]

In UNTAET, though the Gender Affairs Unit (GAU) is credited by some observers as having established "the first effectively functioning gender office in the history of peacekeeping,"[66] others are more critical. Some local East Timorese women's groups claimed the UNTAET GAU was at best "fruitless"[67] and at worst undermined the efforts of local women's organizing. One of the GAU's accomplishments, for example, was the creation of an operational plan for the locally produced "Platform for Action of Women of Timor Loro Sae." However, according to some local women's groups, there were wide discrepancies between the East Timorese document and the GAU "operational" version. In some cases the GAU version altered strategic objectives (adding the development of initiatives "to promote the use of women's traditional knowledge of medicinal plants to advance community health" when the original document contained no such reference); in other cases the GAU document used more general language for very specific concerns (replacing a concern for the needs of orphans in the original document to "at-risk children who are in need of care and protection").[68] As Charlesworth and Wood note, the discrepancies between the two documents were not very important in practical terms but were very significant in symbolic terms, highlighting "a somewhat imperial attitude with which the majority of women's NGOs in Dili associate the GAU."[69]

Gender units yet again reveal the apparently inconsistent treatment that the United Nations makes of its own commitments to mainstream gender in peace operations. On the one hand, their creation seems to signal greater commitment on the part of the UN to mainstream gender issues on peace operations, but on the other hand, the UN provides very few resources to achieve their mandate. For some observers, it is an exceptional accomplishment that gender units have been able to perform any tasks at all, having done so with so little resources and support from the UN.[70] At the same time, though systematic analysis of the impact of gender units has not yet been conducted, existing reports from consultations with local people, and local women, indicate the units have had serious problems in consulting widely with local women's groups, one of their chief mandates.

The "Problem" of Women, Peace, and Security

UN treatments of gender thus have been quite limited and have tended to focus on women as victims of sexual violence and the unique contributions that women can make to peace and peacemaking. Also, the UN has not been able live up to even these more limited understandings of "women, peace, and security." Unless the women's machineries within the UN and women's NGOs push and prod the UN to abide by its commitments to gender, the silence accorded gender concerns is little different in the "1325 era" than it was prior to the adoption of Security Council Resolution 1325. Rather than view UN practices toward women and gender as somehow inconsistent, a more critical engagement with these issues demonstrates that the knowledge claims being produced within the UN has *made possible*[71] certain practices, including the apparently inconsistent treatment of gender itself. Because gender analysis is seen most frequently as a problem-solving activity, the meanings given to women, peace, and security confirm a number of "stories" produced within the UN, including what counts as armed conflict, how those conflicts impact women, who the appropriate actors are in resolving conflicts, and where women fit in terms of the response. As Anne Orford writes, many of these understandings signal the ways in which "a 'gender perspective' can be mapped onto existing ways of doing business without questioning any of the bases upon which peace, security or even the category 'woman' is understood."[72]

One of the "ways of doing business" that the United Nations prides itself in is its understandings of, and responses to, armed conflict. Whatever other activities and programs the UN may be involved in, "to save succeeding generations from the scourge of war" remains, in the words of Secretary-General Kofi Annan, "the cardinal mission of the United Nations."[73] As discussed in Chapter 2, the consensus within the United Nations is that armed conflict has escalated throughout the post–Cold War period and has been predominantly internal in nature.[74] The widespread availability of small arms and light weapons has increased the levels of violence directed at civilians, who by some estimates now account for up to 90 percent of casualties.[75] The targeting of civilians occurs in both direct and indirect ways, with mass displacements, gender-based and sexual violence, ethnic cleansing and genocide, mass exterminations, abductions, and mutilations having become some of the defining characteristics of those conflicts.[76]

Though the causes of conflict are varied, by the UN view, a primary emphasis in UN documents focuses on its political dimensions. Whether the historical legacies of colonialism, competition over scarce resources, political or economic inequities, or ethnic, ideological, or religious differences erupt into outbreaks of violent conflict depends very much on whether "appropriate and effective coping mechanisms exist, including well functioning governance and rule of law institutions."[77] Far less common in UN accounts is any acknowledgment of "the relationship between insecurity and economic liberalization, or the ways in which the international division of labour is itself a violent process."[78] Rather, armed conflict is identified as the moment in which "fighting broke out." It is understood to have "root causes" that preceded the actual "outbreak" of violence but which—even if they are "multidimensional" causes—can be addressed by supporting "the development of national and regional capacities for early warning, conflict prevention and long-term peacebuilding."[79]

Armed conflict, in short, is a problem but it is a problem that can be solved, and the UN has available to it the instruments for doing so: preventive diplomacy, early warning, fact-finding, peacemaking, peacekeeping, confidence-building, and institution-building.[80] Much of the focus on responding to, or preventing, conflicts thus emphasizes the importance of reliable early warning information and a detailed and "deep" understanding of "local circumstances." Sources of conflict may require "long-term structural prevention," which is "ultimately an investment in sustainable development," but this too can be addressed if identified early. If local governments, with international support, "alleviate the conditions that could lead to armed conflict" this will not only prevent the outbreak of violence but will also "help to strengthen the sovereignty of States."[81]

Failures of conflict prevention, by these understandings, are not failures of how the UN comprehends armed conflict or of the instruments they have developed to respond to conflict. Rather, failures result from the resources devoted to those instruments. Insufficient financial resources or properly trained staff, an inability to collect and recognize the right kinds of data, failure of coordination, either within the UN or between the UN and local governments, militaries, and agencies—these are the reasons that account for the failure to prevent conflicts around the world. As Secretary-General Kofi Annan has noted, the outbreak of violence reflects "a failure of the international community to invest in prevention."[82]

United Nations discursive practices thus produce knowledge claims about what counts as armed conflict and how it is to be addressed. Conflicts occur in identifiable moments in time, they entail an "outbreak" of violence, and, in contemporary conflicts, involve both combatants and civilian noncombatants. The sources of conflict may be "multidimensional" and may require "long-term structural prevention," but ultimately the causes of conflict are both knowable and manageable, if the proper information can be garnered about "local circumstances" and the appropriate instruments applied. These understandings convey knowledge about what constitutes armed conflict and its resolution, as well as our appropriate disposition toward both. As discussed in Chapter 2, our attention is concentrated, as Peter Nyers writes, "on the practical ways in which *order* and *normalcy* can be reinstated. Critical questioning of both the unequal power relations and desirability of this order are de-emphasised, marginalised, or ignored."[83]

There is no discussion within UN documents—nor could there be—of alternative understandings of armed conflict, such as those that suggest that contemporary armed conflict is not a departure from "normalcy," as such, but rather a complex configuration of processes of social transformation. This alternative view would see conflict as inextricably connected to the inclusions and exclusions associated with contemporary forms of capitalism.[84] Such an understanding would not be one that celebrated the violence of that social transformation but would understand them differently and, in particular, would be far less optimistic about the application in discrete moments in time of particular "instruments" to achieve their resolution. As A. B. Fetherston writes, within this set of understandings, "peacekeeping becomes another aspect of a system which only seeks stability within the confines of that system, a system which already made the war possible. The unstated job of peacekeeping and other interventions, is to manage a REsolution of the war rather than a transformation of the system itself."[85]

Viewing contemporary conflicts in this way is the difference between "seeing the world as a machine and seeing it as a living system or organism."[86] The former imagines a series of "causes" that can be addressed through instrumental, problem-solving means; the latter envisions a complex totality in the process of transformation. Part of that totality includes UN and other responses to armed conflict, among them the efforts to make women or gender visible within those responses. This view of armed conflict, in short, directs us to the ways the UN's strategies to include women and to apply a "gender perspective" in peace and security operations contribute to the naturalization of UN discursive practices around war, peace, and security. They confirm "the background knowledge that is taken to be true"[87] about contemporary armed conflicts as produced by and through the United Nations.

Women in the UN Gaze

UN knowledge claims about armed conflict and appropriate responses thus make possible the ways in which understandings of women or gender can be inserted into the overall analysis, and these too conform to mechanistic understandings of armed conflict and security. The first, and most common, has been to collect the kind of information about the impact of armed conflict on women that policymakers or those on the ground will need in order to understand better how to respond to conflicts.[88] As noted in previous sections, much of the analysis of women and armed conflict produced by the United Nations focuses on the ways in which women are especially vulnerable during outbreaks of violence.

UN-produced information about the differential impact of armed conflict on women has a number of consequences. The first is that it denies, wittingly or not, the agency of women who face contemporary armed conflicts.[89] They are understood primarily through their vulnerabilities and, in such a position, need to be rescued and protected. Women as vulnerable also supplements and expands what policymakers and bureaucrats already know about armed conflict. War is hell, and it is a particularly devastating hell for women. Acknowledging that armed conflict has a differential impact on women and men does not demand rethinking how the United Nations understands the nature of armed conflict or how to respond to it, it merely adds another "dimension" that should be taken into account by policymakers and workers "in the field."

Once women are understood primarily through their vulnerabilities, and once those vulnerabilities are understood as identifiable, the UN practices of early warning, conflict resolution, peacekeeping, and peace-building become the instruments through which women may be protected or spared from the atrocities they face. Peacekeepers, for example, are reminded that they must "understand local dynamics and . . . not assume that all people have the same experiences of conflict and post-conflict situations."[90] They should be particularly aware of the ways women will need to have issues of sexual assault addressed through the postconflict and reconstruction processes. That the UN in principle is capable of developing appropriate responses to the differential impact of armed conflict on women is never questioned; rather, the consistent focus in all statements, policy pronouncements, and studies is on providing the departments, agencies, or missions of the UN with the sufficient information and resources they require to carry out this function.

When women do appear with agency, as noted above, it is their "uniqueness" that most attracts the attention of UN analyses. As the early study on peacekeeping suggested, women are unique, or different from men, because they have a different approach to conflict resolution and peacekeeping. Women's agency is not only acknowledged insofar as they are unique or different from men, but it is acknowledged primarily when they are involved in, or make themselves available for, the conflict resolution and prevention strategies of the United Nations. When women seem uninterested in UN peace activities—when they ask, for example, "Early warning for whom?"[91]—the response is that a public education campaign is required. Women, in short, can be taught to understand how important early warning, peace negotiations, and the other formal mechanisms of UN peace processes are for them.[92]

Mapping a gender analysis onto UN practices also allows for "gender information" to support existing UN conflict prevention and resolution instruments. Peacekeepers, for example, are told that local women or women's organizations may be sites of expertise about health and education service provision, especially in the areas of reproductive health.[93] Women may also have information on how conflict or emerging conflict affects people on the ground.[94] Knowledge about the gender norms of local contexts can inform early warning efforts: in some settings, women may switch to planting short-cycle crops if a prolonged conflict is anticipated.[95] Encouraging women to participate in formal peace negotiations not only brings a wider set of views "to the table" but increases the likelihood that issues of importance to women, and equality rights provisions, will make it into peace treaties.[96] Understanding women as "different" and "traditional gender practices" in particular local contexts, in short, will support UN peacekeepers and peace negotiators in the tasks that they have been assigned to conduct.

Where gender-informed analysis supplements existing UN practices, the aim is not and cannot be to transform UN instruments because those instruments are taken as given.[97] Rather, the arguments focus directly or indirectly on the promise that taking gender into account will allow UN personnel to perform their already-existing roles more effectively. Adding women, or gender, will promote the incremental and linear progress toward conflict prevention, or its resolution, embedded within UN understandings. It is thus perfectly consistent that the UN would "remember" gender only when it is being pushed to do so by women's machineries within the UN. Gender analyses do not seek to supplant or transform existing knowledge about contemporary armed conflict; they privilege effectiveness. If increased effectiveness is not apparent, if in the moment of a "humanitarian crisis" or "complex political emergency" UN bureaucrats are not convinced that applying a gender analysis will help them to prevent an imminent "outbreak" of violence or bring the "fighting" to an end as quickly as possible, there is simply no compelling reason to do so. Their actions in ignoring gender under such circumstances and within the space of such meanings, given the background knowledge of what is taken to be both true and important, are entirely consistent.

Analyses of women and of gender thus become part of the "programmatic solutions"[98] that form the UN repertoire of responding to conflict and insecurity around the world and, in this way, confirm the appropriateness of that repertoire. This is problematic not only because it makes the apparently inconsistent treatment of women and gender within the UN entirely consistent. It is problematic because it ensures that some critiques will never appear within the UN frame, simply because they are nonsensical in a context that is premised on supporting, not challenging, that frame.[99] There is, for example, no discussion within UN documents of militarism or militarized masculinities or, for that matter, of masculinities more generally.[100] Indeed, the militarized response of the United Nations in its deployment of peacekeeping operations is confirmed rather than challenged. Nowhere is the use of soldiers on peacekeeping missions raised as a point for debate or contention. Likewise, it would be inconceivable, within UN understandings, to present peacekeeping as anything other than a legitimate and benign practice. At best, it is a practice that faces occasional "problems," but these can be resolved. Strategies that are left for feminists are reduced to getting more women into existing practices. Gender experts scramble to provide the UN with advice on how to "gender" the UN's peace practices, and calls regularly go out for lists of eligible and willing specialists who can provide the kind of information, advice, and ideally, lists of "best practices"[101] that the UN requires to gender mainstream peace and security issues.

How the UN "genders" armed conflict also confirms in all instances the narrative authority of the United Nations and its representatives. This is well illustrated by reexamining the issue of gender units on peacekeeping missions. The discrepancies between the platform produced by East Timorese women and that produced by the Gender Affairs Unit might well reflect the attempt by the GAU to make the language of the Women's Platform for Action *useable*[102] within a UN context. From the perspective of the people working within the GAU, it was likely viewed that their job as gender experts was to serve as the transmission belt between local women's groups and the UN. This would have been perfectly consistent with all past gender efforts around peace and security issues within the UN, but it is not an innocent or apolitical act. It could require translating the demands of local women's groups into language that could be "heard" within the UN system. Altering the words of the original platform privileged the GAU *interpretation* as more reliable, more coherent, and more useful than the East Timor Women's Platform itself. East Timorese women in this way were constructed as unreliable, or at least not "understandable" except through the interpretive gaze of a UN staffer working within the gender unit.

UN knowledge claims about women, gender, armed conflict, and peacekeeping are not confined to the corridors of UN buildings or the field operations of DPKO missions. Part of the measure of their hegemony has been their reproduction in venues outside formal UN forums. Numerous studies, for example, have reproduced as authoritative the 1995 DAW study that lists all of the ways women can "make a difference" in peacekeeping missions.[103] NGOs devote considerable energy and resources to producing studies that can help the UN mainstream gender issues around peace and security operations.[104] Scholars not only provide their time as gender experts in the creation of UN documents,[105] but they also craft their analyses in a way that takes UN priorities of "effectiveness" as a given. Suggesting, for example, that it is "easier for female peacekeepers to establish a dialogue with local citizens" or noting that the presence of female peacekeepers "mitigate[s] such security procedures as body searches of women"[106] does not alter (and certainly does not transform) militarized peacekeeping practices. Rather, it simply provides advice on the ways in which understanding gender allows those practices to be conducted more effectively.

UN understandings and priorities have also informed "gender training" efforts by member states. The Canadian and UK governments, for example, have created a "gender and peacekeeping training course" offered both online and through the Pearson Peacekeeping Centre in Canada.[107] The course is organized into separate modules that explain why gender matters, how gender is related to culture, gender in the context of peace support operations, gender and international humanitarian law, and gender during conflict and postconflict situations.

The organizing theme of the course, from its opening welcoming page throughout each of the modules, is a promise that what participants will learn will allow them to enhance their abilities and "improve the overall effectiveness of any PSO" (peace support operation) in which they participate.[108] In the introductory module, participants are told that "The overall aim of this course is to strengthen PSOs."[109] In the "Why Gender Matters" module, we learn that it matters because understanding gender will "facilitate the achievement of mission objectives."[110] Though examples are provided throughout the course of the differential impact of armed conflict on women and men, and the ways in which the arrival of peacekeeping missions can contribute to a rise in prostitution and HIV/AIDS, there is little assessment of the assumptions of masculinity, or of militarized masculinity that may contribute to those issues, nor is there a sustained analysis of the way racism permits and makes possible some acts of violence on peacekeeping missions. Nor could there be in the context of the mandate for the course. The gender problems that arise in peace operations, in short, are understood as problems that can be addressed through proper training and do not require a fundamental rethinking of what those missions seek to accomplish, how they are conducted, or by whom.

Conclusion

As Cynthia Enloe has observed, "A funny thing has happened on the way to international political consciousness: 'gender' has become a safe idea."[111] One of the reasons gender has become a safe idea is that the manner in which it has been used within UN understandings of peace and security issues has transformed it from a critical to a problem-solving tool, which does not challenge prevailing practices in response to armed conflict, peace, and security. The continued lament that the UN needs to contribute greater resources to gender mainstreaming, to add more women into decisionmaking positions, and to produce yet more studies to illustrate how existing UN practices can be "gendered" is missing the point. The practices of the UN were *already* gendered, and in failing to recognize this—and attempt simply to "fit in" to prevailing practices—more critical interventions have been foreclosed. The failure to really live up to its commitments to gender equality and gender mainstreaming is in fact entirely consistent with the gender culture at the UN, and, more generally, with the meanings around peace and security that have been produced within the UN.

One of the most important claims made in the UN context has been to link gender equality to successful outcomes in peace operations. In Secretary-General's Kofi Annan's words: "Just as your work can promote gender equality, so can gender equality make your work more likely to succeed."[112] The question that has been posed throughout this chapter has been one drawn instead from Anne Orford, when she asks: "Does gender work as a category in such situations, and if so, whose work does it do?"[113] The argument here has been that it does the work of the status quo, the traditional focal points of the UN understandings of war, security, states, and territory. These understandings depend upon the absence of women, the marginalization of gender analyses, and the reproduction and reinforcement of militarism.

The work of the status quo also ensures that questions about militarized masculinities do not make it into UN discussions about gender and peacekeeping. But we cannot begin to understand the nature of peacekeeping behavior described in earlier chapters without also interrogating how soldiers are constituted. The following chapter explores this question.

Notes

1. This is not to say that the United Nations only began addressing women's issues and gender issues with the decline of the Cold War. The United Nations had established the Commission on the Status of Women as early as 1946 and held the First World Conference on Women in Mexico in 1975. The Convention on the Elimination of Discrimination Against Women (CEDAW) was adopted in 1979, and other gender-specific instruments included the 1994 UN Declaration on the Elimination of Violence Against Women and a Special Rapporteur on Violence Against Women. Follow-up World Conferences on Women included conferences in Copenhagen and Nairobi and then the Fourth World Conference on Women held in Beijing in 1995, the largest conference in the history of the United Nations to that date. It was in the mid-1990s, after the Beijing Platform for Action, that attention to both gender and women's issues within the UN really intensified, with more extensive mandates provided to the women's machineries within the UN.

2. On "gender balance," see General Assembly Resolution 47/226, April 8, 1993; for "gender mainstreaming, see UN Economic and Social Council, "Economic and Social Council Resolution 1996/310: Mainstreaming a Gender Perspective into All Policies and Programmes of the UN System"; Substantive Session for June 30–July 25, 1997; and UN Office of the Special Adviser on Gender Issues and Advancement of Women (DAW), *Gender Mainstreaming: An Overview* (New York: United Nations, 2001). For a discussion of the impact of "gender mainstreaming" within national women's machineries, see Jacqui True and Michael Mintrom, "Transnational Networks and Policy Diffusion: The Case of Gender Mainstreaming," *International Studies Quarterly* 45 (2001): 27–57, and BRIDGE, "Issue 5: Approaches to Institutionalising Gender," *Development and Gender in Brief* (Brighton: Institute of Development Studies, University of Sussex, 1997). available at www.ids.ac.uk/bridge/dgb5.html.

3. See, for example, United Nations, "Beijing Declaration and the Platform for Action" (New York: United Nations Publications, 1996), paragraphs 44, 135, and 141.

4. UN Department of Peacekeeping Operations Lessons Learned Unit, *Mainstreaming a Gender Perspective in Multidimensional Peace Operations* (New York, July 2000), available at www.un.org/Depts/dpko/lessons/Gender%20Mainstreaming.pdf; UN Department for Disarmament Affairs in Collaboration with the Office of the Special Adviser on Gender Issues and the Advancement of Women, *Gender Perspectives on Disarmament: Briefing Notes* (New York, March 2001). See also UN Department of Peacekeeping Operations Lessons Learned Unit, "Windhoek Declaration and the Namibia Plan of Action on Mainstreaming a Gender Perspective in Multi-Dimensional Peace Support Operations," Namibia, May 31, 2000, available at www.unifem.undp.org/unseccouncil/windhoek.html.

5. UN Report of the Secretary-General, "Women, Peace, and Security," October 16, 2002, S/2002/1154, paragraph 45.

6. UN Department of Peacekeeping Operations and the Joint UN Programme on HIV/AIDS, "Protect Yourself, and Those You Care About, Against HIV/AIDS" (New York: United Nations, April 1998), available at www.un.org/Depts/dpko/training/training_material/training_material_home.htm. While this manual notes the connection between prostitution and HIV/AIDS, its main focus is not on the impact of prostituting local women but rather the impact of contracting HIV/AIDS for the peacekeeper and his own loved ones "at home."

7. UN Secretary-General Study, *Women, Peace, and Security* (New York: United Nations, 2002), p. 81, paragraph 255, available at www.un.org/womenwatch/daw/public/index.html#wps.

8. UN Security Council Resolution 1325 (2000) on "Women, Peace, and Security," October 31, 2000, paragraphs 5 and 6, available at http://ods-dds-ny.un.org/doc/UNDOC/GEN/N00/720/18/PDF/N0072018.pdf?OpenElement.

9. The course is available at www.dfait-maeci.gc.ca/genderandpeacekeeping/intro-e.asp.

10. International Alert, "Gender Mainstreaming in Peace Support Operations: Moving Beyond Rhetoric to Practice," July 2002, p. 1 and passim; Dyan Mazurana, "International Peacekeeping Operations: To Neglect Gender Is to Risk Peacekeeping Failure," in Cynthia Cockburn and Dubravka Zarkov (eds.), *The Postwar Moment: Militaries, Masculinities, and International Peacekeeping* (London: Lawrence and Wishart, 2002), pp. 41–50.

11. Elisabeth Rehn and Ellen Johnson Sirleaf, *Women, War, Peace: The Independent Experts' Assessment on the Impact of Armed Conflict on Women and Women's Role in Peace-building* (New York: UN Development Fund for Women, 2002), p. 5.

12. UN Secretary-General Study, *Women, Peace, and Security,* p. 77, paragraph 237.

13. The idea of "stories" is drawn from Anne Orford's discussion of "intervention stories" in "Muscular Humanitarianism: Reading the Narratives of the New Interventionism," *European Journal of International Law* 10 (1999): 703 and passim. Ken Booth and Steve Smith raise the same point in more general terms, about the ways in which academic engagement with policymakers means speaking on policymakers' terms. As Smith writes: "Those academics who do get involved in talking truth to power must accept that in so doing they must adopt the agenda of those to whom they are talking. They will be involved in problem-solving, and thereby must accept the 'givens' of the policy debate"; Steve Smith, "Power and Truth: A Reply to William Wallace," *Review of International Studies* 23 (1997): 513 and passim. See also Ken Booth, "Discussion: A Reply to Wallace," *Review of International Studies* 23 (1997): 372 and passim.

14. International Alert, "Gender Mainstreaming in Peace Support Operations," p. 1.

15. Orford, "Muscular Humanitarianism," p. 704. Orford's original quote is directed at the language and practice of international lawyers and the new interventionism, but I believe that her critique applies to the UN more generally, as well as to the specific case of gender and peace operations.

16. These kinds of critiques have been examined also by Hester Eisenstein in her discussions of the limitations faced by "femocrats" who seek to promote and advance feminist issues from inside the state. See, for example, Eisenstein, *Inside Agitators: Australian Femocrats and the State* (Philadelphia: Temple University Press, 1996).

17. Trinh T. Minh-ha, *Woman, Native, Other: Writing Postcoloniality and Feminism* (Bloomington: Indiana University Press, 1989), p. 80, cited in Orford, "Muscular Humanitarianism," p. 703.

18. Rehn and Johnson Sirleaf, *Women, War, Peace*, p. 3.

19. Carol Cohn, "Opening Remarks," roundtable on "UN Security Council Resolution 1325: How Women Do (and Don't) Get Taken Seriously in the Construction of International Security," International Studies Association Annual Meetings, Portland, OR, February 26–March 1, 2003.

20. Michael Barnett, *Eyewitness to a Genocide: The United Nations and Rwanda* (Ithaca: Cornell University Press, 2002), p. 7.

21. Hilary Charlesworth, "Transforming the United Men's Club: Feminist Futures for the United Nations," *Transnational Law and Contemporary Problems* 4 (1995): 426.

22. UN Report of the Secretary-General, "Improvement of the Status of Women in the Secretariat," 1985, A/C.5/40/30, cited in ibid., n. 59.

23. These figures are drawn from the UN Office of the Special Adviser on Gender Issues and Advancement of Women web page, available at www.un.org/womenwatch/osagi/fpgenderbalancestats.htm. See also Francine D'Amico, "Women Workers in the United Nations: From Margin to Mainstream?" in M. Meyer and E. Prügl (eds.), *Gender Politics in Global Governance* (Boulder: Rowman and Littlefield, 1999), pp. 19–40.

24. From www.un.org/womenwatch/osagi/fpgenderbalancestats.htm.

25. UN Secretary-General Study, *Women, Peace, and Security*, p. 82, paragraph 262.

26. These figures are all drawn from Mazurana, "International Peacekeeping Operations," p. 43.

27. For example, the Secretary-General formed a Senior Appointments Group comprised of representatives of numerous UN departments and offices, including the Special Adviser on Gender Issues and Advancement of Women. See UN Secretary-General Study, *Women, Peace, and Security*, p. 83, paragraph 264.

28. True and Mintrom, "Transnational Networks and Policy Diffusion," p. 33.

29. DAW, *Gender Mainstreaming: An Overview*, pp. 6–7 and passim. This does not mean that the idea of gender mainstreaming has not been subject to criticism, as will be discussed below. For some observers, gender is used largely to signal women's difference from men, with "men" remaining the standard category of comparison. Elaborations of "mainstreaming" also seem prepared to discuss ethnic and cultural differences as they relate to gender but are conspicuously silent on race or class as categories of analysis, and on racism, globalization, and economic liberalism as contributors to women's and men's differential experiences of security, insecurity, and conflict, as well as their opportunities and access—or lack thereof—to power. These criticisms notwithstanding, however, most acknowledge that, conceptually, gender mainstreaming is a more sophisticated idea and goal than the more straightforward

commitments to "gender balance." See Helen Kinsella, "Approaching the Implementation of Security Council Resolution 1325," roundtable on "UN Security Council Resolution 1325: How Women Do (and Don't) Get Taken Seriously in the Construction of International Security," International Studies Association Annual Meetings, Portland, OR, February 26–March 1, 2003, and Orford, "Feminism, Imperialism, and the Mission of International Law," p. 281.

30. United Nations, "From Beijing to Beijing +5, Report of the Secretary-General, Review and Appraisal of the Implementation of the Beijing Platform for Action" (New York, 2001), p. 106.

31. UN Secretary-General Study, *Women, Peace, and Security,* p. 5, paragraph 16.

32. Ibid., p. 6, paragraph 19; see also General Assembly Resolution 48/104.

33. UN Secretary-General Study, *Women, Peace, and Security,* p. 6, paragraph 18. Two special rapporteurs also were appointed with mandates that directly addressed issues of sexual violence during armed conflict: in 1994 the Commission on Human Rights appointed Ms. Radhika Coomaraswamy as the special rapporteur on "Violence Against Women, Its Causes and Consequences"; and in 1995, Ms. Linda Chavez was appointed as the special rapporteur on "the Question of Systematic Rape and Sexual Slavery and Slavery-like Practices During Wartime," which addressed the use of comfort women during World War II. See UN Secretary-General Study, *Women, Peace, and Security,* p. 7, paragraphs 24 and 25. See also Judith Gardam and Michelle Jarvis, "Women and Armed Conflict: The International Response to the Beijing Platform for Action," *Columbia Human Rights Law Review* 32, no. 1 (fall 2000): 47–52, for a more complete analysis of the special rapporteurs and other UN instruments to address violence against women during armed conflict.

34. UN Division for the Advancement of Women, "Women 2000: Sexual Violence and Armed Conflict: United Nations Response," April 1998, available at www.un.org/womenwatch/daw/public/cover.htm.

35. Ibid.

36. Judith G. Gardam and Michelle J. Jarvis, *Women, Armed Conflict, and International Law* (The Hague: Kluwer Law International, 2001), p. 10.

37. R. Charli Carpenter makes a similar argument, from an antifeminist perspective, regarding the gender norms associated with humanitarian evacuations; "'Women and Children First': Gender, Norms, and Humanitarian Evacuation in the Balkans 1991–95," *International Organization* 57, no. 4 (2003): 661–694.

38. UN Division for the Advancement of Women, "Women 2000: The Role of Women in United Nations Peacekeeping," December 1995, no. 1/1995, available at gopher://gopher.undp.org:70/00/secretar/dpcsd/daw/w2000/1995–1.en.

39. Ibid. The 1995 DAW study and a 1996 study produced by Graça Machel on the "Impact of Armed Conflict on Children" also noted more critically that the arrival of peacekeeping forces could be accompanied by a rise of sexual abuse and mistreatment directed at women and that it had been associated also with a "rapid rise in child prostitution." The DAW study acknowledged some of the charges of sexual harassment described in Chapter 3 of this book, and the Machel report noted that in Mozambique in 1992, soldiers deployed on the UN Operation in Mozambique (ONUMOZ) were directly involved in the recruitment of girls between the ages of twelve and eighteen into prostitution. In addition to the DAW study, see Graça Machel, "The Impact of Armed Conflict on Children: Report of the Expert of the Secretary-General, Ms. Graça Machel, Submitted Pursuant to General Assembly Resolution 48/157," United Nations General Assembly, A/51/306, August 26, 1996, p. 31, paragraph 98; see also Graça Machel, "The Impact of Armed Conflict on

Children: A Critical Review of Progress Made and Obstacles Encountered in Increasing Protection for War-Affected Children," International Conference on War-Affected Children, Winnipeg, MB, September 2000, available at www.unifem. undp.org/machelrep.html.

40. Louise Olsson and Torunn L. Tryggestad, "Introduction," in Louise Olsson and Torunn L. Tryggestad (eds.), *Women and International Peacekeeping* (London: Frank Cass, 2001), p. 2.

41. Judith Hicks Stiehm, "Women, Peacekeeping, and Peacemaking: Gender Balance and Mainstreaming," in Olsson and Tryggestad, *Women and International Peacekeeping*, p. 44.

42. Henry F. Carey, "'Women and Peace and Security': The Politics of Implementing Gender Sensitivity Norms in Peacekeeping," in Olsson and Tryggestad, *Women and International Peacekeeping*, pp. 53–54.

43. Gardam and Jarvis, *Women, Armed Conflict, and International Law*, p. 94. See also Judith Gardam and Hilary Charlesworth, "Protection of Women in Armed Conflict," *Human Rights Quarterly* 22, no. 1 (2000): 160, and "Women and the Law of Armed Conflict: Why the Silence?" *International and Comparative Law Quarterly* 46 (1997): 74.

44. Anne Orford, *Reading Humanitarian Intervention: Human Rights and the Use of Force in International Law* (Cambridge: Cambridge University Press, 2003), p. 62.

45. United Nations, "Report of the Panel on United Nations Peace Operations," August 21, 2000, A/55/305–S/2000/809.

46. For a collection of some of the critiques on the Brahimi report's absence of gender analysis, see Women's Caucus for Gender Justice, "Gender and Frontline Perspectives on Peacekeeping and the Brahimi Report; Report of the Panel Discussion on the Absence of a Gender Perspective in Peacekeeping and in the Brahimi Report," February–March 2001, available at www.iccwomen.org. International Alert provides a brief analysis of the ways in which many of the Brahimi report's recommendations can be "reread" to incorporate gender perspectives; see their *Moving Beyond Rhetoric to Practice*, pp. 46–47.

47. Anuradha Chenoy, "Forever Victims," *Times of India*, December 7, 2001, available at http://timesofindia.indiat . . . ml/uncomp/articleshow?art_id=1442072446; Steven Erlanger, "At Bonn Talks, 3 Women Push Women's Cause," *New York Times*, November 30, 2001, available at www.nytimes.com/2001/11/30/international/asia/ 30WOME.html?ex=1083816000&en=663ab1e76feb6634&ei=5070; "Afghan Rivals Hold Key Talks on Future," *Toronto Star*, November 28, 2001, p. A10.

48. Natasha Walter, "Afghan Women Will Still Be Ignored," *The Independent*, November 15, 2001, available at http://argument.independent.co.uk/regular columnists/natasha walter/story; "Women's Participation Not Negotiable," editorial, *Minnesota Women's Press, Inc.*, December 5, 2001, available at www.womenspress. com/newspaper/2001/17–19edi.html; "Europeans Press Afghan Talks on Women's Rights," Reuters, November 29, 2001, available at www.reliefweb.int/w/rwb.nsf/9ca . . . 171088814885256b13006fe63b?OpenDocument.

49. Of course, to note this is not to forget that the United States', and the West's, sudden interest in the plight of Afghani women was, at best, suspicious. There had long been information available about the systematic abuse of women in Afghanistan—much of it raised by the Revolutionary Association of the Women of Afghanistan—which until September 11 went largely ignored by Western governments and the international media. See Krista Hunt, "The Strategic Co-optation of Women's Rights: Discourses in the 'War on Terrorism,'" *International Feminist*

Journal of Politics 4, no. 1 (2002): 116–121. See also Sandra Whitworth, "11 September and the Aftermath," *Studies in Political Economy* 67 (spring 2002): 33–38.

50. NGO Working Group on Women, Peace, and Security, "Recommendations and Concerns Based on the Afghan Women Leaders Summit in Brussels on 4th and 5th December 2001," available at www.international-alert.org/women/state2.htm.

51. Afghan Women's Summit for Democracy, "The Brussels Proclamation" (Brussels, December 4–5, 2001); Marlise Simons, "Professional Women from Afghanistan Meet to Press for Full Rights in their Country," *New York Times,* December 8, 2001, p. B3.

52. UN Secretary-General Study, *Women, Peace, and Security,* p. 81, paragraph 255.

53. UN Mission in the Democratic Republic of Congo (MONUC), "Activities Report from the Office of Gender Affairs (OGA) of the United Nations Organization Mission in the Democratic Republic of the Congo (MONUC)" (Kinshasa, January 10, 2003), p. 4, available at www.monuc.org/gender/.

54. UN Secretary-General Study, *Women, Peace, and Security,* p. 81, paragraph 255.

55. Hilary Charlesworth and Mary Wood, "Women and Human Rights in the Rebuilding of East Timor," *Nordic Journal of International Law* 71, no. 2 (2002): 340.

56. Ibid., p. 341.

57. Hilary Charlesworth and Mary Wood, "'Mainstreaming Gender' in International Peace and Security: The Case of East Timor," *Yale Journal of International Law* 26 (2001): 316.

58. International Alert, "Gender Mainstreaming in Peace Support Operations," p. 49.

59. Kvinna till Kvinna, *Getting It Right? A Gender Approach to UNMIK Administration in Kosovo* (Stockholm: Kvinna till Kvinna Foundation, 2001), p. 15; see also Chris Corrin, "Gender Audit of Reconstruction Programmes in South Eastern Europe" (Urgent Action Fund and the Women's Commission for Refugee Women and Children, June 2000), available at www.bndlg.de/~wplarre/, and "Post-Conflict Reconstruction and Gender Analysis in Kosova," *International Feminist Journal of Politics* 3, no. 1 (April 2001): 78–98.

60. MONUC, "Activities Report," p. 4.

61. UN General Assembly, "Report of the Secretary-General on Resource Requirements for Implementation of the Report of the Panel on United Nations Peace Operations," October 27, 2000, A/55/507, paragraph 15.

62. International Alert, "Gender Mainstreaming in Peace Support Operations," pp. 47–48.

63. Kvinna till Kvinna, *Getting it Right?* p. 15.

64. Corrin, "Post-Conflict Reconstruction and Gender Analysis in Kosova," p. 86.

65. Carey, "Women and Peace and Security," p. 54.

66. International Alert, "Gender Mainstreaming in Peace Support Operations," p. 49.

67. Charlesworth and Wood, "Women and Human Rights in the Rebuilding of East Timor," p. 338 n. 37.

68. Ibid., p. 343.

69. Ibid. Charlesworth and Wood cite other criticisms of the GAU and the UNTAET mission more generally, including the development of a fairly close relationship between the GAU and only one of the important East Timor women's organizations, to the exclusion of other groups; and, more generally, the problem

that there was little evidence of any attention to gender issues outside the small GAU office (pp. 343, 347).

70. International Alert, "Gender Mainstreaming in Peace Support Operations," p. 49.

71. Though she is discussing different issues, this formulation is drawn directly from Roxanne Lynn Doty, *Imperial Encounters: The Politics of Representation in North-South Relations* (Minneapolis: University of Minnesota Press, 1997), p. 5.

72. Anne Orford, "Feminism, Imperialism, and the Mission of International Law," *Nordic Journal of International Law* 71, no. 2 (2002): 281.

73. UN Report of the Secretary-General, "Prevention of Armed Conflict," June 7, 2001, A/55/985–S/2001/574, p. 9, paragraph 17; UN Report of the Secretary-General, "The Causes of Conflict and the Promotion of Durable Peace and Sustainable Development in Africa," April 13, 1998, A/52/871–S/1998/318, p. 4, paragraph 2; United Nations, *Charter of the United Nations and Statute of the International Court of Justice* (New York, 1945), paragraph 1.

74. UN Report of the Secretary-General, "The Causes of Conflict and the Promotion of Durable Peace and Sustainable Development in Africa," p. 4, paragraphs 3–4; UN Secretary-General Study, *Women, Peace, and Security*, p. 1, paragraph 3; United Nations, "From Beijing to Beijing +5," p. 107. There is a surprising reluctance within UN documents and other sources of information (press releases, web sites, and so on) to indicate the number of conflicts that are currently being waged, or have been waged in the recent past, around the world. Tellingly, Africa is the only place in the world where the UN seems prepared to provide a "number" in support of the general claim that conflicts have been on the rise since the collapse of the Cold War.

75. UN Secretary-General Study, *Women, Peace, and Security*, p. 1, paragraph 3.

76. UN Report of the Secretary-General, "On the Protection of Civilians in Armed Conflict," September 8, 1999, S/1999/957, p. 2, paragraphs 8–20; UN Secretary-General Study, *Women, Peace, and Security*, p. 2, paragraphs 4–5.

77. UN Report of the Secretary-General, "Prevention of Armed Conflict," p. 7, paragraph 7; UN Report of the Secretary-General, "The Causes of Conflict and the Promotion of Durable Peace and Sustainable Development in Africa," p. 5, paragraph 12.

78. Orford, "Feminism, Imperialism, and the Mission of International Law," pp. 281–282.

79. UN Report of the Secretary-General, "Prevention of Armed Conflict," pp. 6–7, paragraphs 1, 2, 7, 9 and 12.

80. Ibid., passim; UN Report of the Secretary-General, "An Agenda for Peace: Preventive Diplomacy, Peacemaking and Peace-keeping," January 31, 1992, A/47/277–S24/11, passim.

81. UN Report of the Secretary-General, "Prevention of Armed Conflict," p. 7, paragraphs 6, 7, 9, passim.

82. Ibid., p. 6, paragraph 3; see also p. 20, paragraph 80.

83. Peter Nyers, "Emergency or Emerging Identities? Refugees and Transformations in World Order," *Millennium: Journal of International Studies* 28, no. 1 (1999): 15.

84. Mark Duffield, *Global Governance and the New Wars: The Merging of Development and Security* (London: Zed Books, 2001), p. 4. See also Robert W. Cox, "Critical Political Economy," in Björn Hettne (ed.), *International Political Economy: Understanding Global Disorder* (Halifax, NS: Fernwood Books, 1995), pp. 39–41, and Robert W. Cox with Michael G. Schechter, *The Political Economy of a Plural World: Critical Reflections on Power, Morals and Civilization* (London: Routledge, 2002), preface and Chaps. 4, 7, and passim.

85. A. B. Fetherston, "Peacekeeping, Conflict Resolution, and Peacebuilding: A Reconsideration of Theoretical Frameworks," *International Peacekeeping* 7, no. 1 (spring 2000): 196–197.

86. Duffy, *Global Governance and the New Wars*, pp. 9–10.

87. Doty, *Imperial Encounters*, p. 10.

88. Anne Orford puts it this way in regard to international law: "Feminists appear authorized to contribute international law in two ways. First, women from 'highly industrialized countries' can gain access to female 'native informants' and produce knowledge about the victimized women of the Third World" (Orford, "Feminism, Imperialism, and the Mission of International Law," p. 278).

89. The UN Secretary-General Study, *Women, Peace, and Security,* also tends to emphasize women as victims and as contributors to peace but in some small way appears to challenge some of these automatic associations. For example, the study points out that "women and girls are not only victims of armed conflict: they are also active agents and participants in conflict. They may actively choose to participate in the conflict and carry out acts of violence because they are committed to the political, religious or economic goals of the parties to the conflict" (p. 3, paragraph 8). The study notes also that "women (just like men) are both actors and victims in armed conflict" and then goes on to provide a series of examples where women have been actors and combatants (p. 13, paragraph 47). Additionally, the study acknowledges that men and boys face sexual-based violence: "Men and adolescent boys are also subject to gender-based and sexual torture. The sexual abuse, torture and mutilation of male detainees or prisoners is often carried out to attack and destroy their sense of masculinity or manhood" (p. 16, paragraph 59). Far from depicting women as active only when they are involved in peace processes, the study emphasizes that "It is important, however, not to generalize about 'women' as not all women work for peace" (p. 54, paragraph 166). While these sentiments are not sufficient to disrupt the prevailing sense of women as victims and promoters of peace found within UN discursive practices, they do suggest a somewhat more complicated account, and one that may be in the process of change.

90. Ibid., p. 75, paragraph 230.

91. International Alert, "Implementing the United Nations Security Council Resolution on Women, Peace and Security: Integrating Gender into Early Warning Systems," report on the First Expert Consultative Meeting, May 7, 2001, Nairobi, Kenya, p. 3.

92. UN Secretary-General Study, *Women, Peace, and Security,* p. 69, paragraph 214.

93. Ibid., p. 76, paragraph 233.

94. Ibid., p. 60, paragraph 185.

95. Ibid., p. 58, paragraph 182. See also International Alert, "Implementing the United Nations Security Council Resolution on Women, Peace and Security."

96. UN Secretary-General Study, *Women, Peace, and Security,* pp. 61–65, paragraphs 190–202, and p. 68, paragraphs 211–213.

97. As Carol Cohn writes, working within the language of mainstream rules and understandings "gets you thinking inside their rules, tacitly accepting all the unspoken assumptions of their paradigms"; Carol Cohn, "Sex and Death in the Rational World of Defense Intellectuals," *Signs: Journal of Women in Culture and Society* 12, no. 4 (1987): 714, cited in Orford, "Muscular Humanitarianism," p. 704.

98. Orford, "Muscular Humanitarianism," p. 704.

99. In Anne Orford's words, any more subversive questioning is "swept away by the promise to increase women's participation in a project the terms of which are already set" ("Feminism, Imperialism and the Mission of International Law," p. 282).

100. Indeed, UN-produced understandings of gender, peace, and armed conflict systematically confirm one of the core precepts of militarism, which is that "in times of crisis, those who are feminine need armed protection"; Cynthia Enloe, "Demilitarization—or More of the Same? Feminist Questions to Ask in the Postwar Moment," in Cockburn and Zarkov, *The Postwar Moment*, p. 23.

101. Mark Duffy writes of the

> huge expansion in the employment of consultant specialists as a quick means of obtaining the information that organisations no longer appear able to produce for themselves. In many respects, however, this has not proved to be a particularly satisfactory response to a changing and mutating environment. Among other things, social advisers and consultants have often been placed in the role of interpreting and, especially, summarising complex problems. Indeed, the claim is often made that unless reports are succinct and easily accessible, busy policy makers will not read them. This creates a situation where, on the one hand, a consensus exists that more in-depth analysis is needed yet, on the other, unless information is pared down to basic essentials, functionaries are unable to absorb it. Under such pressures, demands have grown for summary "good practice" manuals and guides. While promising to show "what works" or provide checklists of essential things to do, these guides reproduce the illusion of a replicable and predictable environment (*Global Governance and the New Wars*, p. 263).

I am grateful to Dyan Mazurana for directing me to this observation.

102. This idea is drawn from Liisa H. Malkki, "Speechless Emissaries: Refugees, Humanitarianism and Dehistoricization," *Cultural Anthropology* 11, no. 3 (1996): 383.

103. See Heidi Hudson, "Mainstreaming Gender in Peacekeeping Operations: Can Africa Learn from International Experience?" *African Security Review* 9, no. 4 (2000): available at www.iss.co.za/Pubs/ASR/9No4/Hudson.html; Anita Helland, Kari Karame, Anita Kristensen, and Inger Skjelsbaek, "Women and Armed Conflict: A Study for the Norwegian Ministry of Foreign Affairs" (Copenhagen: Norwegian Institute of International Affairs, 1999), pp. 82–88.

104. See, for example, International Alert, "Gender Mainstreaming in Peace Support Operations," and "Implementing the United Nations Security Council Resolution on Women, Peace and Security."

105. I have been involved in such consultations myself.

106. Olsson and Tryggestad, "Introduction," p. 2.

107. The online version is available at www.genderandpeacekeeping.org.

108. Ibid.

109. Gender and Peacekeeping training course, module 1, introduction, presentation notes, p. 5, at www.genderandpeacekeeping.org/instroctor-module1-e.asp.

110. Gender and Peacekeeping training course, module 3, "Why Gender Matters, Methodology," p. 3, at www.genderandpeacekeeping.org/instroctor-module3-e.asp.

111. Cynthia Enloe, "Closing Remarks," in Olsson and Tryggestad, *Women and International Peacekeeping*, p. 111.

112. "Annan Urges Security Council to Boost Role of Women in Peacemaking," UN press release, October 28, 2002, available atwww.un.org/apps/news/story.asp?NewsID=5180&Cr=women&Cr1=peace#, cited in Louise Olsson, "Do

Peacekeeping Operations Affect Gender Relations in Host States? Developing a Theoretical Framework for Analyzing Peacekeeping Operations and Gender Relations," presented at the International Studies Association Annual General Meetings, Portland, OR, February 26–March 1, 2003, p. 1.

113. Orford, "Feminism, Imperialism, and the Mission of International Law," p. 28.

6

Militarized Masculinities and Blue Berets

Ask any group of soldiers why they joined the military and you will receive a variety of responses. For some, it is the highest calling: offering one's life in defense of kin and country. Others are following in the steps of fathers or mothers who themselves were members of the military. Some are serving compulsory military service. For others, it is an opportunity to travel, for adventure, or to pursue a career in which athletic skill and physical fitness are part of the routine. Some will answer by pointing to a free university or college education, or to skills training that can be used in the private sector after their military service is complete. For others still it is simply a job, sometimes the best paid job they could find. Often, it is the only job they could find.[1]

For those who will soldier primarily on peace operations, the answers might be even more complicated. In addition to the prospect of making money or facing new military challenges,[2] many respond that they are interested in "helping" people around the world by bringing peace and stability to areas wracked by conflict. They usually anticipate being involved as much in delivering humanitarian aid, rebuilding schools and hospitals, or administering an election as anything that can be properly associated with militaries. Yet, as discussed in earlier chapters, those same soldiers who seem to derive real satisfaction from peace operations might find that the military they have joined views peacekeeping as a less honorable activity than traditional military concerns,[3] and they may express their own disappointment in missing the *main show*—armed conflict and warfare. The military is more than adventure or athleticism, more than a free university degree. It is more than delivering powdered milk to hungry people. It is a strictly ordered hierarchical organization, the main purpose of which is the creation of men—and some women—who will be warriors, who are prepared to kill, and die, for the state. It is, in short, about violence and about preparing people to destroy other human beings by force. As one Canadian soldier aptly commented: "People worry we're too aggressive. But that's what soldiers are supposed to be. You don't go out and give the enemy a kiss. You kill them."[4]

Most people involved in peacekeeping—whether it is the soldiers who are deployed on missions; the political, military, and international actors who send them on those missions; or the academics who study them—argue that soldiers make the best peacekeepers, that the foundation for effective peacekeeping is general purpose combat training.[5] Even some feminist analysts suggest that peacekeeping requires military muscle as much as political will.[6] This is particularly true, proponents of this view argue, of the more complex—and more dangerous—peace missions of the post–Cold War era.

The argument in this book, by contrast, is that we have not spent nearly enough energy asking whether the attitudes and skills associated with soldiering are appropriate to missions dubbed "*peace*keeping." As A. Betts Fetherston writes, "If we only prepare people for war it is far more likely that this is what we will get."[7] The issue, however, goes even deeper than the skills acquired through military training; it involves the very *constitution* of soldiers. The creation of soldiers involves rituals and myths, those that focus on the military itself and other no less subtle messages about masculinity, about manliness, about race, and about belonging. This chapter explores some of the ways in which the soldier is constituted, and the often violently misogynist, racist, and homophobic messages delivered through the basic training, initiation, and indoctrination exercises associated with most national militaries.

The ways soldiers are constituted can have tragic consequences. The sense of entitlement that is inculcated through military indoctrination can be associated with acts of violence within military communities,[8] and with acts of violence outside those communities, directed at the people of countries in which soldiers have been deployed. These are the stories that usually remain invisible within official accounts of soldiering and peacekeeping. Ironic, though often just as invisible, are the ways in which the constitution of soldiering also has had sometimes tragic consequences for peacekeepers themselves: soldiers devastated by their missions and emotionally immobilized as a result of post-traumatic stress disorder are as much a liability to militaries and the United Nations as is news that soldiers are violently abusive with family members or that peacekeepers deployed abroad have run brothels, assaulted local women, or killed local citizens.

The argument of this chapter therefore is that it is not only *explosions* of militarized masculinity, but also its *implosions* that disturb and unsettle prevailing visions of the heroic warrior. Both illustrate well the fragile and contradictory base upon which peacekeeping is built.

Masculinities and the Making of a Soldier

Essentialist accounts of men, and of masculinity, suggest a certain natural-
ness to male aggressive behavior in militaries or society more generally.
The much-cited "End of History" commentator Francis Fukuyama, for
example, has argued that men are more closely associated with aggression,
violence, war, and intense competition for dominance, and these attitudes
are "rooted in biology."[9] Bob Connell, an Australian intellectual who is a
strong critic of essentialist views, summarizes essentialism as follows:

> The vast majority of the world's soldiers are men. So are most of the
> police, most of the prison warders, and almost all of the generals, admi-
> rals, bureaucrats and politicians who control the apparatus of coercion and
> collective violence. Most murderers are men. Almost all bandits, armed
> robbers, and muggers are men; all rapists, most domestic bashers; and
> most people involved in street brawls, riots and the like. . . . The same
> story, then, appears for both organised and unorganised violence [and]
> there is surprisingly widespread belief that this is all "natural." Human
> males are genetically programmed to be hunters and killers.[10]

By this account, man's appetite for violence and aggression needs to be har-
nessed, and historically, this has been best accomplished by directing it outward, toward "others." For Fukuyama, "The basic social problem that any
society faces is to control the aggressive tendencies of its young men. . . .
Older men in the community have generally been responsible for socializ-
ing younger ones by ritualizing their aggression, often by directing it
toward enemies outside the community."[11]

Soldiering thus becomes the natural activity of young males, who are
drawn to it by instinct and encouraged by older men (and women) who see
it as a proper way to channel potentially violent and disruptive behavior
into the defense of community and state. Whereas by this view men are naturally aggressive, women, by contrast, are more peaceful, more cooperative, more in touch with the cycle of life.[12] For essentialists—some feminists and many nonfeminists and antifeminists—women's more peaceful
views are a biological given and so might usefully be brought into the public sphere of governance, decisionmaking, even war-making. Sociobiolo-
gists Lionel Tiger and Robin Fox, in a manner that echoes many radical
feminist arguments, contend that "if all the menial and mighty military
posts in the world were taken over by women, there would be no war."[13]
In the end, however, essentialism is a deeply pessimistic position because
most essentialists assume that the possibilities for individual, institutional,
or societal transformation are so limited. Men, after all, according to
Fukuyama, Tiger, Fox, and their adherents, will not soon relinquish their

positions of power to women, but even more importantly, man's naturally aggressive tendencies are seen as largely unchangeable.[14] As Fukuyama writes:

> The realms of war and international politics in particular will remain controlled by men for longer than many feminists would like. Most important, the task of resocializing men to be more like women—that is, less violent—will run into limits. *What is bred in the bone cannot be altered easily by changes in culture and ideology.*[15]

While such characterizations may appeal to prevailing stereotypes about men and women, the essentialist argument by itself is difficult to sustain. Among other things, essentialism has always been troubled by the exceptions: those men who prefer peace and those women who are perfectly comfortable with violence, power, and war. There is ample historical evidence of men who have resisted violence—in both its organized and unorganized forms—as well as women who have embraced it. Many men have been at the forefront of peace activism around the globe, and many have refused, or sought to avoid, taking up arms. As Barbara Ehrenreich writes, "Throughout Western history, individual men have gone to near-suicidal lengths to avoid participating in wars—cutting off limbs or fingers or risking execution by deserting."[16] In contrast to women's depiction as universally peaceful and nonviolent, Katha Pollitt notes that "Women commit infanticide, abuse and kill children, mutilate the genitals of little girls, and cruelly tyrannize daughters, daughters-in-law, servants, and slaves. . . . Historically, cultures organized around war and displays of cruelty have had women's full cooperation: Spartan and Roman women were famed for their 'manly' valor."[17] Essentialism thus is unable to address, or even to recognize, the variation that exists among both women and men in terms of their attitudes toward, and participation in, acts of violence.

Rather than think in terms of the simple dichotomies presented by essentialists, it is more useful to note that there is no single masculinity or femininity but rather multiple masculinities and femininities. There are forms of masculinity, for example, that privilege physical strength and "machismo" attitudes and those that privilege rational thought and objectivity, or entrepreneurial spirit and commercial risk-taking, or technological expertise and restraint.[18] There are visions of masculinity that acknowledge the "gender straightjackets" existing in many social contexts and that seek to break the connection between masculinity and violence.[19] In different times or places, communities or institutions, any one vision of masculinity may predominate over others or, in Bob Connell's terms, become "culturally exalted" or hegemonic.[20] Where one form of masculinity is exalted, alternative masculinities will be culturally discredited or despised.[21] The form different masculinities take, and whether one of the competing forms becomes hegemonic, is not determined in advance as a result of some natural characteristics. Rather, it is the result of social practices.[22] Masculinities—like femininities—are, in short, created.

Critics of essentialism offer another valuable caveat. They point out that whatever "natural" instinct some men may have for violence, it is not nearly so widespread or trustworthy an instinct that military decisionmakers have counted on it alone to produce the kinds, and quantity, of warriors they require. As Clark McCauley writes, "The hypothesis of a killer instinct is not so much wrong as irrelevant."[23] The qualities demanded by militaries—the requisite lust for violence (when needed) and a corresponding willingness to subordinate oneself to hierarchy and authority (when needed)[24]—must be self-consciously cultivated. Few new male recruits arrive as ready-made soldiers and, as Ehrenreich notes, "The difference between an ordinary man or boy and a reliable killer, as any drill sergeant could attest, is profound. A transformation is required."[25]

Historically, that transformation has been accomplished in different ways, sometimes through drinking wine or liquor or taking drugs, and in other instances through social pressure or ceremonies designed to urge young men to fight.[26] By the seventeenth century in Europe, as Ehrenreich describes it, the process had become more organized:

> New recruits and even seasoned veterans were endlessly drilled, hour after hour, until each man began to feel himself part of a single, giant fighting machine. The drill was only partially inspired by the technology of firearms. It's easy enough to teach a man to shoot a gun: the problem is to make him willing to get into situations where guns are being shot and to remain there long enough to do some shooting of his own. . . . In the fanatical routines of boot camp, a man leaves behind his former identity and is reborn as a creature of the military—an automaton and also, ideally, a willing killer of other men.[27]

The contemporary practices of boot camp are remarkably similar across most modern state militaries. They entail a carefully designed and executed process by senior officers and often supporting civilian specialists. It is a tightly choreographed process aimed at breaking down the individuality of the recruits and replacing it with a commitment to, and dependence on, the "total" institution of which they are now a part.[28] The goal of boot camp, in short, is to inculcate recruits into the norms and values—the ideas—that constitute the imagined community of military institutions.

As Christian Appy describes 1970s-era U.S. basic training: "Every detail of life was prescribed, regulated, and enforced. Every moment was accounted for. There was a method and time for every action. Even using the bathroom was limited to short, specified times or required special permission. . . . Some men went for a full week before they were able to defecate in the time allotted."[29] By its end, recruits should conform to the official attitudes of military conduct, be able to follow orders instantly and without question, and commit themselves to the larger group (whether that is co-recruits, barrack, regiment, battalion, military, or state) over any personal or individual commitments they previously held.[30]

The process of military indoctrination begins immediately upon arrival, when all evidence of the recruit's civilian life is stripped away: clothing, hair, and most belongings. New recruits are separated from families, undergo tests of physical endurance and sleep deprivation, and are forced to participate in numerous arbitrary, often mundane, and apparently irrelevant tasks. All have the same shaved heads, the same uniforms, eat the same food, sleep in the same uncomfortable beds, and must conform to the same expectations and follow the same rules.[31] They learn how to march in unison—a task aimed entirely at teaching them that they are no longer individuals but members of a group.[32] As one male U.S. Marine described it: "They tore you down. They tore everything civilian out of your entire existence—your speech, your thoughts, your sights, your memory—anything that was civilian they tore out and then they re-built you and made you over."[33] New recruits are being trained for the same purpose, and they are reminded repeatedly that it is the most important and most challenging purpose any individual may ever face—warfare.

The new soldier also faces the humiliation strategies that are common to most national militaries. The new recruit might face a drill instructor who screams in his ear: "You no good fucking civilian maggot. . . . You're worthless, do you understand? And I'm gonna kill you."[34] The tactics used to humiliate and degrade the recruit will vary depending on the military. In some, physically brutalizing new recruits remains an acceptable strategy, whether by officers or more senior recruits. In other militaries where physical punishment in principle is prohibited, drill sergeants often have at their official disposal only the threat of violence and verbal assaults. Here the new recruit is not only reminded constantly of his or her incompetence, but faces a variety of gendered and raced insults crafted to play on her or his specific feminine or masculine anxieties, including "whore," "faggot," "sissies," "cunt," "ladies," "abortion," "pussies," "nigger," "Indian," and sometimes simply "you woman."[35]

Even in militaries that ostensibly outlaw physical violence toward new recruits, unofficial initiation rituals, or "hazing," is still common and regularly conducted in the presence of superior officers.[36] Soldiers who do not conform or perform tasks exactly as demanded face a variety of punishments, usually some physical ordeal or humiliation, such as being forced to exercise until they drop, eat garbage, or put their heads in urinals.[37] Kate Muir, who has researched recent British military training practices, comments that it is astounding that people who are not conscripted would put themselves through the brutalities of boot camp, which in any other setting would be tantamount to a form of torture:

> Take an average day at boot camp . . . as new recruits learn the awful truth: they are in the army now. In summer they will be sweating, pallid and inevitably cleaning the linoleum of their barracks, inch by inch, with a very small scrubbing brush, as a sergeant of unparalleled viciousness bawls them out. In winter, they will be ordered on three-mile runs before dawn in sub-zero temperatures, wearing scarves over their mouths to stop their breath freezing. Next they will be taken on exercise in the field, on short rations, and go sleepless until they start to hallucinate. On parade ground, if asked a question, their only permitted responses will be "Yes, Sir," "No, Sir," and "No excuse, Sir."[38]

This is not Britain in 1690. This is Britain in 1990.

After breaking down new recruits, the training aims slowly to rebuild them as soldiers. While new recruits have been told repeatedly that they are worthless by themselves, they soon learn that through the military, in concert with drill instructor and fellow soldier, they can achieve almost any goal. The early litany of insults and complaints from superior officers is gradually replaced with occasional words of praise or encouragement for tasks well done, especially if done in concert with others.[39] As Donna Winslow writes of the Canadian military's current strategies, "The military does things quite deliberately to intensify the power of group pressure within its ranks as recruits are taught the need for teamwork."[40] Individuals who fail will bring down their entire squad, platoon, company, or regiment, but those who succeed, succeed together as a team.[41] Deborah Harrison and Lucie Laliberté, close observers of Canadian military practices and policies, note that "The ensuing emotional roller coaster also produces dependence on the instructor's strokes. The instructor takes on the character of a parent whom the child wants to please. He or she becomes the source of all reward and punishment, the passionately revered leader."[42] As one former soldier reminisces:

> Our instructors at the school made a tremendous impression on me. . . . Most were prematurely gray with rugged features brought on by years of hard living. All of them carried a long list of injuries, and we could see their discomfort after nights spent out training under the stars. Yet each one of them, in their late twenties or thirties, could run a group of cocky youngsters into the ground or shoulder twice the weight of any of us. Their physical toughness, matched with unbreakable self-confidence, was an example of what a man could achieve if he set his sights high enough. To have been counted amongst them, as a peer, is probably my greatest accomplishment.[43]

Leaders are admired by new recruits, whether they are officers or drill sergeants, or leaders who emerge from within their own ranks. Once peers recognize and respect a leader, as another Canadian soldier comments, those recruits will follow him to any length: "We're so connected physically and mentally, that if there's one person that we admire . . . the others will group around him. If he incites his group to racist behaviour, they'll follow, even if they don't agree, because they won't distinguish themselves from the group. Because the group's all you've got."[44]

Sanctioned and nonsanctioned initiation rituals not only break the new recruit's sense of individuality but also accomplish the broader goals of militarized transformation: to enforce obedience, underline the importance of the chain of command, and promote an intense bonding among soldiers who may need to depend on one another in battle.[45] Recruits come to accept that the rules and regimens into which they are trained have been established to enhance their chances of survival.[46] Soldiers need to see also that they are part of a chain of command that follows clear and highly structured lines of authority from which no one, at any level, is allowed to deviate. They have been trained, in short, to become "a disciplined cog within the military machine."[47]

Perhaps most important to the new soldier's sense of self is the intense bonding among soldiers that is inculcated through the training regimen. It is not only the drill sergeant or commander who is eventually revered but fellow soldiers as well. New recruits come to see whom they can count on (the military and their fellow soldiers) and who cannot be counted on (the civilian world and political leaders). The bond is one that many soldiers report is stronger than any relationship they had previously experienced,[48] including familial and intimate relations. Some will not extend their sense of community to the military in its entirety, but only to the soldiers closest to them.[49] Most, however, have come to see themselves as members of a new family, a warrior brotherhood, which is very distinct from the larger world around them.

That distinct new world is quite literally separated from the society around it, usually fenced off and patrolled by armed guards, with any movement in or out strictly controlled. The military world has its own unique set of norms of behavior and dress, its own judicial system, and its own rights and responsibilities. It is for these reasons that militaries are described as "total" institutions—they regulate almost every aspect of their members' lives. But neither is this an entirely coercive relationship, for an important element of the total institution is the military's pledge to support and care for its members, to actually become the soldier's new family. Harrison and Laliberté describe how the Canadian military, for example, provides medical, dental, and educational services to its members. It provides housing for both single and married soldiers and emergency funds if a recruit is short of cash. Members are encouraged to socialize with one another, and good food and cheap liquor are readily available in the company mess. Visitors are sent to ensure that families are not left entirely alone when soldiers are deployed abroad. When a family member dies, the military family is there to offer support and grieve, and when babies are born they are there to celebrate. As Harrison and Laliberté note, the "caring military community [is] often cherished by members and their families."[50]

The sense of the military as a "family" helps to inculcate the conformity expected of soldiers, a conformity new recruits eventually embrace. While they may have joined up or been conscripted as members of different regional, ethnic, class, or language groups, most recruits come to identify primarily with the military. The bond is easier and perhaps more strongly established when some level of conformity existed already. As one member of the Canadian forces commented: "The best is having the same colour, the same haircut, the same religion, the same colour of eyes, the same height, the same weight. Because everybody outside of that—we don't like difference."[51] One soldier writes:

> As our graduation neared, some press-hungry officers decided Gosel [a Sikh recruit] should wear a turban for graduation. Gosel had never worn one while he was in the Forces and refused to wear anything but his green beret for our ceremony. He had been with us since day one in Basic and he had become his own man, not a Sikh or anything but a soldier.[52]

"Difference," in short, can be accommodated, but that accommodation involves the erasure of difference.

Myths, Militaries, and Violence

Part of the process of transforming young men into warriors involves the lure of masculinity itself, and more specifically, in the words of Sherene Razack, white masculinity.[53] In many societies, both historical and contemporary, men are expected to undergo some sort of ritual or rite of passage in order to prove their "manhood" and to satisfy prevailing myths of appropriate masculinity. In some settings, this may involve simply a male adolescent's first sexual experience. In other settings, it may involve a collective rite of passage through participation in some form of physical ordeal, for example the practice in some hunter-gatherer societies of participating in a particularly dangerous or difficult hunt, or in other societies of the infliction of pain, sometimes through male adolescent circumcision. For societies centered on warfare or militarism, that ordeal has typically involved proving oneself in battle.[54] A contemporary lament in many Western societies is that few suitable rites of passage or collective initiation rituals exist anymore to transform boys into men, and that absence is blamed for increasing insecurity among men about their sense of manhood and masculinity.[55] Indeed, the only remaining collective initiation ritual that exists for many men is enlistment in national militaries.[56]

Militaries thus have long promised to "make a man out of you,"[57] and indeed some observers have suggested that the military's *first* job is to teach manhood and only secondarily to teach soldiering.[58] Theorists of both militarism and of masculinity have pointed to the intimate connection between military organizations and hegemonic representations of masculinity. David Morgan describes it this way:

> Of all the sites where masculinities are constructed, reproduced, and deployed, those associated with war and the military are some of the most direct. Despite far-reaching political, social, and technological changes, the warrior still seems to be a key symbol of masculinity. In statues, heroic paintings, comic books, and popular films the gendered connotations are inescapable. The stance, the facial expressions, and the weapons clearly connote aggression, courage, a capacity for violence, and, sometimes, a willingness for sacrifice. The uniform absorbs individualities into a generalized and timeless masculinity while also connoting a control of emotion and a subordination to a larger rationality.[59]

Even before joining up or being conscripted, young men normally have been socialized into ideas associated with soldiering, and of being a warrior, through family norms, movies, male role models, books, military recruitment campaigns, television programs, and children's games.[60] Many of these ideas may convey conflicting and confusing messages, but in numerous societies it is notable how stubbornly pervasive is the prescriptive moral tale: join a military, young man, and you will confirm your manliness, both to others and to yourself.

Young men have been socialized, in short, into myths associated with militarized masculinity. Myths, according to Jim McKay, "are partial truths that emphasize specific versions of reality and conceal or overlook others. In all cultures myths are crucial in defining what is natural, normal and legitimate. They are inextricably involved in relations of power, because they ensure that some accounts of reality count more than others."[61] Myths are carried through rituals that, as Varda Burstyn notes, "encode and transmit information about basic, ideal social arrangements."[62]

The myths of manhood into which the new soldier is inculcated throughout basic training are highly specific and privileged: courage and endurance; physical and psychological strength; rationality; toughness; obedience; discipline; patriotism; lack of squeamishness; avoidance of certain emotions such as fear, sadness, uncertainty, guilt, remorse, and grief; and heterosexual competency.[63] The information conveyed through the rituals of military initiation encode a fundamental connection between masculinity, physical strength, and violence captured well by a 1990s U.S. recruiting poster that declared: "Pain Is Weakness Leaving the Body."[64] The hardened body of the soldier warrior is now a real or potential weapon.[65] As one U.S. soldier commented: "What they did is they took a seventeen-year-old kid and put him through all this training and turn[ed] me into what I deem to be a *perfect killing machine.*"[66] The new soldier is both physically and emotionally tough—betraying little emotion, with the possible exceptions of anger and aggression.[67] The soldier learns to "deny all that is 'feminine' and soft in himself,"[68] and any who depart from the ideal are neither men nor soldiers. Soldiers who quit basic training or the military prematurely can anticipate being shouted down: "You're not a man, right? You're a little boy, aren't you? You can't be trusted."[69]

Some of the techniques involved in creating soldiers, as noted above, include constant harassment and the promotion of elitist attitudes, including "in-group" language. They also include dehumanizing "the enemy," rewarding obedience, and severely punishing noncooperation. Violence is modeled, as is the gradual exposure to repugnant acts in order to make them routine. As Janice Gibson writes, "Military training, after all, is designed to create soldiers obedient to all orders, even when those orders require them to commit acts that they were taught throughout their lives to be repugnant."[70] For people close to the new soldier, these changes can be disturbing. Harrison and Laliberté describe one fighter pilot's wife's account of her husband's transformation:

> When I first met Pete, I said to him one day, "Could you fly over a village and bomb?" . . . And he said to me, "No, I couldn't do that." And about midway through fighter weapons school, I noticed . . . something changing. And he was becoming this fighting machine. And I don't know how they did it, but they did it. And I said to him, "Could you fly over a village and bomb?" He said, "If I was ordered to, yes." That cold and simple. And I went, "My God, what have I married?"[71]

Just as often, however, instead of shock and concern, new recruits report the pride their families express at the transformation they have undergone. As one mother exclaims at her son's graduation from basic training: "He's a man now. . . . I'm so proud. He's a real beauty."[72]

Basic military training helps to nurture the exaggerated ideals of manhood and masculinity demanded by national militaries. But this transformation is most effectively accomplished through the denigration of everything marked by difference, whether that be women, people of color, or homosexuality. It is not by coincidence that the insults most new recruits face are gendered, raced, and homophobic insults: young soldiers are learning to deny, indeed to obliterate, the "other" within themselves. Difference can include race or ethnic differences; it can even include simply having attended university or college.[73] Soldiers must, in particular, deny all that is deemed to be feminine, and this is accomplished throughout the training process.[74] The practice of shaving heads, for example, not only exposes the new recruit to the discipline and uniformity of military life but is aimed also at "removing the extra frills of longer hair often associated with individual vanity (vanity believed to be the prerogative of women)."[75] The chants to which soldiers march, either denigrating women or linking their militarized masculinity to an aggressive and violent heterosexuality, are widely documented, including the call while holding one hand to rifle and the other to crotch: "This is my rifle. This is my gun. This is for pleasure. This is for fun."[76]

The discursive and material practices to which the new recruit is exposed "fix" meaning, or produce a truth, in which all soldiers are expected to participate. Put another way, the representational practices involved in the creation of a soldier simultaneously construct the "other" (woman, homosexual, black, Indian, Tamil, Tutsi, Somali, Kurd) and also construct the "self" vis-à-vis this other.[77] In order for truths that are fixed through these processes to remain intact, self and other must remain both distinct and separate.

It is for this reason that militaries have long been so resistant to the inclusion of the "other" within their ranks, whether that be members of "other" ethnic or racial groups, gay men and lesbians, or women. The presence of the "other" makes the strategies of recruitment, basic training, and the inculcation of an appropriate militarized masculinity all the more difficult to accomplish, and those involved in recruiting and training have long understood this. Whenever militaries marked by racial segregation have been faced with racial integration, for example, the arguments used to resist that integration usually focus on the ways in which mixed-raced regiments or battalions could never be trained to fight together.

Today, more often it is the prospect of including women or openly gay men and lesbians that provoke those same forms of resistance.[78] For some observers, the presence of women within militaries is both a symptom and a cause of the "decline" of the advanced military.[79] By this view, it will be difficult to attract young men to join militaries that include women, gay men, and lesbians, and more difficult still to train them to bond with their fellow soldiers. One author notes that by including more women, the U.S. military "is now paying a heavy penalty for the folly of the responsible politicians and voters as cohesion suffers, training becomes almost impossible, and some of its best personnel are forced out by 'sexual harassment' claims which may or may not be well founded."[80] As Suzanne E. Hatty writes of women's involvement in militaries: "According to this fearful perspective, the presence of women dilutes the masculine character of the institution, erodes the solidarity of the body of fighting men, and introduces confusion and conflict to the system of loyalties."[81] In an era during which conscription has been eliminated for many national militaries, this is considered a very serious problem.

After the 1993 removal of the ban on at least fully closeted gays and lesbians in the U.S. Navy, for example, one retired naval commander, exasperated by the new compromise informed by what he saw as merely "political correctness," predicted that:

> Because of "women-in-charge" ads, fewer blue-collar teenaged boys will join. The last thing that many of our prospective male recruits need is another matriarch. Plus, as my 19-year-old nephew told me . . . "How hard can the Navy be if all you have is sissies and girls in it?" A harsh perspective—but for teenagers perceptions equal reality. The perception in working-class America . . . is that the Navy is now a haven for gays and women. Their attitude is: What self-respecting teenaged guy would join the Navy?[82]

For military decisionmakers, then, attracting the mostly young men they require who will be willing give up their individuality, and to kill and die for the state, involves a series of promises and myths: the promise of turning boys into men; the myth of a male-dominated and exclusively heterosexual world; the promise of a place in which force, and even violence, can be celebrated; and the myth that a soldier's superiority will never be questioned. The presence of "the other" among them makes it far more difficult for militaries to sustain these myths and to deliver on these promises. Cynthia Enloe describes the angry reaction of some active and veteran military professionals to the civilian outcry against male pilots' sexually harassing behavior at the infamous 1991 Tailhook Convention:

> If male aircraft pilots can't have a few drinks and send women down a hotel corridor gauntlet, how are they supposed to militarily bond with one another? If women are allowed not just to speak out against the hotel gauntlet tradition, but to join the fighter squadron itself, then who will be left at home for the manly pilot to take pride in protecting? And if a woman who isn't sexually attracted to even benign versions of male heterosexuality is permitted to openly express her sexual indifference to masculinized pilots, then what's the prize waiting at the end of the war?[83]

However, it is not only the "other" hoping to join their ranks that disrupts the myths and promises new recruits have been weaned on. Perhaps even more difficult is when a soldier faces resistance to his authority, and to his sense of privilege, from those "others" around him, family members who do not buy in to the entitlements associated with militarized masculinity. As Doreen Drewry Lehr notes, "The myth of male superiority is hard to maintain when military men are obliged to work equally alongside, or for, military females. It is officially mandated that men cannot display their frustration in the workplace, but no such restrictions apply to home life."[84] Studies into the levels of spousal abuse and violence within military communities draw the link between the degree of power and control a soldier has been promised, and his sometimes violent reaction when partners and children do not grant him that control within personal and familial relationships.[85]

Soldiers faced with a lack of control in their personal relationships—a spouse who wants to socialize with friends, who wants to end the relationship, or even a family "that generally has been functioning successfully without them"[86] when they have been deployed abroad—may react by feeling threatened and may respond by reasserting their control through physical violence or psychological abuse. That reaction to loss of control appears to be alarmingly widespread within military communities. In the United States by the mid-1990s, for example, it was reported that "an average of one child or spouse dies each week at the hand of a relative in uniform."[87]

The norms and expectations within militaries about the appropriate roles of husbands and wives within a family can also contribute to a male soldier's desire to control spouses and families through violence and abuse. Though most contemporary militaries officially disapprove of domestic violence, it is not at all uncommon, as Deborah Harrison notes, for military members "to receive specific admonishments from their superiors to 'Keep your wife in line!'"[88] Military wives who do not behave appropriately in official functions or public venues—who themselves cannot be "counted on"—can prove an embarrassment to militaries and an impediment to their husband's career advancement as much as or even more than his own behavior and actions.[89] At the same time, militaries do not often like to air their own dirty laundry in public, and have long sought to keep quiet incidents of domestic violence within their ranks. Even in situations where superior officers are aware of physical violence within an officer's home, a "good soldier" or "good officer" can normally rely on the military family to take care of him, not his abused spouse or children.[90]

Many observers argue that the problem of family violence within military communities results from the fundamental contradiction of military training itself: it is difficult to "turn it off" in settings where that training is no longer appropriate. As a 1979 report of the U.S. inspector general noted:

> Social workers and other persons working with battered women in [U.S.] military families agree that military service is probably more conducive to violence at home than at any other occupation because of the military's authoritarianism, its use of physical force in training and the stress produced by perpetual moves and separations. In addition, those men in the civilian population most likely to physically abuse the women with whom they live are men who have had prior military service.[91]

Likewise, a Canadian army officer notes: "We're the only people who train people to go out and attack somebody else and kill them. And that is a difficult thing to get around. . . . How do you say, 'Okay guys, turn in your gear and turn off that switch and go home and have a nice life?' And I'm not sure we're ever going to get around that 100 percent."[92]

Lending credence to this observation, anecdotal evidence suggests that the incidence of spousal and family violence within militaries increases after soldiers return home from being deployed into combat situations. In the United States, for example, the 2002 murder of four wives by their soldier husbands, who had just returned from deployment to Afghanistan and were all stationed at Fort Bragg in North Carolina, attracted considerable media attention across North America.[93] Likewise, both during and immediately after the Gulf War, battered women's shelters and rape crisis centers in Israel reported a sharp increase in violence against women.[94] Men trained in the conduct of war, by this view, are not reluctant to apply those "skills" to family members who do not submit themselves properly to the control and sense of superiority that the soldier has been promised he can expect.

The problem of family violence within military communities, however, likely goes deeper than a simple failure to "turn off" the training soldiers receive; rather, it is a symptom of the fundamental fragility of the construction of militarized masculinity and the ways in which its myths and promises must be constantly confirmed and reconfirmed in order to appear naturalized or stable. Despite all the effort that goes into the constitution of soldiers, that identity is never fixed, closure is never really accomplished. So the process of constituting soldiers remains an incomplete and ongoing one.[95] Masculinity in general is a fragile construct, as Michael Kaufman notes:

> The personal insecurities conferred by a failure to make the masculine grade, or simply, the threat of failure, is enough to propel many men, particularly when they are young, into a vortex of fear, isolation, anger, self-punishment, self-hatred and aggression. Within such an emotional state, violence becomes a compensatory mechanism. It is a way of re-establishing the masculine equilibrium, of asserting to oneself one's masculine credentials.[96]

Militarized masculinity may be particularly fragile, in part because the hypermasculinized entitlements associated with it require more vigilant and consistent confirmation.

The kinds of promises made through the processes of military indoctrination, moreover, are fundamentally an illusion, and eventually many soldiers come to recognize this. The power and control the newly constituted soldier has been told is rightfully his, for example, is available to only a select few, and in fact the vast majority of soldiers have few opportunities to control even the most basic elements of their lives. As Deborah Harrison writes, "It may be that military organizations implant the desire to exert power among all their members but provide the experience of doing so significantly only to a few."[97] Or as the former wife of a Canadian noncommissioned officer, and an abuse survivor, describes it: "[The military controls] everything. They control every action that comes, every word that comes, everything you do in your life is [in] their control. And I think because these guys are so controlled . . . then they come home and they want to control at home. And if you have any type of an opinion, or you don't agree with them, then you're the bad guy and you get beat on."[98] The discrepancy between the myths and promises associated with militarized masculinity on the one hand and on the other the actual conditions of militarized men's lives can be so enormous that some of those men resort to violence directed at family members in an effort to reestablish for themselves the equilibrium of their militarized masculine credentials. They are, in short, attempting to "fix" an identity that can never be fixed, and so must be involved in a constant denigration and violence directed at "others" who undermine the privileges and entitlements, the ultimately unfulfilled promises on which militarized masculinity rests.

Killing the Woman in Them

The violence that informs militarized masculinity, however, is not only directed outward toward "others" who resist, impede, or otherwise do not confirm its entitlements. Sometimes that violence is directed at the "others" within. According to U.S. conservative writer George Gilder: "When you want to create a solidaristic group of male killers, that is what you do: you kill the woman in them."[99] This captures well the way in which the goal of militarized masculinity is understood by those anxious to promote it: soldiers must demonstrate an absence of emotion and a willingness to use violence; they must excise all that is perceived to be "feminine." As already suggested, however, many soldiers cannot reconcile the warrior myths into which they have been trained with their own lived experiences as individual men.[100] This is true not only when soldiers kill the women close to them but also when "the woman *in* them" is not killed. As Lisa Vetten writes, the masculinity affirmed by the process of most contemporary military training "is a fragile one, entirely unable to tolerate traces of femininity."[101] Where militaries—and individual soldiers—face an ironic set of challenges is when "traces of femininity" reemerge. When the stoic, tough, emotionless soldier begins to feel and react, when he feels pain, fear, anxiety, guilt, shame, and despair as a result of the activities he must participate in as a soldier. When he can no longer fulfill, or sometimes even participate in, the myths of militarized manhood that have shaped him.[102]

When "traces of femininity" reemerge, soldiers react in a variety of ways. Some become angry, hostile, and violent.[103] Some want to die, and many do attempt suicide. Others are ostracized by their comrades or are treated as though they are contagious. Others are dismissed, as "fakers." Until recently, militaries have largely ignored the psychological impact of combat and combat-like situations on soldiers. Yet what is now known as post-traumatic stress disorder (PTSD) is something that has long affected soldiers. One recent study showed that almost half the Canadian soldiers who survived the battle of Dieppe during World War II still suffer post-traumatic stress.[104] In the United States, 53.4 percent of male Vietnam War veterans experienced stress reaction symptoms, either full or partial PTSD.[105] As one soldier recalls: "Bodies without heads; bodies without arms and the smell, the horrible, horrible smell of death. . . . That's the kind of thing that stays with you."[106] A related form of psychiatric distress in battle, combat stress reaction (CSR), constituted 23 percent of all Israeli casualties in the 1982 Lebanon War.[107]

PTSD is both widespread and has a long history, even if it has not always been acknowledged by either medical or military communities. As Peter Neary and Jack Granatstein write:

> Folk memory and literature, if not formal history, are full of examples of the returned soldier who became a burnt-out case, the promising young man who was never the same again, the chronic alcoholic who couldn't get over the war. The universal character of this phenomenon is easy enough to establish. What requires investigation are the intellectual and ultimately social constructs developed to explain the persistence of pain and the reality of chronic neurosis.[108]

Part of the social constructs involved in the chronic neurosis and persistent pain of many soldiers who return from battle or peacekeeping duties may well be associated with their own sense—confirmed by the reactions of those around them—of failing to live up to the military ethos of appropriate masculinity. Some of the first medical accounts of PTSD, reports of "shell shock" in British soldiers after World War I, treated it as a male form of female "hysteria." As Sandra Gilbert writes, "paradoxically . . . the war to which so many men had gone in hope of becoming heroes, ended up emasculating them."[109] For soldiers to give expression to their pain, fear, and doubt, not only have they failed to live up to the ideals of militarized masculinity but they are participating in the culturally discredited and despised "other" of femininity.

The manifestation of a soldier's breakdown usually involves a wide variety of symptoms, including acute anxiety, fear of death, anger, nightmares, vivid intrusive reliving of their most horrible experiences, intense distress, hypervigilance, exaggerated startle response, and crying.[110] Clinical studies into PTSD and CSR have noted a number of other revealing patterns. One is that the incidence of PTSD appears to be higher among soldiers who participated in armed conflicts that resulted in an ambiguous military outcome, or in which they faced a less appreciative societal homecoming at the end of the hostilities. Thus the rates of PTSD among U.S. veterans seems to be higher for veterans of either the Vietnam War or Korean conflict than it was for veterans of World War II.[111]

Some initial investigations into PTSD among soldiers serving as peacekeepers indicate that the ambiguity of peacekeeping duty may have a similar impact on rates of PTSD. That ambiguity is important not only in terms of the "outcome" of peacekeeping missions—which is never a clear-cut military "victory"—but also because of the very nature of the missions themselves. As one study notes, peacekeepers are "repeatedly exposed to dangerous, provoking, or humiliating situations" with "limited possibilities to express feelings of anger and frustration" because a peacekeeper "is not expected to engage in regular war activities."[112] When deployed on a peacekeeping mission, a soldier cannot vent his anger in a way he was trained would be both permitted and encouraged: "The exercise of restraint in the face of danger is likely to be quite troubling for combat-trained soldiers, contributing to feelings of helplessness and increased anxiety."[113] The contradiction of being denied the opportunity to participate in some of the basic entitlements associated with soldiering, in short, may be linked to higher rates of PTSD.

Another important pattern that has emerged in U.S. studies is the higher incidence of PTSD among Hispanic, African American, and Native American Vietnam veterans. Here, factors may include the perception among people of color that their ethnicity directly increased their exposure to combat, with Native Americans, African Americans, or Latinos often chosen over white soldiers for the most difficult, dangerous, and life-threatening tasks.[114] When it came to actual combat, in other words, the tight-knit military family broke down along racialized lines, and those faced with the contradiction and betrayal were less able to remain the tough heroic warrior they had been trained to be. Native American Vietnam veterans also noted "a profoundly troubling identification with the enemy," with some reporting being shot at by their own troops, and others describing their sense of connection to Vietnamese nationals:

> We entered this [village] . . . destroyed by artillery, we had called in. It was horrible, bodies everywhere . . . children, women, old people. This mamasan staggered from a hut, hurt really bad. She looked at me, grabbed my hand, pointed at it, and said: "Same, Same." My skin, of course. Same shade as her, as all of them. . . . Looking at the children and elders here, on our reservation, I see the faces of those who died there, then. That happened over and over.[115]

Soldiers thus experienced greater emotional pain when they were no longer able to dehumanize "the enemy," when they saw the "other" in themselves, and when the myths they had been trained to believe began to break down in the face of alternative experiences or readings of the war in which they were engaged.

Militaries can accommodate physical injuries, most especially those sustained in battle; but the traumatic reactions that result from battle, or result from being witness to or participant in horrible acts of carnage and destruction, are injuries most militaries find it difficult, if not impossible, to reconcile. During World War I, for example, the response was relatively straightforward: "A man was shot for cowardice" and any officers who failed to carry out such executions were themselves arrested.[116] When soldiers were not executed for having human emotions, for betraying and acting on their fear and dread, they were usually simply ignored.

Having been trained into the ideals of hypermasculinity, there is little place in the military family to raise emotions or reactions that do not accord with those ideals.[117] Even soldiers who suffer PTSD have claimed "sometimes I wish I had lost a leg instead of having all those brain cells screwed up."[118] Many soldiers report that although they share a closeness with fellow soldiers that is unmatched, that closeness does not extend to discussions of emotional topics, such as relationship difficulties with wives or girlfriends. It certainly does not extend to discussions of fear and emotional pain. As one U.S. Vietnam veteran commented:

> When you was over there you was a macho figure, that was all you was taught to be, a macho figure, you know, nothing can hurt you, you're scared of nothing, no feelings, no pain, you know, just kill, okay? And everybody has got that feeling so you don't relate to the next guy, "Hey man, you know I'm really scared that this is happening." . . . You don't say that to the next guy because in return he would probably laugh at you, you know, or call you a wimp or puss or whatever and then it gets around and everybody points a finger at this guy, you know, well he's a wimp or he's a puss or queer or whatever.[119]

Soldiers who do experience debilitating fear or anguish during battle or as witness to situations of armed conflict thus risk being ostracized from their brotherhood for betraying the ideals of manhood and allowing "the feminine" within to express itself. Emotional pain and fear fundamentally contradict the ideals of hypermasculinity so carefully inculcated into the soldier recruit.

A recent Canadian study into PTSD confirms that members of the Canadian Forces with PTSD find little support within their units and face often widespread resentment from colleagues. Soldiers who experienced PTSD said that they long resisted coming forward to avoid the humiliation and stigma associated with mental illness. Many will not admit to post-traumatic stress out of fear of their brethren's reaction. As one soldier described it: "To be quite honest, I would rather tell my peer group that I got the dose at a whore house than PTSD."[120] Getting "the dose at a whore house" would not contradict the norms of militarized masculinity, whereas acknowledging feelings of fear, pain, and trauma would.

Many in the military also refuse to acknowledge that they might be ill because, as one psychologist reported, to do so would be to admit you are "weak." One soldier commented: "Nobody fucked with me, and here I was having a mental health problem. Soldiers aren't supposed to have that."[121] Many soldiers also treated colleagues who had come forward and acknowledged their illness as though they might be contagious—in the Canadian military it is "a latter-day leprosy."[122] Another said it was as though "I was the person with the bubonic plague."[123] One senior noncommissioned member described his colleagues' reactions:

> I was completely ostracized by the battalion . . . because most of them were afraid to have anything to do with us. . . . I remember a guy came up to me going, You know . . . I don't want to say this, but I can't be caught talking to you. . . . [If I went into the Sergeants' mess] I would probably be asked to leave. . . . When I was coming back [from treatment for PTSD], there was a Sergeant Major sitting right there, right across from me. I looked at him. He looked away. . . . These were all people I used to work with.[124]

Indeed, by unsettling the norm that militarized masculinity is a *fixed* identity, the risks of PTSD, if not PTSD itself, might well be contagious: once hypermasculine men begin to experience and share feelings of fear and horror, the myth of the heroic soldier warrior is seen as groundless. This may be a more terrifying idea than PTSD itself.

PTSD is such a profound betrayal of the norms of hypermasculinity militarized men have been trained into that the stigma associated with it also extends to family members: several spouses told investigators they too were ostracized once their spouse's condition became known. As one military wife described it: "It's just ugly. . . . We're not treated as human beings. We lost all our friends, military and civilian."[125] What many members of the military and their families discovered was that the idea of a military family "that would look after its own through thick and thin" did not exist for members with PTSD.[126]

Many members of the Canadian forces also reported to the ombudsman's investigators that PTSD could be faked and claim that its increasingly prominent coverage only brings disrepute to the military. In the Canadian case, that increased coverage is associated in part with the public acknowledgment by retired Canadian general Roméo Dallaire of his own

PTSD resulting from his service as UN commander in Rwanda. Although his warnings of a coming genocide in Rwanda were ignored by political leaders at the United Nations, Dallaire feels both a personal and professional responsibility for the deaths of ten Belgian peacekeepers, fifty-six Red Cross personnel, two million people displaced, and nearly a million Rwandans killed.[127] Despite calls for more troops, Dallaire was ordered to protect the evacuation of foreign nationals, including his own troops, leaving Rwandans targeted for genocide with no protection.[128]

Dallaire's guilt afterward was debilitating, and he was given a medical discharge in April 2000. He was discharged in part because his struggles with depression, alcoholism, and attempts at suicide had made it practically impossible to function in his work. But the discharge came also as a result of his refusal to let go of what had happened in Rwanda—when he was able, he used every opportunity available to him to speak out about the failure of the UN and members of the Security Council to prevent the genocide in Rwanda.[129] For his superiors, Dallaire's inability to "let it go" was simply a further sign of his illness.

Dallaire's public accounting of his own PTSD received mixed reaction. On the one hand, it was an important acknowledgment that allowed other soldiers to come forward and seek treatment, but on the other hand, some accused Dallaire of "getting preferential treatment. If a rank-and-file soldier confessed to such a condition . . . they would be treated with suspicion and not concern. Breaking down is seen as a betrayal of the codes of soldiering."[130] As one member of the Canadian military commented: "I have heard comments ranging from 'Roméo Dallaire was the worst thing that happened to the Forces' to 'I bet if you looked at the . . . list [of soldiers on medical leave], every one of them is a below average soldier. They are just faking it.'"[131] For many members of the military, then, the only way to "make sense" of emotional pain and trauma on the part of militarized men is to locate it either in their attempts at deception, or in their failure as a soldier.

That Dallaire may have failed as a soldier is certainly something that haunts him to this day, and it also formed part of the reaction to his mission when he returned from Rwanda. A Belgian inquiry into the deaths of their peacekeepers laid the blame firmly with Dallaire, and some commentators within Canada, for a time, tended to agree. Some suggested that his "failure was a complete disappointment to the military." As one retired Canadian colonel wrote: "Personal intervention, even if suicidal, would have been in the best military tradition, and may even have been successful in saving lives."[132] Dallaire, in short, had failed to live up to the ideals of military life, and he continues to pay an enormous emotional price. As Anne Orford writes, "Both protectors and protected suffer when they believe that international intervention is a mission of salvation."[133]

Conclusion

Militaries depend on attracting young people, but especially young men, to the idea of becoming "real men" through the initiation rituals associated with soldiering. As Judith Stiehm has written: "all militaries have . . . regularly been rooted in the psychological coercion of young men through appeals to their (uncertain) manliness."[134] Militaries replace that uncertainty with a hegemonic representation of idealized norms of masculinity that privilege the tough, stoic, emotionless warrior, capable and willing to employ violence to achieve whatever ends he may be ordered into. Militaries work hard to fix the identities of young men in these terms and have worked equally hard to deny the fragility of this construction.

Numerous consequences may flow from the construction of militarized masculinity: the sense of license to sexually assault and exploit women when deployed on peacekeeping missions; the hyperviolence against men understood as "foreign" and less than human; the high rates of domestic violence recorded within military communities; and incidence of post-traumatic stress disorder and, importantly, militaries' reactions to PTSD in soldiers who fail to live up to military ideals. One of the ways that the fundamentally contradictory—and ultimately fragile—base on which militarized masculinity has been constructed can be observed is through the treatment of and reaction to soldiers who do express feelings of fear, terror, and emotional pain in situations of armed conflict, who do not "live up to" the ideals of militarized masculinity, and who permit traces of "the feminine" to reemerge. Caring, emotive human beings who feel a connection with other human beings are not, it seems, what most militaries are looking for. The ultimate irony, of course, is that these may be the very qualities that are required of anyone involved in missions aimed at keeping, creating, promoting, or maintaining something called *peace*.

Notes

1. In the U.S. army, for example, African American women comprise almost 50 percent of all women in the enlisted ranks, even though they make up only 12 percent of the general U.S. population. As Cynthia Enloe writes, these figures "do suggest that thousands of young black women have decided that the best way to cope with an economy distorted by militarism is to join the military"; Cynthia Enloe, "The Right to Fight: A Feminist Catch-22," *Ms.*, July–August 1993, pp. 84–87. In Canada, between 20 and 35 percent of new recruits come from the Maritime provinces—a region with relatively few employment options beyond part-time, seasonal, and factory work—even though these provinces represent only 10 percent of the national population. Other recruits often come from single-industry towns that offer limited employment opportunities. A 1975 study indicated that of the 2,567 applicants to the Canadian forces that summer, 51 percent were unemployed compared to only

7.5 percent of the Canadian population in general. See Deborah Harrison and Lucie Laliberté, *No Life Like It: Military Wives in Canada* (Toronto: James Lorimer, 1994), pp. 17–18.

2. See, for example, Eva Johansson and Gerry Larsson, "Swedish Peacekeepers in Bosnia and Herzegovina: A Quantitative Analysis," *International Peacekeeping* 8, no. 1 (spring 2001): 64–76.

3. Morris Janowitz, *The Professional Soldier* (Glencoe, IL: Free Press, 1960), p. 418, cited in David R. Segal, Jesse J. Harris, Joseph M. Rothberg, and David H. Marlowe, "Paratroopers as Peacekeepers," *Armed Forces and Society* 10, no. 1 (summer 1984): 488.

4. David Pugliese, "Airborne Again," *Ottawa Citizen*, April 15, 1996, p. A1.

5. Allen G. Sens, *Somalia and the Changing Nature of Peacekeeping: The Implications for Canada,* prepared for the Commission of Inquiry into the Deployment of Canadian Forces to Somalia (Ottawa: Government Services Canada, 1997), p. 111. At the United Nations, the Department of Peacekeeping Operations recognizes only those missions that involve a military component as formally part of peacekeeping and does not include electoral or observer missions on their list of past and current peacekeeping missions; available at www.un.org/Depts/dpko/dpko/ops.htm.

6. Judith Hicks Stiehm has written that "might without right may be monstrous, but right without might is ridiculous." See her "Peacekeeping and Peace Research: Men's and Women's Work," *Women and Politics* 18, no. 1 (1997): 50; for a general discussion of the use of force in peacekeeping operations, see Alex Morrison, Douglas Fraser, and James D. Kiras (eds.), *Peacekeeping with Muscle: The Use of Force in International Conflict Resolution* (Cornwallis, NS: Canadian Peacekeeping Press, 1997).

7. A. Betts Fetherston, "Voices from Warzones: Implications for Training UN Peacekeepers," in Edward Moxon-Browne (ed.), *A Future for Peacekeeping?* (Basingstoke, UK: Macmillan, 1998), p. 172; see also A. B. Fetherston, *Towards a Theory of United Nations Peacekeeping* (Basingstoke, UK: Macmillan, 1994).

8. See Harrison and Laliberté, *No Life Like It*, Chap. 6, and Deborah Harrison, *The First Casualty: Violence Against Women in Canadian Military Communities* (Toronto: James Lorimer, 2002).

9. Francis Fukuyama, "Women and the Evolution of World Politics," *Foreign Affairs,* September–October 1998, p. 27 and passim. This type of argument has a long history, in a variety of literatures, from sociobiology to psychology, through to feminism. A number of feminist citations include Pam McAllister (ed.), *Reweaving the Web of Life: Feminism and Nonviolence* (Philadelphia: New Society Publishers, 1982); Betty A. Reardon, *Feminism and the War System* (New York: Teachers College Press, 1985); and Brian Easlea, *Fathering the Unthinkable: Masculinity, Scientists, and the Nuclear Arms Race* (London: Pluto Press, 1983), pp. 5, 11, and Chap. 1 passim. See also Diana E. H. Russell, "The Nuclear Mentality: An Outgrowth of the Masculine Mentality," *Atlantis* 12, no. 1 (1987): 10–17. For a summary and critique of these views, see Lynne Segal, *Is the Future Female? Troubled Thoughts on Contemporary Feminism* (London: Virago Press, 1987), Chap. 5, and Sandra Whitworth, *Feminism and International Relations: Towards a Political Economy of Gender in Interstate and Non-Governmental Institutions* (Basingstoke, UK: Macmillan, 1997), Chap. 1. The sociobiology literature includes Lionel Tiger and Robin Fox, *The Imperial Animal* (Toronto: McClelland and Stewart, 1971), Chap. 8 and passim, and Lionel Tiger, *Men in Groups,* 2nd ed. (New York: Marion Boyars, 1984).

10. Bob Connell, "Masculinity, Violence, and War," in Michael S. Kimmel and Michael A. Messner (eds.), *Men's Lives*, 3rd ed. (Boston: Allyn and Bacon, 1995), p. 125. See also R. W. Connell, "Masculinities, the Reduction of Violence, and the Pursuit of Peace," in Cynthia Cockburn and Dubravka Zarkov (eds.), *The Postwar Moment: Militaries, Masculinities, and International Peacekeeping* (London: Lawrence and Wishart, 2002), pp. 33–40.

11. Fukuyama, "Women and the Evolution of World Politics," p. 34. For a more detailed account of this view, see Tiger and Fox, *The Imperial Animal*, and Tiger, *Men in Groups*.

12. For a brief summary of this view, see Whitworth, *Feminism and International Relations*, pp. 16–20.

13. Tiger and Fox, *The Imperial Animal*, p. 213.

14. As Bob Connell notes, when many of the arguments and popular understandings associated with masculinity rely on notions of a natural or true masculinity, the suggestion that men can changed is depicted as not only futile, but dangerous; R. W. Connell, *Masculinities* (Berkeley: University of California Press, 1995), p. 45.

15. Fukuyama, "Women and the Evolution of World Politics," pp. 27–28. Emphasis added.

16. Barbara Ehrenreich, "Fukuyama's Follies: So What If Women Ruled the World?" *Foreign Affairs*, January–February 1999, pp. 118–119.

17. Katha Pollitt, "Father Knows Best," *Foreign Affairs*, January–February 1999, p. 123. See also Binta Mansaray, "Women Against Weapons: A Leading Role for Women in Disarmament," in Anatole Ayissi and Robin-Edward Poulton (eds.), *Bound to Cooperate: Conflict, Peace, and People in Sierra Leone* (Geneva: UN Institute for Disarmament Research, December 2000), pp. 144–149.

18. For accounts of different notions or forms of masculinity, see, for example, R. W. Connell, *Gender and Power* (Stanford: Stanford University Press, 1987), esp. Part 3; Connell, *Masculinities;* Charlotte Hooper, "Masculinist Practices and Gender Politics: The Operation of Multiple Masculinities in International Relations," in Marysia Zalewski and Jane Parpart (eds.), *The "Man" Question in International Relations* (Boulder: Westview, 1998), pp. 28–53; Craig N. Murphy, "Six Masculine Roles in International Relations and Their Interconnection: A Personal Investigation," in ibid., pp. 93–108; and Steve Niva, "Tough and Tender: New World Order Masculinity and the Gulf War," in ibid., pp. 109–128. Some arguments about masculinity note not only the ways in which qualities such as objectivity are *associated* with masculinity but also that "objectivity itself pre-supposes the masculine asceticism of the scientist"; Marieke de Goede, "Mastering 'Lady Credit': Discourses of Financial Crisis in Historical Perspective," *International Feminist Journal of Politics* 2, no. 1 (2000): 73. This kind of argument has been made with reference to economics and the natural sciences in particular. For an excellent account of the association of risk-taking and masculinity in financial markets, see Stacey Mayhall, *Riding the Bull, Wrestling the Bear: Sex and Identity in the Discourses of Global Finance* (Ph.D. diss., York University, 2002).

19. William Pollack, *Real Boys: Rescuing Our Sons from the Myths of Boyhood* (New York: Random House, 1998); Michael Kaufman, "Working with Men and Boys to Challenge Sexism and End Men's Violence," in Ingeborg Breines, Robert Connell, and Ingrid Eide (eds.), *Male Roles, Masculinities, and Violence: A Culture of Peace Perspective* (Paris: UNESCO Publishing, 2000), pp. 213–222. See also Michael Kaufman, *Cracking the Armour: Power, Pain, and the Lives of Men* (Toronto: Viking, 1993) and "Men, Feminism, and Men's Contradictory Experi-

ences of Power," in Harry Brod and Michael Kaufman (eds.), *Theorizing Masculinities* (Thousand Oaks, CA: Sage, 1994), pp. 142–163.

20. Connell, *Gender and Power,* pp. 183–188; Connell, *Masculinities,* pp. 76–81 and passim. It is important to note as well that for Connell and others who have picked up on the notion of hegemonic masculinity, while there may be multiple masculinities and femininities, there can be no corresponding hegemonic *femininity*—all forms of femininity are in some ways subordinate.

21. R. W. Connell, "Masculinities, the Reduction of Violence, and the Pursuit of Peace," in Cockburn and Zarkov, *The Postwar Moment,* p. 35.

22. Connell, *Masculinities,* p. 72. See also Varda Burstyn, *The Rites of Men: Manhood, Politics, and the Culture of Sport* (Toronto: University of Toronto Press, 1999), Chap. 1.

23. Clark McCauley, "Conference Overview," in Jonathan Haas (ed.), *The Anthropology of War* (Cambridge: Cambridge University Press, 1990), p. 2, cited in Barbara Ehrenreich, *Blood Rites: Origins and History of the Passions of War* (New York: Metropolitan Books, 1997), p. 10.

24. Charlotte Hooper notes the way in which soldiering also involves many traditional "feminine" traits such as "total obedience and submission to authority, the attention to dress detail, and the endless repetition of mundane tasks that enlisted men as opposed to officers are expected to perform." But these activities are not emphasized in representations of soldiering, illustrating the way in which, for Hooper, "it is not the actions themselves but the gendered interpretations placed on them that are crucial in determining which activities count as masculine and valued and which count as feminine and devalued"; Charlotte Hooper, *Manly States: Masculinities, International Relations, and Gender Politics* (New York: Columbia University Press, 2001), pp. 47–48.

25. Ehrenreich, *Blood Rites,* p. 10. See also Ehrenreich, "Fukyhama's Follies," p. 118.

26. As Ehrenreich writes:

Tahitian warriors were browbeaten into fighting by functionaries called Rauti, or "exhorters who ran around the battlefield urging their comrades to mimic "the devouring wild dog." The ancient Greek hoplites drank enough wine, apparently, to be quite tipsy when they went to battle; Aztecs drank pulque; Chinese troops at the time of Sun Tzu got into the mood by drinking wine and watching "gyrating sword dancers" perform. Almost any drug or intoxicant has served, in one setting or another, to facilitate the transformation of man into warrior. Yanomamo Indians of the Amazon ingest a hallucinogen before battle; the ancient Scythians smoked hemp, while a neighboring tribe drank something called "hauma," which is believed to have induced a frenzy of aggression. So, if there is a destructive instinct that impels men to war, it is a weak one, and often requires a great deal of help (*Blood Rites,* p. 11).

See also her sources: Georges Dumézil, *Destiny of the Warrior* (Chicago: University of Chicago Press, 1969), p. 140; Hilda Ellis Davidson, *Myths and Symbols in Pagan Europe: Early Scandinavian and Celtic Religions* (New York: Syracuse University Press, 1988), p. 84; Lawrence H. Keeley, *War Before Civilization: The Myth of the Peaceful Savage* (New York: Oxford University Press, 1996), p. 146; Victor Davis Hanson, *The Western Way of War: Infantry Battle in Classical Greece* (New York: Knopf, 1989), p. 126; Samuel B. Griffith, introduction to Sun Tzu, *The*

Art of War (London: Oxford University Press, 1971), p. 37; Renate Rolle, *The World of the Scythians* (Berkeley: University of California Press, 1989), pp. 94–95. For a summary of these arguments, see Joshua S. Goldstein, *War and Gender* (Cambridge: Cambridge University Press, 2001), Chap. 5.

27. Ehrenreich, *Blood Rites,* pp. 11–12.

28. For an excellent summary of the goals and procedures of basic training, see Harrison and Laliberté, *No Life Like It,* Chap. 1. See also James Davis, *The Sharp End: A Canadian Soldier's Story* (Vancouver: Douglas and McIntyre, 1997), Chap. 2; Goldstein, *War and Gender,* Chap. 5; William Arkin and Lynne R. Dobrofsky, "Military Socialization and Masculinity," *Journal of Social Issues* 34, no. 1 (1978): 151–168; Tracy Xavia Karner, "Engendering Violent Men: Oral Histories of Military Masculinity," in Lee H. Bowker (ed.), *Masculinities and Violence* (Thousand Oaks, CA: Sage, 1998), pp. 214–216; Janice T. Gibson, "Training People to Inflict Pain: State Terror and Social Learning," *Journal of Humanistic Psychology* 31, no. 2 (spring 1991): 72–87; Alfred W. McCoy, "'Same Banana': Hazing and Honor at the Philippine Military Academy," *Journal of Asian Studies* 54, no. 3 (August 1995): 689–726; Alfred McCoy, "Ram Boys: Changing Images of the Masculine in the Philippine Military," presented at the International Studies Association Annual Meetings, Toronto, March 18–22, 1997; Lesley Gill, "Creating Citizens, Making Men: The Military and Masculinity in Bolivia," *Cultural Anthropolgy* 12, no. 4 (1997): 527–550; and Cynthia Enloe, *The Morning After: Sexual Politics at the End of the Cold War* (Berkeley: University of California Press, 1993), Chap. 3.

29. Christian G. Appy, *Working-Class War: American Combat Soldiers and Vietnam* (Chapel Hill: University of North Carolina Press, 1993), p. 88.

30. Arkin and Dobrofsky, "Military Socialization and Masculinity," p. 158.

31. Gill, "Creating Citizens, Making Men," p. 15.

32. As Gwynn Dyer notes, it has been over one hundred years since mass formations were any use on the battlefield, but all militaries still make soldiers march in unison, especially in basic training (Gwynn Dyer, *Anybody's Son Will Do,* National Film Board of Canada, 1983).

33. Appy, *Working-Class War,* p. 86.

34. Ibid.

35. Gill, "Creating Citizens, Making Men," p. 15; Davis, *The Sharp End,* p. 14; Appy, *Working-Class War,* p. 101. Linda Bird Francke notes that the same techniques are sometimes also applied to women: at Fort Jackson in the United States, a 1991 strategy was to shout at female recruits: "You wuss, you baby, you goddamn female." Reverse psychology, by contrast, doesn't seem to work: a female instructor who yelled "You boy!" at a straggler discovered, in the context of basic training, that it sounded more like a compliment than an insult; Linda Bird Francke, *Ground Zero: The Gender Wars in the Military* (New York: Simon and Schuster, 1997), pp. 155–156.

36. Jonathan S. Landay, "Hazing Rituals in Military Are Common—and Abusive," *Christian Science Monitor,* February 11, 1997, p. 1. Donna Winslow notes that a 1908 U.S. Secretary of War Board of Inquiry at West Point military academy indicated that the practice of hazing—a continued period of abuse during an initial entry period into the military—had been going on since the 1860s. See Donna Winslow, "Rites of Passage and Group Bonding in the Canadian Airborne," *Armed Forces and Society* 25, no. 3 (spring 1999): 440.

37. Appy, *Working-Class War,* pp. 88–89.

38. Kate Muir, *Arms and the Woman* (London: Sinclair-Stevenson, 1992), p. 4.

39. Gwynn Dyer notes that most of the hurdles of basic training are low enough that most people can reach them, and as each recruit accomplishes another

task, the group together begins to feel more confident, more like "real men" (Dyer, *Anybody's Son Will Do*).

40. Donna Winslow, "Misplaced Loyalties: The Role of Military Culture in the Breakdown of Discipline in Peace Operations," *Canadian Review of Sociology and Anthropology* 35, no. 3 (1998): 353.

41. Arkin and Dobrofsky, "Military Socialization and Masculinity," p. 163.

42. Harrison and Laliberté, *No Life Like It*, p. 22. An issue not discussed at length here, but worth noting, is the way that the role of drill sergeant or commander as "father figure" is a particularly potent mix in situations where children, and in particular boy children, join or are forcibly conscripted into fighting forces. As Judith Large recounts, "This can lead to armies manipulating children's loyalty to authority figures to force them to commit atrocities: 'as fighters, these boys excelled. Their commanders served as father figures, and the children followed orders without hesitation or moral qualm'"; Judith Large, "Disintegration Conflicts and the Restructuring of Masculinity," *Gender and Development* 5, no. 2 (June 1997): 26, citing A. Purvis, "Beware the Children," *Time*, December 4, 1995.

43. Davis, *The Sharp End*, pp. 14–15.

44. Interview conducted by Winslow, "Misplaced Loyalties," p. 353.

45. Harrison and Laliberté, *No Life Like It*, pp. 22–34.

46. Karner, "Engendering Violent Men," p. 215.

47. Arkin and Dobrofsky, "Military Socialization and Masculinity," p. 158.

48. Harrison and Laliberté, *No Life Like It*, pp. 27–28.

49. Donna Winslow explores the problems that emerged in the Canadian Airborne regiment where group bonding at the regimental level far exceeded the bonding soldiers felt for the Canadian military as a whole. See Winslow, "Misplaced Loyalties," passim.

50. Harrison and Laliberté note the ways in which "supporting the mess" is not only considered an important element of each soldier's annual assessments but contributes to problem drinking and spousal abuse, which the "military family" is also keen to cover up; Harrison and Laliberté, *No Life Like It*, pp. 29–33.

51. Ibid., pp. 36–37.

52. Davis, *The Sharp End*, pp. 16–17.

53. According to Razack, "Through the practices of othering women, homosexuals and racial minorities . . . they learn to be white men." Sherene Razack, "From the 'Clean Snows of Petawawa': The Violence of Canadian Peacekeepers in Somalia," *Cultural Anthropology* 15, no. 1 (2000): 138.

54. Goldstein, *War and Gender*, p. 264. See Lynne Segal, *Slow Motion: Changing Masculinities, Changing Men* (London: Virago, 1990), pp. 130–131, and Goldstein, *War and Gender*, p. 265.

55. Goldstein, *War and Gender*, p. 265.

56. In addition to military service, organized sport is also a site for many modern-day manhood initiation rituals. Excellent studies (which also examine the relationship between sport and militarized masculinity) include Burstyn's *The Rites of Men;* Michael A. Messner and Donald F. Sabo (eds.), *Sport, Men, and the Gender Order: Critical Feminist Perspectives* (Champaign, IL: Human Kinetics Books, 1990); and Greg Malszecki and T. Cavar, "Men, Masculinities, War, and Sport," in Nancy Mandell (ed.), *Feminist Issues: Race, Class, and Sexuality* (Toronto: Pearson Educational, 2000), pp. 166–192.

57. Arkin and Dobrofsky, "Military Socialization and Masculinity," p. 154. Or, as Ehrenreich notes, not only do men make wars but "wars make men"; Barbara Ehrenreich, "Foreword" to Klaus Theweleit, *Male Fantasies*, vol. 1 (Minneapolis:

University of Minnesota Press, 1987), p. xvi. See also Jacklyn Cock, *Women and War in South Africa* (London: Open Letters, 1992), p. 58.

58. Loren Baritz, *Backfire: A History of How American Culture Led Us into Vietnam and Made Us Fight the Way We Did* (New York: William Morrow, 1985), pp. 22–23, cited in Burstyn, *The Rites of Men*, p. 171.

59. Morgan, "Theater of War," p. 165.

60. David R. Segal, Mady Wechsler Segal, and Dana P. Eyre, "The Social Construction of Peacekeeping in America," *Sociological Forum* 7, no. 1 (1992): 121. See also Lynda E. Boose, "Techno-Muscularity and the 'Boy Eternal': From the Quagmire to the Gulf," in Miriam Cooke and Angela Woollacott (eds.), *Gendering War Talk* (Princeton: Princeton University Press, 1993).

61. Jim McKay, "Sport and the Social Construction of Gender," in Gillian Lupton, Patricia M. Short, and Rosemary Whip (eds.), *Society and Gender: An Introduction to Sociology* (Sydney: Macmillan, 1992), p. 247, cited in Burstyn, *The Rites of Men*, p. 22.

62. Burstyn, *The Rites of Men*, p. 20.

63. This list of characteristics is drawn from both Cristina Masters, "Cyborg Soldiers and Militarized Masculinities" (M.A. research paper, York University, October 2000), p. 9, and S. A. Stouffer et al., *The American Soldier*, vol. 2: *Combat and Its After-Math* (Princeton: Princeton University Press, 1949), cited in Arkin and Dobrofsky, "Military Socialization and Masculinity," p. 156.

64. Lieutenant Commander Thomas Strother, U.S. Navy (ret.), "The Recruiting Problem We *Don't* Talk About," *U.S. Naval Institute Proceedings* 125, no. 5 (May 1999): 192.

65. Suzanne E. Hatty, *Masculinities, Violence, and Culture* (Thousand Oaks, CA: Sage, 2000), Chap. 4.

66. Karner, "Engendering Violent Men," p. 215. Emphasis in original.

67. Ibid., p. 217; Davis, *The Sharp End*, p. 14; Goldstein, *War and Gender*, Chap. 5.

68. Cited in Goldstein, *War and Gender*, p. 266.

69. Dyer, *Anybody's Son Will Do*.

70. Janice T. Gibson, "Teaching People to Inflict Pain: State Terror and Social Learning," *Journal of Humanistic Psychology* 31, no. 2 (spring 1991): 80–82. Gibson notes that many of the same techniques used to train torturers are those used to train soldiers.

71. Harrison and Laliberté, *No Life Like It*, p. 20.

72. Dyer, *Anybody's Son Will Do*.

73. Christian Appy describes an encounter between a drill instructor and a new recruit who confesses that he "wasted four years in college." From that point on, the recruit was called "College Fag" (Appy, *Working-Class War*, p. 100).

74. There are a number of studies that describe the ways in which, despite their own experiences of racism within a military, a common bond can be inculcated among soldiers of ethnic and racial minorities through the intense denigration of women and homosexuals. See, for example, Katharine H. S. Moon, *Sex Among Allies: Military Prostitution in U.S.-Korea Relations* (New York: Columbia University Press, 1997).

75. Arkin and Dobrofsky, "Military Socialization and Masculinity," p. 159.

76. Ibid., p. 160. One variation on this chant goes "This is my rifle, this is my gun; this one's for killing, this one's for fun." Others include "I don't know but I've been told. Eskimo pussy is mighty cold"; "Momma's on the bottom, Poppa on the top. Baby in the middle yelling give it to her pop!"

77. Though she uses it in a different way, this idea is taken from Roxanne Lynn Doty, *Imperial Encounters: The Politics of Representation in North-South Relations* (Minneapolis: University of Minnesota Press, 1996), p. 10.

78. Two examples of the many excellent works that explore this issue are Randy Shilts, *Conduct Unbecoming: Gays and Lesbians in the U.S. Military* (New York: Fawcett Columbine, 1994), and Francine D'Amico and Laurie Weinstein (eds.), *Gender Camouflage: Women and the U.S. Military* (New York: New York University Press, 1999).

79. Martin van Creveld, "The Great Illusion: Women in the Military," *Millennium: Journal of International Studies* 29, no. 2 (2000): 429. See also the responses to this article: Jean Bethke Elshtain, "'Shooting' at the Wrong Target: A Response to Van Creveld," and Christopher Croker, "Humanising Warfare, or Why Van Creveld May Be Missing the 'Big Picture,'" both in *Millennium: Journal of International Studies* 29, no. 2 (2000): 443–448, 449–460.

80. Van Creveld, "The Great Illusion," p. 442.

81. Hatty, *Masculinities, Violence, and Culture*, p. 129. See also Marcia Kovitz, "The Roots of Military Masculinity," in Paul R. Higate (ed.), *Military Masculinities: Identity and the State* (Westport, CT: Praeger, 2003), pp. 1–14.

82. Strother, "The Recruiting Problem We *Don't* Talk About," p. 192.

83. Enloe, "The Right to Fight," pp. 84–85.

84. Doreen Drewry Lehr, "Military Wives: Breaking the Silence," in D'Amico and Weinstein, *Gender Camouflage*, p. 123.

85. Harrison, *The First Casualty*, pp. 14, 48–49.

86. "'Disturbing': Veterans of Afghanistan Kill Wives at Fort Bragg," *NewsMax.com Wires*, July 27, 2002, available at www.newsmax.com/cgi-bin/ (accessed September 11, 2002).

87. Eric Schmitt, "Military Struggling to Stem an Increase in Family Violence," *New York Times*, May 23, 1994, quoted in Enloe, *Maneuvers*, p. 189.

88. Harrison, *The First Casualty*, pp. 18–19.

89. Ibid., and Lehr, "Military Wives," p. 124; see also Enloe, *Maneuvers*, Chap. 5.

90. Harrison, *The First Casualty*, Chap. 2; Lehr, "Military Wives," p. 124 and passim; Enloe, *Maneuvers*, pp. 189–191.

91. Cited in Enloe, *Maneuvers*, p. 189.

92. Harrison, *The First Casualty*, p. 16.

93. "Fort Bragg Murders Expose Domestic Violence in Military," *Ms. News*, July 30, 2002, available at www.msmagazine.com/news/printnews.asp?id=6744 (accessed September 11, 2002); Jon Elliston and Catherine Lutz, "Hidden Casualties: An Epidemic of Violence When Troops Return from War," *The Nation*, October 14, 2002.

94. Simona Sharoni, *Gender and the Israeli-Palestinian Conflict: The Politics of Women's Resistance* (Syracuse: Syracuse University Press, 1995), p. 126.

95. I am grateful to Cristina Masters for helping me to think through this point.

96. Kaufman, "Working with Men and Boys to Challenge Sexism and End Men's Violence," pp. 214–215.

97. Harrison, *The First Casualty*, p. 49.

98. Interview conducted by Harrison, *The First Casualty*, p. 48.

99. Cited in Francke, *Ground Zero*, p. 155.

100. Hatty, *Masculinities, Violence, and Culture*, p. 128.

101. Lisa Vetten, "War and the Making of Men and Women," Centre for the Study of Violence and Reconciliation, South Africa, available at www.csvr.org.za/articles/artwarl.htm (accessed May 18, 2002).

102. Dubravka Zarkov makes an interesting argument about PTSD, quite different from the one presented here, in her analysis of the post-traumatic stress experienced by Dutch soldiers after Srebrenica. Zarkov argues that only by describing the experiences of Dutch soldiers as "trauma" could the powerlessness of one's own military men be made public. The depiction of Dutch helplessness over, and even facilitation of, the Bosnian Serb massacre of Muslim men in Srebrenica was the only way, in short, that both members of the Dutch military and the Dutch public could reconcile the military's inability to stop the atrocities. See Dubravka Zarkov, "*Srebrenica Trauma:* Masculinity, Military and National Self-Image in Dutch Daily Newspapers," in Cockburn and Zarkov, *The Postwar Moment,* pp. 183–203.

103. Raymond W. Novaco and Claude M. Chemtob, "Anger and Combat-Related Posttraumatic Stress Disorder," *Journal of Traumatic Stress* 15, no. 2 (April 2002): 123; Patrick S. Calhoun, Jean C. Beckham, Michelle E. Feldman, John C. Barefoot, Thom Haney, and Hayden B. Bosworth, "Partners' Ratings of Combat Veterans' Anger," *Journal of Traumatic Stress* 15, no. 2 (April 2002): 133.

104. Canadian Broadcasting Corporation, "The Unseen Scars: Post Traumatic Stress Disorder," *The National Features,* available at www.tv.cbc.ca/national/gpminfo/ptsd/wounds.html (accessed May 16, 2002).

105. Richard A. Kulka, William E. Schlenger, John A. Fairbank, Richard L. Hough, B. Kathleen Jordan, Charles R. Marmar, and Daniel S. Weiss, *Trauma and the Vietnam War Generation: Report of Findings from the National Vietnam Veterans Readjustment Study* (New York: Brunner/Mazel, 1990), p. 63.

106. Canadian Broadcasting Corporation, "The Unseen Scars."

107. Zahava Solomon, Nathaniel Laor, and Alexander C. McFarlane, "Acute Posttraumatic Reactions in Soldiers and Civilians," in Bessel A. van der Kolk, Alexander C. McFarlane, and Lars Weisaeth (eds.), *Traumatic Stress: The Effects of Overwhelming Experience on Mind, Body, and Society* (New York: Guilford Press, 1996), p. 104.

108. Peter Neary and J. L. Granatstein, *The Veterans Charter and Post–World War II Canada* (Montreal: McGill-Queen's University Press, 1998), p. 149, cited in André Marin, Canada's Military Ombudsman, *Special Report: Systemic Treatment of CF Members with PTSD* (Ottawa: Government of Canada, February 5, 2002), p. 32.

109. Sandra Gilbert, "Soldier's Heart: Literary Men, Literary Women, and the Great War," *Signs* 8 (1983): 447. See also Elaine Showalter, "Male Hysteria: W. H. R. Rivers and the Lessons of Shell Shock," Chap. 7 of *The Female Malady: Women, Madness and English Culture, 1830–1980* (New York: Penguin, 1985), pp. 167–194.

110. Solomon, Laor, and McFarlane, "Acute Posttraumatic Reactions," p. 105; Gibson, "Training Torturers," p. 84; Kulka et al., *Trauma and the Vietnam War Generation,* p. 33.

111. Edward W. McCranie and Leon A. Hyer, "Posttraumatic Stress Disorder Symptoms in Korean Conflict and World War II Combat Veterans Seeking Outpatient Treatment," *Journal of Traumatic Stress* 13, no. 3 (2000): 435.

112. Lars Mehlum and Lars Weisæth, "Predictors of Posttraumatic Stress Reactions in Norwegian U.N. Peacekeepers 7 Years After Service," *Journal of Traumatic Stress* 15, no. 1 (February 2002): 17–26.

113. Brett T. Litz, Lynda A. King, Daniel W. King, Susan M. Orsillo, and Matthew J. Friedman, "Warriors as Peacekeepers: Features of the Somalia Experience and PTSD," *Journal of Consulting and Clinical Psychology* 65, no. 6 (December 1997): 1001–1010. See also Eva Johansson and Gerry Larsson, "A Model for Understanding Stress and Daily Experiences Among Soldiers in Peacekeeping

Operations," *International Peacekeeping* 5, no. 3 (autumn 1998): 129, where they note the frustration of Swedish peacekeepers serving in Bosnia who were not allowed to "hit back": "Somewhere a safety valve was needed, a possibility of venting the successively growing frustration and aggression."

114. Janette Beals, Spero M. Manson, James H. Shore, Matthew Friedman, Marie Ashcraft, John A. Fairbank, and William E. Schlenger, "The Prevalence of Posttraumatic Stress Disorder Among American Indian Vietnam Veterans: Disparities and Context," *Journal of Traumatic Stress* 15, no. 2 (April 2002): 89–97.

115. Ibid., p. 95.

116. Solomon, Laor, and McFarlane, "Acute Posttraumatic Reactions in Soldiers and Civilians," p. 111.

117. Carol Cohn has discussed the ways discursive strategies in military think tanks make it almost impossible to discuss conflict, war, or strategy in a manner that resembles anything that can be characterized as "feminine." See Carol Cohn, "Sex and Death in the Rational World of Defense Intellectuals," *Signs* 12, no. 4 (summer 1987): 687–718, and "Wars, Wimps, and Women: Talking Gender and Thinking War," in Miriam Cooke and Angela Woollacott (eds.), *Gendering War* (Princeton: Princeton University Press, 1993), pp. 227–246.

118. Canadian Broadcasting Corporation, "The Unseen Scars."

119. Karner, "Engendering Violent Men," pp. 217–218.

120. Quoted from Marin, *Special Report: Systemic Treatment of CF Members with PTSD*, p. 60.

121. Ibid., pp. 62, 91.

122. Ibid., p. 71.

123. Ibid., p. 70.

124. Ibid., pp. 71–72.

125. Ibid., p. 62.

126. Ibid., p. 92.

127. Carol Off, *The Lion, the Fox, and the Eagle: A Story of Generals and Justice in Rwanda and Yugoslavia* (Toronto: Random House Canada, 2000), p. 114.

128. See Roméo Dallaire, *Shake Hands with the Devil: The Failure of Humanity in Rwanda* (Toronto: Random House, 2003), and Samantha Power, *"A Problem from Hell": America and the Age of Genocide* (New York: Basic Books, 2002), Chap. 10. See also Anne Orford, *Reading Humanitarian Intervention: Human Rights and the Use of Force in International Law* (Cambridge: Cambridge University Press, 2003), pp. 198, 205–206.

129. Off, *The Lion, the Fox and the Eagle*, p. 94 and Chap. 5 passim.

130. Ibid., p. 100.

131. Ibid., p. 78.

132. Ibid., p. 94 and Chap. 5 passim.

133. Orford, *Reading Humanitarian Intervention*, p. 201.

134. Judith Hicks Stiehm, *Arms and the Enlisted Woman* (Philadelphia: Temple University Press, 1989), p. 226.

7

Conclusion:
Do Warriors Make the Best
Peacekeepers?

In 2001, the "Lessons Learned Unit" in the United Nations Department of Peacekeeping Operations, through a bureaucratic amalgamation, was transformed into the "Best Practices Unit." For anyone wanting to raise critical questions about peacekeeping missions, it was an ominously symbolic move. Even within departmental nomenclature, the suggestion now is that there are no more lessons to be learned, except from practices that worked "best."

For the United Nations and many of its member states, what works best when confronted with the horrors of contemporary armed conflict and political violence is the deployment of third-party military forces to serve as peacekeepers and peace-builders. As has been argued throughout this book, these best practices and their associated meanings have implications that far exceed the missions and the official accounts made of them. Chapter 2 discussed a number of the state militaries that contribute to such missions with enthusiasm, countries like Canada, Ireland, India, Nigeria, Fiji, and the Netherlands. It examined also some of the newcomers to peacekeeping such as Japan, Germany, and Argentina. Peacekeeping provides a rationale for the militaries of these countries, and through those militaries gives meaning to these states as nations. Some states also quite self-consciously use involvement in peacekeeping to promote, or shore up, international reputations. In the construction of both state and military, peacekeeping is a widely effective tool and is involved in the production of meanings well beyond strictly "keeping" the peace.

Yet not all militaries are quick to embrace peacekeeping. Not only does the United States rarely contribute to peacekeeping missions, but many U.S. commentators have pointed to the problems of using combat-capable trained soldiers on missions of peace. Most of those commentators, however, are not concerned about the kinds of issues raised in this book—the impacts on local populations that were discussed in Chapters 3 and 4 that

183

result from deploying militarized men on peacekeeping missions: the dramatic increase in prostitution to service UN personnel, the rise of HIV/AIDS, and the widespread sexual harassment and sexual violence that we saw in Cambodia; or the denigration, loathing, and racialized violence perpetrated against local men, as we saw in Somalia. Rather, the concern raised about peacekeeping by conservative observers in countries like the United States focuses on the ways peacekeeping duty blunts the skills of military men. As one U.S. soldier commented (a view shared by soldiers of many national militaries, even those who are involved in peacekeeping): "I think [peacekeeping missions] should be handled by [military police]. . . . Otherwise you are trying to teach the grunt the exact opposite of what we have been learning, which is to kill. When it does come down to real war, you're going to see a lot more dead soldiers."[1]

This signals another issue that has been thread throughout this book: despite the enthusiasm that many countries and their militaries feel for peacekeeping, for many soldiers, it is a poor approximation of real soldiering. As Ruth Wedgwood writes, "Peacekeepers are soldiers as a matter of appearance more than function."[2] When deployed on UN peacekeeping missions, soldiers are supposed to be lightly armed and fire their weapons only in self-defense. Although this is what contributes to the many prevailing images of peacekeepers as benign and altruistic, for many of the soldiers, it is also considered a second-rate set of duties that do not fulfill the expectations they had been given in becoming soldiers. Peacekeeping is a lesser warrior purpose, so unsoldierly it can be almost shameful. As one American's comments describing the deaths of ten Belgian peacekeepers in Rwanda captures: "Well, at least, you know, our rangers died fighting in Somalia. These guys, with their blue berets, were slaughtered, without getting a shot off."[3]

This is the fundamental contradiction of using individuals (mostly men) trained to fight wars in order to conduct peace missions. The tension between being trained as a warrior and then being told to keep a lid on warrior traits can contribute to some of the explosions of hypermasculinity that were described in Chapters 3 and 4. As discussed in Chapter 6, it can contribute also to what has been called *implosions* of hypermasculinity: not only are soldiers serving on peacekeeping missions witness to horrific acts of violence, they sometimes must stand by and do nothing to intervene. Everything a soldier has been told about being the tough, capable warrior collapses, and if they compound that by openly experiencing emotions such as grief and pain, they wear the "badge of dishonor" of post-traumatic stress disorder.

For many, however, the fact of the matter is that whatever problems might be associated with sending soldiers on peacekeeping missions, there simply isn't anyone else who can do it. In simple organizational terms, there are no other large "contingents" of people who could be deployed relatively quickly to zones of conflict around the world. If sending soldiers is not the "best practice," it is the *only* practice. Military analyst Charles Moskos wrote as early as 1976 that "Peacekeeping is not a soldier's job, but only a soldier can do it."[4] Moreover, there is an increasingly widespread call for peacekeeping to become even *more* militarized than it already is. The complex nature of contemporary armed conflicts, it is argued by proponents of this view, demands that UN peacekeeping rethink some of its early cherished principles. In the language of the UN's 2000 Brahimi report on peace operations, the United Nations needs more "robust" peacekeeping.[5]

Part of the call for a more militarized approach to peacekeeping comes from the sense that contemporary conflicts are more brutally violent, and that the brutality is borne primarily by civilian populations. But it also comes from an understanding of the places in which those conflicts occur, "conflict-prone third world countries," which are defined by what they lack: the institutions, the liberalism, the rationality, and the order of Western states. Peacekeeping, as part of the contemporary *"mission civilatrice,"* is the means by which that "lack" can be addressed, bringing meaning and order where there are none. Peacekeeping is, in short, part of the "subject-constituting project"[6] of the colonial encounter.

One of the ways these kinds of questions are deflected is to point to the enormity of the issues associated with contemporary armed conflict, with international responses normally undertaken on the basis of crisis management.[7] Moreover, UN understandings of conflict, as discussed in Chapter 5, envision conflict as occurring in particular points in time with identifiable, if multiple, "causes." Those causes, inevitably by these understandings, are local causes. UN responses to conflict thus envision the application of the appropriate "techniques," such as peacekeeping, in order to create the right conditions for conflict resolution, bring a conflict to an end, or simply maintain a peace once one has been secured.

With responses being demanded on an emergency basis, and soldiers being the only game in town, it is little wonder that, as discussed in Chapter 5, most attempts to insert a gender analysis into UN practices concerning peace and security focus on helping policymakers and those in the field perform their jobs better. Most work on gender, peace, and security being produced by, or for, the United Nations focuses on "gendering" its existing practices. So, for example, calls are made to help the UN to "gender" early warning or to "gender" preventative diplomacy. Or training courses are developed to assist peacekeepers in understanding how "gender competence" will help them to better perform their tasks once deployed. All of this work may on occasion help a UN staffer, but it does not transform existing practices; it ignores the ways in which those practices are already gendered, and it does not ask the difficult questions, such as: Do soldiers make the best peacekeepers? Is peacekeeping a form of the colonial encounter? Not only do these questions remain unasked within this problem-solving terrain, they remain practically *unaskable*.

But despite these concerns—and despite the ways in which configurations of both knowledge and power in particular state and military contexts, and within the UN itself, are lined up against raising critical questions about peacekeeping—this is precisely the time to ask, and to keep asking, the unaskable questions. The reactionary response to this line of reasoning will be that it is a call for "inaction" or "isolationism," a retreat from responsibility.[8] By contrast, this is a call to think more carefully about what responsibility means and to act in the world in ways that "do not perpetuate the violence they seek to avoid."[9] It is time to insist on the ideas that will be dismissed as impractical and idealistic by the United Nations.[10] Alternatives that are based, in the words of Anne Orford, on an ethics of intervention "not grounded quite so brutally in a politics of violence and exclusion."[11] Critics have to imagine alternatives that do not simply try to "fit" into existing practices; they must suggest wild and impractical solutions.

Some of these solutions might actually begin by listening to the people who have lived through both contemporary conflict and the peacekeeping missions deployed there, those who remember peacekeepers for the parks, the hospitals, the schools, and the health services they provided. Those who remember peacekeepers not for their warrior qualities but for the moments in which they could contribute to "those tiny, cumulative efforts by which individuals and families reclaim their lives—a shutter repaired, a class taught, a palm-tree tended."[12] When the people of countries in conflict call for contributions (as opposed to when they are constructed as requiring salvation), wildly impractical but responsible ideas might include contributing not platoons of warriors but contingents of doctors, feminists, linguists, and engineers; regiments of construction workers and carpenters; armies of midwives, cultural critics, anthropologists, and social workers; battalions of artists, musicians, poets, writers, and social critics.[13]

It is time to do this because militarized peacekeeping results in greater insecurity for far too many people, women and men, who through the exclusionary practices of militarism and armed intervention become targets of sexual abuse and racist violence. Militarized peacekeeping is founded on a series of contradictions, such that it cannot deliver on the promises it makes to those who are subject to the missions or even to those who are deployed on peacekeeping missions.

Thankfully, there is an increasing chorus of feminist and other critical voices that are interrogating peacekeeping practices and insist on posing the tough questions. That there is a sudden proliferation of such writing at this time[14] signals the way in which many observers of peacekeeping, writing from different perspectives and from different parts of the world, are coming to the same conclusions: "best practices" are simply *not* good enough.

Notes

1. Laura L. Miller, "Do Soldiers Hate Peacekeeping? The Case of Preventive Diplomacy Operations in Macedonia," *Armed Forces and Society* 23, no. 3 (spring 1997): 426–427.
2. Ruth Wedgwood, "The Evolution of United Nations Peacekeeping," *Cornell International Journal of Law* 28 (1995): 637.
3. Cited in Samantha Power, *"A Problem from Hell": America and the Age of Genocide* (New York: Basic Books, 2002), p. 333.
4. Charles Moskos, *Peace Soldiers* (Chicago: University of Chicago Press, 1976), p. 139.
5. United Nations, "Report of the Panel on United Nations Peace Operations," August 21, 2000, A/55/305–S/2000/809.
6. Anne Orford, *Reading Humanitarian Intervention: Human Rights and the Use of Force in International Law* (Cambridge: Cambridge University Press, 2003), p. 64.
7. This is paraphrased from Peter Nyers, "Emergency or Emerging Identities? Refugees and Transformations in World Order," *Millennium: Journal of International Studies* 28, no. 1 (1999): 14.
8. See Orford, *Reading Humanitarian Intervention,* p. 14, on "action and inaction"; see also David Campbell, *Politics Without Principle: Sovereignty, Ethics, and the Narratives of the Gulf War* (Boulder: Lynne Rienner, 1993), p. 94, on "isolationism."
9. Campbell, *Politics Without Principle,* p. 98.
10. Anne Orford, "Muscular Humanitarianism: Reading the Narratives of the New Interventionism," *European Journal of International Law* 10, no. 4 (1999): 704. Orford's original quote is directed at the language and practice of international lawyers and the new interventionism.
11. Orford, *Reading Humanitarian Intervention,* p. 218.
12. Amitav Ghosh, "The Global Reservation: Notes Toward an Ethnography of International Peacekeeping," *Cultural Anthropology* 9, no. 3 (1994): 415.
13. Barbara Ehrenreich suggests thinking about these and other ways in which "militaries" might be rethought to become engaged in peacekeeping. Barbara Ehrenreich, "Peacekeeping," *Z Magazine,* January 1997, p. 6.
14. See, for example, these forthcoming books: Dyan Mazurana, Angela Raven-Roberts, and Jane Parpart (eds.), *Gender, Conflict, and Peacekeeping* (Boulder: Rowman and Littlefield), and Sherene H. Razack, *Dark Threats and White Knights: The Somalia Affair, Peacekeeping, and the New Imperialism* (Toronto: University of Toronto Press). See also these recently published books: Orford, *Reading Humanitarian Intervention,* and Cynthia Cockburn and Dubravka Zarkov (eds.), *The Postwar Moment: Militaries, Masculinities and International Peacekeeping* (London: Lawrence and Wishart, 2002).

ACRONYMS

ASEAN	Association of Southeast Asian Nations
CPP	Cambodian People's Party
CSR	combat stress reaction
DAW	Division for the Advancement of Women
DDA	Department of Disarmament Affairs
DDR	disarmament, demobilization, and reintegration
DND	Department of National Defence
DPKO	Department of Peacekeeping Operations
DRC	Democratic Republic of Congo
ECOMOG	Monitoring Group of the Economic Community of West African States
ECOWAS	Economic Community of West African States
FUNCINPEC	Front Uni National pour un Cambodge Indépendant, Neutre, Pacifique et Coopératif (National United Front for an Independent, Neutral, Peaceful and Cooperative Cambodia)
GAU	Gender Affairs Unit
ICRC	International Committee of the Red Cross
IFIs	international financial institutions
IGOs	international governmental organizations
KPNLF	Khmer People's National Liberation Front
MONUC	UN Mission in the Democratic Republic of Congo
NATO	North Atlantic Treaty Organization
NGOs	nongovernmental organizations
ONUC	UN Operation in the Congo
ONUMOZ	UN Operation in Mozambique
PSO	peace support operation
PTSD	post-traumatic stress disorder
SDF	Self-Defense Forces

SNC	Supreme National Council
SOC	State of Cambodia
UNAMIC	UN Advance Mission in Cambodia
UNAMIR	UN Assistance Mission for Rwanda
UNAMSIL	UN Assistance Mission in Sierra Leone
UNBRO	UN Border Relief Operation
UNEF I	UN Emergency Force I
UNFICYP	UN Peacekeeping Force in Cyprus
UNHCR	UN High Commission for Refugees
UNIFEM	UN Development Fund for Women
UNITAF	Unified Task Force
UNMBIH	UN Mission to Bosnia Herzegovina
UNMIK	UN Mission in Kosovo
UNMOGIP	UN Military Observer Group in India and Pakistan
UNOSOM I and II	UN Operation in Somalia
UNPROFOR	UN Protection Force
UNTAC	UN Transitional Authority in Cambodia
UNTAET	UN Transitional Administration in East Timor
UNTSO	UN Truce Supervision Organization
WHO	World Health Organization

BIBLIOGRAPHY

Abdela, Lesley. "Kosovo: Missed Opportunities, Lessons for the Future." Report by Lesley Abdela, Former Deputy-Director Democratisation, OSCE Mission, Kosovo. Available at www.peacewomen.org/un/pkwatch/abdela.html.

Acharya, Amitav, Pierre Lizée, and Sorpong Peou (eds.). *Cambodia—The 1989 Paris Peace Conference. Background Analysis and Documents.* Millwood, NY: Kraus International, 1991.

Adibe, Clement E. "Learning from the Failure of Disarmament and Conflict Resolution in Somalia." In Edward Moxon-Browne (ed.), *A Future for Peacekeeping?* Basingstoke: Macmillan, 1998, pp. 118–157.

"Afghan Rivals Hold Key Talks on Future." *Toronto Star,* November 28, 2001, p. A10.

Afghan Women's Summit for Democracy. "The Brussels Proclamation." Brussels, December 4–5, 2001.

"AIDS May Claim Highest UNTAC Toll." *Cambodia Daily,* October 25, 1993, p. 5.

"Airborne No More." *Ottawa Citizen,* January 30, 1995, p. A8.

Akaha, Tsuneo. "Japan's Security Policy in the Posthegemonic World: Opportunities and Challenges." In Tsuneo Akaha and Frank Langdon (eds.), *Japan in the Posthegemonic World.* Boulder: Lynne Rienner, 1993, pp. 91–112.

"Akashi Responds to Community Concerns." *Phnom Penh Post,* November 20–December 3, 1992, p. 2.

Akashi, Yasushi. "To Build a New Country: The Task of the U.N. Transitional Authority in Cambodia." *Harvard International Review* 16, no. 1 (winter 1993): 34–37.

"Allegations of Sexual Harassment Hit U.N. Peacekeeping Forces in Cambodia." *Business Wire,* January 11, 1993.

Amer, Ramses. "The United Nations' Peacekeeping Operation in Cambodia: Overview and Assessment." *Contemporary Southeast Asia* 15, no. 2 (September 1993): 211–231.

Anderlini, Sanam. *Women at the Peace Table: Making a Difference.* New York: United Nations Development Fund for Women, 2000.

Anderson, Benedict. *Imagined Communities.* Rev. ed. London: Verso, 1991.

"Annan Urges Security Council to Boost Role of Women in Peacemaking." UN Press Release, October 28, 2002. Available at www.un.org/apps/news/story. asp?NewsID=5180&Cr=women&Cr1=peace#.

Appy, Christian G. *Working-Class War: American Combat Soldiers and Vietnam.* Chapel Hill: University of North Carolina Press, 1993.

Arkin, William, and Lynne R. Dobrofsky. "Military Socialization and Masculinity." *Journal of Social Issues* 34, no. 1 (1978): 151–168.

"Army Commander Probes Report of Lepine Dinner." *Ottawa Citizen,* November 10, 1995, p. A3.

Arnvig, Eva. "Women, Children and Returnees." In Peter Utting (ed.), *Between Hope and Insecurity: The Social Consequences of the Cambodian Peace Process.* Geneva: UN Research Institute for Social Development, 1994, pp. 143–182.

Asian Recorder, February 5–11, 1993, p. 22903.

———, April 16–22, 1993, p. 23060.

———, May 21–27, 1993, p. 23144.

Aungkana Kamonpetch. "The Progress of Preliminary Phase of Khmer Repatriation." Occasional Paper Series, no. 6. Bangkok: Indochinese Refugee Information Center, Institute of Asian Studies, Chulalongkorn University, May 1993, pp. 25–40.

Barber, Benjamin J. *Jihad vs. McWorld.* New York: Ballantine, 1996.

Baritz, Loren. *Backfire: A History of How American Culture Led Us into Vietnam and Made Us Fight the Way We Did.* New York: William Morrow, 1985.

Barnett, Michael. *Eyewitness to a Genocide: The United Nations and Rwanda.* Ithaca: Cornell University Press, 2002.

Barrington, Kevin. "Massacre Condemned But . . ." *Phnom Penh Post,* March 26–April 8, 1993, p. 1.

———. "Pay Dispute Undermines UNTAC Morale." *Phnom Penh Post,* March 12–25, 1993, p. 13.

Beals, Janette, Spero M. Manson, James H. Shore, Matthew Friedman, Marie Ashcraft, John A. Fairbank, and William E. Schlenger. "The Prevalence of Posttraumatic Stress Disorder Among American Indian Vietnam Veterans: Disparities and Context." *Journal of Traumatic Stress* 15, no. 2 (April 2002): 89–97.

Benhabib, Seyla, and Drucilla Cornell. "Introduction: Beyond the Politics of Gender." In S. Benhabib and D. Cornell (eds.), *Feminism as Critique.* Minneapolis: University of Minnesota Press, 1987, pp. 1–15.

Bercuson, David. *Significant Incident: Canada's Army, the Airborne, and the Murder in Somalia.* Toronto: McClelland and Stewart, 1996.

Berdal, Mats R. "Whiter UN Peacekeeping?" Adelphi Paper, no. 281. London: IISS, 1993.

Berman, Eric G., and Katie E. Sams. *Peacekeeping in Africa: Capabilities and Culpabilities.* Geneva: UN Institute for Disarmament Research, 2000.

"Better Restaurants." *Asian Recorder,* February 19–25, 1993, p. 22934.

Bilgin, Pinar, Ken Booth, and Richard Wyn Jones. "Security Studies: The Next Stage?" *Naçâo Defesa* 84, no. 2 (1998): 131–157.

Black, David, and Claire Turenne Sjolander. "Multilateralism Re-constituted and the Discourse of Canadian Foreign Policy." *Studies in Political Economy* 49 (spring 1996): 7–36.

Blodgett, John Q. "The Future of UN Peacekeeping." *Washington Quarterly* 14, no. 1 (winter 1991): 207–220.

Boose, Lynda E. "Techno-Muscularity and the 'Boy Eternal': From the Quagmire to the Gulf." In Miriam Cooke and Angela Woollacott (eds.), *Gendering War Talk.* Princeton: Princeton University Press, 1993, pp. 67–106.

Booth, Ken. "Discussion: A Reply to Wallace." *Review of International Studies* 23 (1997): 371–377.

——— (ed.). *Critical Security Studies and World Politics*. Boulder: Lynne Rienner, forthcoming 2005.

Boua, Chanthou. "Cotton Wool and Diamonds." *New Internationalist* 242 (April 1993): 20–21.

Boutros-Ghali, Boutros. "Introduction." In *The United Nations and Cambodia, 1991–1995*. The United Nations Blue Book Series, vol. 2. New York: UN Department of Public Information, 1995.

BRIDGE. "Issue 5: Approaches to Institutionalising Gender." *Development and Gender in Brief*. Brighton: Institute of Development Studies, University of Sussex, 1997. Available at www.ids.ac.uk/bridge/dgb5.html.

Brod, Harry, and Michael Kaufman (eds.). *Theorizing Masculinities*. London: Sage, 1994.

Brodeur, Jean-Paul. "Violence and Racial Prejudice in the Context of Peacekeeping." Study Prepared for the Commission of Inquiry into the Deployment of Canadian Forces to Somalia. Ottawa: Minister of Public Works and Government Services Canada, 1997.

Brown, Frederick Z., and David G. Timberman (eds.). *Cambodia and the International Community: The Quest for Peace, Development, and Democracy*. New York: Asia Society, 1998.

Bullion, Alan. "India and UN Peacekeeping." In Edward Moxon-Browne (ed.), *A Future for Peacekeeping?* Basingstoke, UK: Macmillan, 1998, pp. 58–72.

Burslem, Chris. "UNTAC Bubble Economy Set to Burst." *Phnom Penh Post,* May 7–20, 1993, p. 16.

Burstyn, Varda. *The Rites of Men: Manhood, Politics, and the Culture of Sport*. Toronto: University of Toronto Press, 1999.

Calhoun, Patrick S., Jean C. Beckham, Michelle E. Feldman, John C. Barefoot, Thom Haney, and Hayden B. Bosworth. "Partners' Ratings of Combat Veterans' Anger." *Journal of Traumatic Stress* 15, no. 2 (April 2002): 133–136.

Cambodian Women's Development Association. "Prostitution Survey Results." Phnom Penh: Cambodian Women's Development Association, 1994.

Campbell, David. *Politics Without Principle: Sovereignty, Ethics, and the Narratives of the Gulf War*. Boulder: Lynne Rienner, 1993.

———. *Writing Security: United States Foreign Policy and the Politics of Identity*. Minneapolis: University of Minnesota Press, 1992.

Canadian Broadcasting Corporation. "The Unseen Scars: Post Traumatic Stress Disorder." *The National Features*. Available at http://www.tv.cbc.ca/national/gpminfo/ptsd/wounds.html.

CARE International in Cambodia. "'Men Are Gold, Women Are Cloth': A Report on the Potential for HIV/AIDS Spread in Cambodia and Implications for HIV/AIDS Education." Draft copy. Phnom Penh: CARE, 1993.

Carey, Henry F. "'Women and Peace and Security': The Politics of Implementing Gender Sensitivity Norms in Peacekeeping." In Louise Olsson and Torunn L. Tryggestad (eds.), *Women and International Peacekeeping*. London: Frank Cass, 2001, pp. 49–68.

Carpenter, R. Charli. "'Women and Children First': Gender, Norms, and Humanitarian Evacuation in the Balkans 1991–95." *International Organization* 57, no. 4 (2003): 661–694.

Chanda, Nayan, and Rodney Tasker. "The Gem Stampede: Round-the-Clock Mining by Thai Companies." *Far Eastern Economic Review,* July 30, 1992, p. 20.

Chanda, Nayan, and Nate Thayer. "Rivers of Blood." *Far Eastern Economic Review,* April 8, 1993, p. 22.

Chandler, David P. *The Tragedy of Cambodian History: Politics, War, and Revolution Since 1945.* New Haven: Yale University Press, 1991.

Channo, Mang. "Sex Trade Flourishing in Capital." *Phnom Penh Post,* February 12–25, 1993, p. 6.

———. "Women's Day Highlights Gender Inequalities." *Phnom Penh Post,* March 12–25, 1993.

Channo, Mang, and Sara Colm. "Glut of Small Banknotes Creates a Riel Problem." *Phnom Penh Post,* August 7, 1992, p. 1.

Charlesworth, Hilary. "Transforming the United Men's Club: Feminist Futures for the United Nations." *Transnational Law and Contemporary Problems* 4 (1995): 421–463.

Charlesworth, Hilary, and Mary Wood. "'Mainstreaming Gender' in International Peace and Security: The Case of East Timor." *Yale Journal of International Law* 26 (2001): 313–317.

———. "Women and Human Rights in the Rebuilding of East Timor." *Nordic Journal of International Law* 71, no. 2 (2002): 325–348.

Chatterjee, Partha. "Whose Imagined Community?" In Gopal Balakrishnan (ed.), *Mapping the Nation.* London: Verso, 1996, pp. 214–225.

Cheney, Peter. "Canada . . . Canada." *Toronto Star,* July 10, 1994, p. F1.

Chenoy, Anuradha. "Forever Victims." *Times of India,* December 7, 2001. Available at http://timesofindia.indiat...ml/uncomp/articleshow?art_id=1442072446.

Chesterman, Simon. "Introduction: Global Norms, Local Contexts." In Simon Chesterman (ed.), *Civilians in War.* Boulder: Lynne Rienner, 2001, pp. 1–6.

Chopra, Jarat. "United Nations Authority in Cambodia." Occasional paper no. 15. Providence: Thomas J. Watson Jr. Institute for International Studies, 1994.

——— (ed.). *The Politics of Peace Maintenance.* Boulder: Lynne Rienner, 1998.

Chopra, Jarat, John Mackinlay, and Larry Minear. *Report on the Cambodian Peace Process.* Oslo: Norwegian Institute of International Affairs, 1993.

Chou, Meng Tarr. "The Vietnamese Minority in Cambodia." *Race and Class* 34, no. 2 (1992): 33–47.

Chowdhry, Geeta, and Sheila Nair. "Introduction: Power in a Postcolonial World: Race, Gender and Class in International Relations." In Geeta Chowdhry and Sheila Nair (eds.), *Power, Postcolonialism and International Relations: Reading Race, Gender, and Class.* London: Routledge, 2002.

Cock, Jacklyn. *Women and War in South Africa.* London: Open Letters, 1992.

Cockburn, Cynthia, and Dubravka Zarkov (eds.). *The Postwar Moment: Militaries, Masculinities, and International Peacekeeping.* London: Lawrence and Wishart, 2002.

Cohn, Carol. "Opening Remarks." Roundtable on "UN Security Council Resolution 1325: How Women Do (and Don't) Get Taken Seriously in the Construction of International Security." International Studies Association Annual Meetings, Portland, OR, February 26–March 1, 2003.

———. "Sex and Death in the Rational World of Defense Intellectuals." *Signs: Journal of Women in Culture and Society* 12, no. 4 (summer 1987): 687–718.

———. "Wars, Wimps, and Women: Talking Gender and Thinking War." In Miriam Cooke and Angela Woollacott (eds.), *Gendering War.* Princeton: Princeton University Press, 1993, pp. 227–246.

Cohn, Carol, and Sara Ruddick. "A Feminist Ethical Perspective on Weapons of Mass Destruction." In Steven Lee and Sohail Hashmi (eds.), *Ethics and*

Weapons of Mass Destruction: Religious and Secular Perspectives. New York: Cambridge University Press, 2004.

Colm, Sara. "U.N. Agrees to Address Sexual Harassment Issue." *Phnom Penh Post,* October 11, 1992, p. 1.

———. "What's in a Name? A Not So Neighborly Debate." *Phnom Penh Post,* November 6–19, 1992, p. 9.

Commission of Inquiry into the Deployment of Canadian Forces to Somalia. *Document Book no. 1: Hewson Report.* Ottawa, 1995.

———. *Document Book no. 8: Racism.* Ottawa, 1995.

Connell, R. W. *Gender and Power.* Stanford: Stanford University Press, 1987.

———. *Masculinities.* Berkeley: University of California Press, 1995.

———. "Masculinities, the Reduction of Violence, and the Pursuit of Peace." In Cynthia Cockburn and Dubravka Zarkov (eds.), *The Postwar Moment: Militaries, Masculinities, and International Peacekeeping.* London: Lawrence and Wishart, 2002, pp. 33–40.

———. "Masculinity, Violence, and War." In Michael S. Kimmel and Michael A. Messner (eds.), *Men's Lives.* 3d ed. Boston: Allyn and Bacon, 1995.

Cook, Maria. "Bloomberg Blames Canada." *Ottawa Citizen,* August 15, 2003, p. A11.

Cooper, Andrew F. *Canadian Foreign Policy: Old Habits and New Directions.* Scarborough: Prentice Hall-Canada, 1997.

Corrin, Chris. "Gender Audit of Reconstruction Programmes in South Eastern Europe." Urgent Action Fund and the Women's Commission for Refugee Women and Children, June 2000. Available at www.bndlg.de/~wplarre/.

———. "Post-Conflict Reconstruction and Gender Analysis in Kosova." *International Feminist Journal of Politics* 3, no. 1 (April 2001): 78–98.

Coulon, Jocelyn. *Soldiers of Diplomacy: The United Nations, Peacekeeping, and the New World Order.* Toronto: University of Toronto Press, 1998.

Cox, Robert W. "Critical Political Economy." In Björn Hettne (ed.), *International Political Economy: Understanding Global Disorder.* Halifax: Fernwood, 1995, pp. 31–45.

———. "Social Forces, States, and World Orders: Beyond International Relations Theory (1981)." In Robert W. Cox, with Timothy J. Sinclair. *Approaches to World Order.* Cambridge: Cambridge University Press, 1996, pp. 85–123.

Cox, Robert W., with Michael G. Schechter. *The Political Economy of a Plural World: Critical Reflections on Power, Morals, and Civilization.* London: Routledge, 2002.

Cox, Wayne, and Claire Turenne Sjolander. "Damage Control: The Politics of National Defence." In Leslie Pal (ed.), *How Ottawa Spends, 1998–99: Balancing Act: The Post-Deficit Mandate.* Toronto: Oxford University Press, 1998, pp. 217–242.

Croker, Christopher. "Humanising Warfare, or Why Van Creveld May Be Missing the 'Big Picture.'" *Millennium: Journal of International Studies* 29, no. 2 (2000): 449–460.

Curtis, Grant. *Cambodia: A Country Profile.* Stockholm: Swedish International Development Agency, 1980.

———. *Cambodia Reborn? The Transition to Democracy and Development.* Geneva: UN Research Institute for Social Development, 1998.

———. "Transition to What? Cambodia, UNTAC, and the Peace Process." In Peter Utting (ed.), *Between Hope and Insecurity: The Social Consequences of the Cambodian Peace Process.* Geneva: UN Research Institute for Social Development, 1994, pp. 41–69.

"Dag Hammarskjöld: The UN Years, 1956." Available at www.un.org/Depts/dhl/ dag/time1956.htm.

Dale, Stephen. "Guns n' Poses: The Myths of Canadian Peacekeeping." *This Magazine* 26 (March–April 1993): 11–16.

Dallaire, Roméo. *Shake Hands with the Devil: The Failure of Humanity in Rwanda.* Toronto: Random House Canada, 2003.

D'Amico, Francine. "Women as Warriors: Feminist Perspectives." Paper presented at the Annual General Meetings of the International Studies Association, Vancouver, March 20–23, 1992.

———. "Women Workers in the United Nations: From Margin to Mainstream?" In M. Meyer and E. Prügl (eds.), *Gender Politics in Global Governance.* Boulder: Rowman and Littlefield, 1999, pp. 19–40.

D'Amico, Francine, and Laurie Weinstein (eds.). *Gender Camouflage: Women and the U.S. Military.* New York: New York University Press, 1999.

Dauphinee, Elizabeth Allen. "You Can't Get There from Here: The Political Economy of Peace Operations." Paper presented at the Canadian Political Science Association Annual Meetings, May 29, 2002, Toronto.

Davenport, Paul, Sr., Joan Healy, and Kevin Malone. "'Vulnerable in the Village': A Study of Returnees in Battambang Province, Cambodia, with a Focus on Strategies for the Landless." Phnom Penh: Lutheran World Service, UNHCR, Japan Sotoshu Relief Committee, 1995.

Davidson, Hilda Ellis. *Myths and Symbols in Pagan Europe: Early Scandinavian and Celtic Religions.* New York: Syracuse University Press, 1988.

Davies, Robin. "Blue Berets, Green Backs: What Was the Impact?" *Phnom Penh Post,* October 22–November 4, 1993, p. 16.

———. "Economic Warfare, or a Riel Crisis of Confidence." *Phnom Penh Post,* March 26–April 8, 1993, p. 1.

———. "UNTAC and the Cambodian Economy: What Impact?" *Phnom Penh Post,* January 29–February 11, 1993, pp. 4–5.

Davis, James R. *The Sharp End: A Canadian Soldier's Story.* Vancouver: Douglas and McIntyre, 1997.

Debrix, François. *Re-Envisioning Peacekeeping: The United Nations and the Mobilization of Ideology.* Minneapolis: University of Minnesota Press, 1999.

de Goede, Marieke. "Mastering 'Lady Credit': Discourses of Financial Crisis in Historical Perspective." *International Feminist Journal of Politics* 2, no. 1 (2000): 58–81.

de Leeuw, Marc. "A *Gentle*men's Agreement: Srebrenica in the Context of Dutch War History." In Cynthia Cockburn and Dubravka Zarkov (eds.), *The Postwar Moment: Militaries, Masculinities, and International Peacekeeping.* London: Lawrence and Wishart, 2002, pp. 162–182.

Derks, Annuska. "Perspectives on Gender in Cambodia: Myths and Realities." *Cambodia Report* (publication of the Center for Advanced Study, Phnom Penh) 2, no. 3 (1996): 6–10.

———. "Vietnamese Prostitutes in Cambodia." *Cambodia Report* (publication of the Preah Sihanouk Raj Academy, Phnom Penh) 2, no. 1 (1996): 4–6.

Desbarats, Peter. *Somalia Cover-Up: A Commissioner's Journal.* Toronto: McClelland and Stewart, 1997.

Diehl, Paul F. *International Peacekeeping.* Baltimore: Johns Hopkins University Press, 1994.

"'Disturbing': Veterans of Afghanistan Kill Wives at Fort Bragg," *NewsMax.com Wires,* July 27, 2002. Available at www.newsmax.com/cgi-bin/.

Dornan, Christopher. "Scenes from a Scandal." *Globe and Mail,* January 21, 1995, p. D1.

Doty, Roxanne Lynn. *Imperial Encounters: The Politics of Representation in North-South Relations.* Minneapolis: University of Minnesota Press, 1996.

———. "Sovereignty and the Nation: Constructing the Boundaries of National Identity." In Thomas J. Biersteker and Cynthia Weber (eds.), *State Sovereignty as Social Construct.* Cambridge: Cambridge University Press, 1996.

Doyle, Michael W. *UN Peacekeeping in Cambodia: UNTAC's Civil Mandate.* Boulder: Lynne Rienner, 1995.

Doyle, Michael W., Ian Johnstone, and Robert C. Orr (eds.). *Keeping the Peace: Multidimensional UN Operations in Cambodia and El Salvador.* Cambridge: Cambridge University Press, 1997.

Doyle, Michael W., and Nishkala Suntharalingam. "The UN in Cambodia: Lessons for Complex Peacekeeping." *International Peacekeeping* 1, no. 2 (summer 1994): 117–147.

Dudink, Stefan. "The Unheroic Men of a Moral Nation: Masculinity and Nation in Modern Dutch History." In Cynthia Cockburn and Dubravka Zarkov (eds.), *The Postwar Moment: Militaries, Masculinities, and International Peacekeeping.* London: Lawrence and Wishart, 2002, pp. 146–151.

Duffey, Tamara. "Cultural Issues in Contemporary Peacekeeping." *International Peacekeeping* 7, no. 1 (spring 2000): 142–168.

Duffield, Mark. *Global Governance and the New Wars: The Merging of Development and Security.* London: Zed Books, 2001.

———. "Globalization, Transborder Trade, and War Economies." In Mats Berdal and David Malone (eds.), *Greed and Grievance: Economic Agendas in Civil Wars.* Boulder: Lynne Rienner, 2000.

Dumézil, Georges. *Destiny of the Warrior.* Chicago: University of Chicago Press, 1969.

Dyer, Gwynn. *Anybody's Son Will Do.* National Film Board of Canada, 1983.

Easlea, Brian. *Fathering the Unthinkable: Masculinity, Scientists, and the Nuclear Arms Race.* London: Pluto Press, 1983.

Ehrenreich, Barbara. *Blood Rites: Origins and History of the Passions of War.* New York: Metropolitan Books, 1997.

———. "Foreword" to Klaus Theweleit, *Male Fantasies.* Minneapolis: University of Minnesota Press, 1987, vol. 1, pp. ix–xvii.

———. "Fukuyama's Follies: So What If Women Ruled the World?" *Foreign Affairs,* January–February 1999, pp. 118–122.

———. "Peacekeeping." *Z Magazine,* January 1997, pp. 5–6.

Eisenstein, Hester. *Inside Agitators: Australian Femocrats and the State.* Philadelphia: Temple University Press, 1996.

Elliston, Jon, and Catherine Lutz. "Hidden Casualties: An Epidemic of Violence When Troops Return from War." National Sexuality Resource Center. Available at www.nsrc.sfsu.edu/htmlArticle.cf...=1&SID=AD8DFA464A318A5C615F 8158C135C346. Reprinted in *The Nation,* October 14, 2002.

Elshtain, Jean Bethke. "'Shooting' at the Wrong Target: A Response to Van Creveld." *Millennium: Journal of International Studies* 29, no. 2 (2000): 443–448.

Eng, Peter. "Little Sympathy for Vietnamese Victims." *Phnom Penh Post,* August 7, 1992, p. 4.

Enloe, Cynthia. *Bananas, Beaches, and Bases: Making Feminist Sense of International Politics.* Berkeley: University of California Press, 1990.

————. "Closing Remarks." In Louise Olsson and Torunn L. Tryggestad (eds.), *Women and International Peacekeeping*. London: Frank Cass Publishers, 2001, pp. 111–113.

————. "Demilitarization—or More of the Same? Feminist Questions to Ask in the Postwar Moment." In Cynthia Cockburn and Dubravka Zarkov (eds.), *The Postwar Moment: Militaries, Masculinities, and International Peacekeeping*. London: Lawrence and Wishart, 2002, pp. 22–32.

————. *Maneuvers: The International Politics of Militarizing Women's Lives*. Berkeley: University of California Press, 2000.

————. *The Morning After: Sexual Politics at the End of the Cold War*. Berkeley: University of California Press, 1993.

————. "The Right to Fight: A Feminist Catch-22." *Ms.*, July–August 1993, pp. 84–87.

Erlanger, Steven. "At Bonn Talks, 3 Women Push Women's Cause." *New York Times*, November 30, 2001. Available at www.nytimes.com/2001/11/30/international/asia/30WOME.html?ex=1083816000&en=663ab1e76feb6634&ei=5070.

"Europeans Press Afghan Talks on Women's Rights." Reuters, November 29, 2001. Available at www.reliefweb.int/w/rwb.nsf/9ca...171088814885256b13006fe63b?OpenDocument.

Farmanfarmaian, Abouali. "Did You Measure Up? The Role of Race and Sexuality in the Gulf War." In Cynthia Peters (ed.), *Collateral Damage: The "New World Order" at Home and Abroad*. Boston: South End, 1992, pp. 111–138.

Fetherston, A. B. "Peacekeeping, Conflict Resolution, and Peacebuilding: A Reconsideration of Theoretical Frameworks." *International Peacekeeping* 7, no. 1 (spring 2000): 190–218.

————. "Putting the Peace Back into Peacekeeping: Theory Must Inform Practice." *International Peacekeeping* 1, no. 1 (spring 1994): 3–29.

————. *Towards a Theory of United Nations Peacekeeping*. Basingstoke, UK: Macmillan, 1994.

————. "UN Peacekeepers and Cultures of Violence." *Cultural Survival Quarterly* 19, no. 1 (1995): 19–23.

————. "Voices from Warzones: Implications for Training UN Peacekeepers." In Edward Moxon-Browne (ed.), *A Future for Peacekeeping?* Basingstoke, UK: Macmillan, 1998, pp. 158–175.

Fisher, Matthew, and Sean Rayment. "The Photographs That Shocked the World: Britain, U.S. Try to Quell Scandal." *Ottawa Citizen*, May 2, 2004, p. A1.

Fisk, Robert. "New Crises, Old Lessons." *The Independent*, January 15, 2003. Available at http://news.independent.co.uk/world/politics/story.jsp?story=368408.

"Fort Bragg Murders Expose Domestic Violence in Military." *Ms. News*, July 30, 2002. Available at www.msmagazine.com/news/printnews.asp?id=6744.

Francis, Daniel. *National Dreams: Myth, Memory, and Canadian History*. Vancouver: Arsenal Pulp Press, 1997.

Francke, Linda Bird. *Ground Zero: The Gender Wars in the Military*. New York: Simon and Schuster, 1997.

Fukuyama, Francis. "Women and the Evolution of World Politics." *Foreign Affairs*, September–October 1998, pp. 24–40.

Gardam, Judith. "Women and the Law of Armed Conflict: Why the Silence?" *International and Comparative Law Quarterly* 46 (1997): 55–80.

Gardam, Judith, and Hilary Charlesworth. "Protection of Women in Armed Conflict." *Human Rights Quarterly* 22, no. 1 (2000): 148–166.

Gardam, Judith, and Michelle Jarvis. "Women and Armed Conflict: The International Response to the Beijing Platform for Action." *Columbia Human Rights Law Review* 32, no. 1 (fall 2000): 1–65.

———. *Women, Armed Conflict, and International Law.* The Hague: Kluwer Law International, 2001.

George, Jim. *Discourses of Global Politics: A Critical (Re)introduction to International Relations.* Boulder: Lynne Rienner, 1994.

Ghosh, Amitav. "The Global Reservation: Notes Toward an Ethnography of International Peacekeeping." *Cultural Anthropology* 9, no. 3 (1994): 412–422.

Gibson, Janice T. "Teaching People to Inflict Pain: State Terror and Social Learning." *Journal of Humanistic Psychology* 31, no. 2 (spring 1991): 72–87.

Gilbert, Martin. *A History of the Twentieth Century,* vol. 3: *1952–1999.* New York: William Morrow, 1999.

Gilbert, Sandra. "Soldier's Heart: Literary Men, Literary Women, and the Great War." *Signs* 8 (1983): 422–450.

Giles, Wenona, Malathi de Alwis, Edith Klein, and Neluka Silva (eds.). *Feminists Under Fire: Exchanges Across War Zones.* Toronto: Between the Lines, 2003.

Gill, Lesley. "Creating Citizens, Making Men: The Military and Masculinity in Bolivia." *Cultural Anthropolgy* 12, no. 4 (1997): 527–550.

Goldstein, Joshua S. *War and Gender.* Cambridge: Cambridge University Press, 2001.

Government of Canada. *Canada in the World, Government Statement.* Ottawa, 1995.

———. *Canada's Foreign Policy: Principles and Priorities for the Future, Report of the Special Joint Committee Reviewing Canadian Foreign Policy.* Ottawa, 1994.

———. *The Dilemmas of a Committed Peacekeeper: Canada and the Renewal of Peacekeeping.* Standing Committee on National Defence and Veterans Affairs. Ottawa, June 1993.

———. *Dishonoured Legacy: The Lessons of the Somalia Affair.* Ottawa: Minister of Public Works and Government Services Canada, 1997.

———. *1994 Defence White Paper.* Ottawa: Canada, 1994.

———. *Security in a Changing World, 1994.* Ottawa: Special Joint Committee on Canada's Defence Policy, 1994.

Griffith, Samuel B. "Introduction" to Sun Tzu, *The Art of War.* London: Oxford University Press, 1971.

Hagi, Jiro. "Japan and Peacekeeping: Starting from Zero." In Alex Morrison (ed.), *The Changing Face of Peacekeeping.* Toronto: Canadian Institute of Strategic Studies, 1993, pp. 59–70.

Halliday, Fred. *Rethinking International Relations.* Vancouver: University of British Columbia Press, 1994.

Hamilton, Andrea. "Murders of Party Officials Continue." *Phnom Penh Post,* July 2–15, 1993, p. 1.

Hampson, Fen Osler. *Madness in the Multitude: Human Security and World Disorder.* Don Mills: Oxford University Press, 2002.

Han, Sonia K. "Building a Peace That Lasts: The United Nations and Post–Civil War Peace-Building." *New York University Journal of International Law and Politics* 26 (1994): 837–892.

Hanson, Victor Davis. *The Western Way of War: Infantry Battle in Classical Greece.* New York: Alfred A. Knopf, 1989.

Harrison, Deborah. *The First Casualty: Violence Against Women in Canadian Military Communities.* Toronto: James Lorimer, 2002.

Harrison, Deborah, and Lucie Laliberté. *No Life Like It: Military Wives in Canada.* Toronto: James Lorimer, 1994.

Hatty, Suzanne E. *Masculinities, Violence, and Culture.* Thousand Oaks, CA: Sage, 2000.

Hayes, Michael. "Indibatt Gets High Marks for Civic Work." *Phnom Penh Post,* September 24–October 7, 1993, p. 8.

———. "With a Little Help from the Troops." *Phnom Penh Post,* April 23–May 6, 1993, p. 16.

Hein, Laura, and Mark Selden. "Learning Citizenship from the Past: Textbook Nationalism, Global Context, and Social Change." *Bulletin of Concerned Asian Scholars* 30, no. 2 (1998): 3–15.

Heininger, Janet E. *Peacekeeping in Transition: The United Nations in Cambodia.* New York: Twentieth Century Fund Press, 1994.

Heje, Claus. "United Nations Peacekeeping—An Introduction." In Edward Moxon-Browne (ed.), *A Future for Peacekeeping?* Basingstoke, UK: Macmillan, 1998, pp. 1–25.

Helland, Anita, Kari Karame, Anita Kristensen, and Inger Skjelsbaek. "Women and Armed Conflict: A Study for the Norwegian Ministry of Foreign Affairs." Copenhagen: Norwegian Institute of International Affairs, 1999.

Herdt, Gilbert H. "Rituals of Manhood: Male Initiation in Papua New Guinea." In Caroline B. Brettell and Carolyn F. Sargent (eds.), *Gender in Cross-Cultural Perspective.* Englewood Cliffs, NJ: Prentice Hall, 1993, pp. 111–115.

Hiebert, Murray. "Baht Imperialism: Thai Investors Pour into Cambodia." *Far Eastern Economic Review,* June 25, 1992, pp. 46–47.

Higate, Paul R. (ed.). *Military Masculinities: Identity and the State.* Westport, CT: Praeger, 2003.

Hobsbawm, E. J. *Nations and Nationalism Since 1789: Programme, Myth, Reality.* Cambridge: Cambridge University Press, 1990.

Hooper, Charlotte. *Manly States: Masculinities, International Relations, and Gender Politics.* New York: Columbia University Press, 2001.

———. "Masculinist Practices and Gender Politics: The Operation of Multiple Masculinities in International Relations." In Marysia Zalewski and Jane Parpart (eds.), *The "Man" Question in International Relations.* Boulder: Westview Press, 1998.

Horkheimer, Max. "Traditional and Critical Theory." In *Critical Theory: Selected Essays.* New York: Continuum, 1982.

Hudson, Heidi. "Mainstreaming Gender in Peacekeeping Operations: Can Africa Learn from International Experience?" *African Security Review* 9, no. 4 (2000). Available at www.iss.co.za/Pubs/ASR/9No4/Hudson.html.

Human Rights Task Force on Cambodia. "Prostitution and Sex Trafficking: A Growing Threat to Women and Children in Cambodia." Phnom Penh, n.d.

Human Rights Vigilance of Cambodia. "Combating Women Trafficking and Child Prostitution," March–April 1995. In Appendix 2 of UNICEF, "The Trafficking and Prostitution of Children in Cambodia." Phnom Penh, 1995.

Hunt, Krista. "The Strategic Co-optation of Women's Rights: Discourses in the 'War on Terrorism.'" *International Feminist Journal of Politics* 4, no. 1 (2002): 116–121.

Huntington, Samuel P. "The Clash of Civilizations? The Next Pattern of Conflict." *Foreign Affairs* 72, no. 3 (summer 1993): 22–28.

Information Legacy: A Compendium of Source Material from the Commission of Inquiry into the Deployment of Canadian Forces to Somalia. Ottawa: Government of Canada, 1997.

International Alert. "Gender Mainstreaming in Peace Support Operations: Moving Beyond Rhetoric to Practice." London, July 2002.

———. "Implementing the United Nations Security Council Resolution on Women, Peace and Security: Integrating Gender into Early Warning Systems." Report on the First Expert Consultative Meeting, May 7, 2001, Nairobi, Kenya.

"An Introduction to United Nations Peacekeeping." UN Department of Peacekeeping Operations website. Available at www.un.org/Depts/dpko/intro/index.htm.

Jacobs, Susie, Ruth Jacobson, and Jennifer Marchbank (eds.). *States of Conflict: Gender, Violence, and Resistance.* London: Zed Books, 2000.

James, Alan. "Peacekeeping in the Post–Cold War Era." *International Journal* 50, no. 2 (spring 1995): 241–265.

Janowitz, Morris. *The Professional Soldier.* Glencoe, IL: Free Press, 1960.

"Japanese UNTAC Troops Contracted AIDS Virus." *Cambodia Daily,* October 22–24, 1993, p. 1.

Jennar, R. M. "UNTAC: 'International Triumph' in Cambodia?" *Security Dialogue* 25, no. 2 (1994): 145–156.

Jockel, Joseph T. *Canada and International Peacekeeping.* Washington, DC: Center for Strategic and International Studies, 1994.

Johansson, Eva, and Gerry Larsson. "A Model for Understanding Stress and Daily Experiences Among Soldiers in Peacekeeping Operations." *International Peacekeeping* 5, no. 3 (autumn 1998): 124–141.

———. "Swedish Peacekeepers in Bosnia and Herzegovina: A Quantitative Analysis." *International Peacekeeping* 8, no. 1 (spring 2001): 64–76.

Jordens, Jay. "The Ethnic Vietnamese Community in Cambodia: Prospects Post-UNTAC." Association for Asian Studies Annual Meeting, Boston, March 27, 1994.

Kaplan, Robert. "The Coming Anarchy." *Atlantic Monthly,* February 1994, pp. 44–76.

Karner, Tracy Xavia. "Engendering Violent Men: Oral Histories of Military Masculinity." In Lee H. Bowker (ed.), *Masculinities and Violence.* Thousand Oaks, CA: Sage, 1998, pp. 197–232.

Kaufman, Michael. *Cracking the Armour: Power, Pain and the Lives of Men.* Toronto: Viking, 1993.

———. "Men, Feminism, and Men's Contradictory Experiences of Power." In Harry Brod and Michael Kaufman (eds.), *Theorizing Masculinities.* Thousand Oaks, CA: Sage, 1994, pp. 142–163.

———. "Working with Men and Boys to Challenge Sexism and End Men's Violence." In Ingeborg Breines, Robert Connell, and Ingrid Eide (eds.), *Male Roles, Masculinities, and Violence: A Culture of Peace Perspective.* Paris: UNESCO, 2000, pp. 213–222.

Keeley, Lawrence H. *War Before Civilization: The Myth of the Peaceful Savage.* New York: Oxford University Press, 1996.

Keo Keang and Im Phallay, Human Rights Task Force on Cambodia. "Notes on the March–April 1995 Rapid Appraisal of the Human Rights Vigilance of Cambodia on Child Prostitution and Trafficking." In Appendix 2 of UNICEF, "The Trafficking and Prostitution of Children in Cambodia." Phnom Penh, 1995.

Kernic, Franz. "The Soldier and the Task: Austria's Experience of Preparing Peacekeepers." *International Peacekeeping* 6, no. 3 (autumn 1999): 113–128.

Kien Serey Phal. "The Lessons of the UNTAC Experience and the Ongoing Responsibilities of the International Community for Peacebuilding and Development in Cambodia." *Pacifica Review* 7, no. 2 (1995): 129–133.

Kiernan, Ben. "Review Essay: William Shawcross, Declining Cambodia." *Bulletin of Concerned Asian Scholars* 18, no. 1 (January–March 1986): 56–63.

————. "The Cambodian Crisis, 1990–1992: The UN Plan, the Khmer Rouge, and the State of Cambodia." *Bulletin of Concerned Asian Scholars* 24, no. 2 (April–June 1992): 3–24.

Kinsella, Helen. "Approaching the Implementation of Security Council Resolution 1325." Roundtable on "UN Security Council Resolution 1325: How Women Do (and Don't) Get Taken Seriously in the Construction of International Security." International Studies Association Annual Meetings, Portland, OR, February 26–March 1, 2003.

Kirshenbaum, Gayle. "In U.N. Peacekeeping, Women Are an Untapped Resource." *Ms.,* January–February 1997, pp. 20–21.

————. "Who's Watching the Peacekeepers?" *Ms.,* May–June 1994, pp. 10–15.

Klein, Uta. "'Our Best Boys': The Gendered Nature of Civil-Military Relations in Israel," *Men and Masculinities* 2, no. 1 (July 1999): 47–65.

Klintworth, Gary. "United Nations: A Poor Job in Cambodia." *International Herald Tribune,* February 2, 1993.

Knox, Paul. "Peacebuilding Concept Imperilled, Conference Told." *Globe and Mail,* March 21, 1997, p. A12.

Kovitz, Marcia. "The Roots of Military Masculinity." In Paul R. Higate (ed.), *Military Masculinities: Identity and the State.* Westport, CT: Praeger, 2003, pp. 1–14.

Kratochwil, Friedrich. "The Monologue of 'Science.'" *International Studies Review* 5, no. 1 (March 2003): 124–128.

Krause, Keith, and Michael C. Williams (eds.). *Critical Security Studies.* Minneapolis: University of Minnesota Press, 1997.

Krousar Thmey. "Child Prostitution and Trafficking in Cambodia: A New Problem." March–October 1995. In Appendix 2 of UNICEF, "The Trafficking and Prostitution of Children in Cambodia." Phnom Penh, 1995.

Kulka, Richard A., William E. Schlenger, John A. Fairbank, Richard L. Hough, B. Kathleen Jordan, Charles R. Marmar, and Daniel S. Weiss. *Trauma and the Vietnam War Generation: Report of Findings from the National Vietnam Veterans Readjustment Study.* New York: Brunner/Mazel, 1990.

Kumar, Chetan. *Building Peace in Haiti.* Boulder: Lynne Rienner, 1998.

Kvinna till Kvinna. *Engendering the Peace Process: A Gender Approach to Dayton— and Beyond.* Stockholm: Kvinna till Kvinna Foundation, 2000.

————. *Getting It Right? A Gender Approach to UNMIK Administration in Kosovo.* Stockholm: Kvinna till Kvinna Foundation, 2001.

Landay, Jonathan S. "Hazing Rituals in Military Are Common—and Abusive." *Christian Science Monitor,* February 11, 1997, p. 1.

Large, Judith. "Disintegration Conflicts and the Restructuring of Masculinity." *Gender and Development* 5, no. 2 (June 1997): 23–30.

Last, Alex. "Porn Scandal Rocks Eritrean Peace Force." *BBC News World Edition,* December 20, 2002. Available at http://news.bbc.co.uk/2/hi/africa/2595003.stm.

Ledgerwood, Judy. *Analysis of the Situation of Women in Cambodia.* Phnom Penh: UNICEF, February–June 1992.

————. "Gender Symbolism and Culture Change: Viewing the Virtuous Woman in the Khmer Story 'Mea Yoeng.'" In May M. Ebihara, Carol A. Mortland, and Judy Ledgerwood (eds.), *Cambodian Culture Since 1975: Homeland and Exile.* Ithaca: Cornell University Press, 1994, pp. 119–128.

————. "UN Peacekeeping Missions: The Lessons from Cambodia." *Analysis from the East-West Center,* no. 11. Honolulu: East-West Center, March 1994.

Ledgerwood, Judy, May M. Ebihara, and Carol A. Mortland. "Introduction," In Ebihara, Mortland, and Ledgerwood (eds.), *Cambodian Culture Since 1975: Homeland and Exile.* Ithaca: Cornell University Press, 1994, pp. 1–26.

Lehr, Doreen Drewry. "Military Wives: Breaking the Silence." In Francine D'Amico and Laurie Weinstein (eds.), *Gender Camouflage: Women and the U.S. Military.* New York: New York University Press, 1999, pp. 117–131.

Leitch, Richard D., Jr., Akira Kato, and Martin E. Weinstein. *Japan's Role in the Post–Cold War World.* Westport, CT: Greenwood, 1995.

Leonard, Christine. "Becoming Cambodian: Ethnic Identity and the Vietnamese in Kampuchea." *Cambodia Report* (publication of the Preah Sihanouk Raj Academy, later the Center for Advanced Study, Phnom Penh) 2, no. 1 (January–February 1996): 15–18.

Ling, Lily. "Cultural Chauvinism and the Liberal International Order: 'West Versus Rest' in Asia's Financial Crisis." In G. Chowdhry and S. Nair (eds.), *Power, Postcolonialism, and International Relations: Reading Race, Gender, Class.* London: Routledge, 2002, pp. 115–141.

———. "Hypermasculinity." *Routledge International Encyclopedia of Women's Studies.* London: Routledge, 2001, pp. 1089–1091.

———. "Hypermasculinity on the Rise, Again: A Response to Fukuyama on Women and World Politics." *International Feminist Journal of Politics* 2, no. 2 (2000): 278–286.

Litz, Brett T., Lynda A. King, Daniel W. King, Susan M. Orsillo, and Matthew J. Friedman. "Warriors as Peacekeepers: Features of the Somalia Experience and PTSD." *Journal of Consulting and Clinical Psychology* 65, no. 6 (December 1997): 1001–1010.

Lizée, Pierre. *Peace, Power, and Resistance in Cambodia: Global Governance and the Failure of International Conflict Resolution.* Basingstoke, UK: Macmillan, 2000.

Lupi, Natalia. "Report by the Enquiry Commission on the Behaviour of Italian Peacekeeping Troops in Somalia." *Yearbook of International Humanitarian Law,* vol. 1. The Hague: T. M. C. Asser, 1998.

Macdonald, Laura. "Unequal Partnerships: The Politics of Canada's Relations with the Third World." *Studies in Political Economy* 47 (summer 1995): 111–114.

Macdonald, Oliver A. K. "Recent Developments in Peacekeeping—The Irish Military Experience." In Edward Moxon-Browne (ed.), *A Future for Peacekeeping?* Basingstoke, UK: Macmillan, 1998, pp. 40–57.

Machel, Graça. "The Impact of Armed Conflict on Children: A Critical Review of Progress Made and Obstacles Encountered in Increasing Protection for War-Affected Children." International Conference on War-Affected Children, Winnipeg, MB, September 2000. Available at www.unifem.undp.org/machelrep.html.

———. "The Impact of Armed Conflict on Children: Report of the Expert of the Secretary-General, Ms. Graça Machel, Submitted Pursuant to General Assembly Resolution 48/157." UN General Assembly, A/51/306, August 26, 1996.

MacKenzie, Lewis. "Airborne Never Received a Sliver of the Credit It Earned." *Ottawa Citizen,* July 15, 2000, p. A6.

———. *Peacekeeper: The Road to Sarajevo.* Vancouver: Douglas and McIntyre, 1993.

MacQueen, Norrie. *United Nations Peacekeeping in Africa Since 1960.* London: Pearson Education, 2002.

Makinda, Samuel M. *Seeking Peace from Chaos: Humanitarian Intervention in Somalia.* Boulder: Lynne Rienner, 1993.

Malkki, Liisa H. "Speechless Emissaries: Refugees, Humanitarianism, and Dehistoricization." *Cultural Anthropology* 11, no. 3 (1996): 377–404.

Malone, David M., and Karin Wermester. "Boom and Bust? The Changing Nature of UN Peacekeeping." *International Peacekeeping* 7, no. 3 (autumn 2000): 37–54.

Malszecki, Greg, and T. Cavar. "Men, Masculinities, War, and Sport." In Nancy Mandell (ed.), *Feminist Issues: Race, Class and Sexuality.* Toronto: Pearson Educational, 2000, pp. 166–192.

Mansaray, Binta. "Women Against Weapons: A Leading Role for Women in Disarmament." In Anatole Ayissi and Robin-Edward Poulton (eds.), *Bound to Cooperate: Conflict, Peace, and People in Sierra Leone.* Geneva: UN Institute for Disarmament Research, December 2000, pp. 139–162.

Manson, General Paul D. "Peacekeeping in a Changing World." Address to the Empire Club of Canada, Toronto, November 17, 1988. In *Canadian Speeches* 2, no. 8 (December 1988): 35–41.

Marin, André (Canada's Military Ombudsman). *Special Report: Systemic Treatment of CF Members with PTSD.* Ottawa: Government of Canada, February 5, 2002.

Martin, Pierre, and Michel Fortmann. "Canadian Public Opinion and Peacekeeping in a Turbulent World." *International Journal* 50, no. 2 (spring 1995): 370–400.

Masters, Cristina."Cyborg Soldiers and Militarized Masculinities." M.A. research paper, York University, September 2000.

Mayhall, Stacey. "Riding the Bull, Wrestling the Bear: Sex and Identity in the Discourses of Global Finance." Ph.D. diss., York University, December 2002.

Mazurana, Dyan. "International Peacekeeping Operations: To Neglect Gender Is to Risk Peacekeeping Failure." In Cynthia Cockburn and Dubravka Zarkov (eds.), *The Postwar Moment: Militaries, Masculinities and International Peacekeeping.* London: Lawrence and Wishart, 2002, pp. 41–50.

Mazurana, Dyan, Susan McKay, Khristopher Carlson, and Janel Kasper. "Girls in Fighting Forces: Their Recruitment, Participation, Demobilization, and Reintegration." *Peace and Conflict* 8, no. 2 (2002): 97–123.

Mazurana, Dyan, Angela Raven-Roberts, and Jane Parpart (eds.). *Gender, Conflict, and Peacekeeping.* Boulder: Rowman and Littlefield, forthcoming.

McAllister, Pam (ed.). *Reweaving the Web of Life: Feminism and Nonviolence.* Philadelphia: New Society Publishers, 1982.

McCarthy, Tom. "Slaughter of Vietnamese in Phum Taches Was Cold and Calculated." *Phnom Penh Post,* January 15–28, 1993, p. 3.

McCauley, Clark. "Conference Overview." In Jonathan Haas (ed.), *The Anthropology of War.* Cambridge: Cambridge University Press, 1990.

McCoy, Alfred W. "Ram Boys: Changing Images of the Masculine in the Philippine Military." Presented at the International Studies Association Annual Meetings, Toronto, March 18–22, 1997.

———. "'Same Banana': Hazing and Honor at the Philippine Military Academy." *Journal of Asian Studies* 54, no. 3 (August 1995): 689–726.

McCranie, Edward W., and Leon A. Hyer. "Posttraumatic Stress Disorder Symptoms in Korean Conflict and World War II Combat Veterans Seeking Outpatient Treatment." *Journal of Traumatic Stress* 13, no. 3 (2000): 427–438.

McDermott, Anthony. "Japan's Financial Contribution to the UN System: In Pursuit of Acceptance and Standing." *International Peacekeeping* 6, no. 2 (summer 1999): 64–88.

McKenna, Magin. "Sins of the Peacekeepers." *Sunday Herald* (London), June 30, 2002. Available at www.sundayherald.com/print25914.

McNulty, Sheila. "Returning Khmer Opting for Cash Grants, Mine-Free Land Scarcer Than First Thought." *Phnom Penh Post,* August 27, 1992, p. 3.

———. "SOC Heeds U.N. Call to Stop Runaway Inflation." *Phnom Penh Post,* October 23, 1992, p. 13.

———. "UN Investigation Concludes KR Slayed Vietnamese Families." *Phnom Penh Post,* August 27, 1992, p. 3.

Mearsheimer, John J. "Why We Will Soon Miss the Cold War." *Atlantic Monthly,* August 1990, pp. 35–50.

Mehlum, Lars, and Lars Weisaeth. "Predictors of Posttraumatic Stress Reactions in Norwegian U.N. Peacekeepers 7 Years After Service." *Journal of Traumatic Stress* 15, no. 1 (February 2002): 17–26.

Mehta, Mona. "Gender Dimensions of Poverty in Cambodia: A Survey Report." Phnom Penh: Oxfam, 1993.

Messner, Michael A., and Donald F. Sabo (eds.). *Sport, Men, and the Gender Order: Critical Feminist Perspectives.* Champaign, IL: Human Kinetics Books, 1990.

Miller, Laura L. "Do Soldiers Hate Peacekeeping? The Case of Preventive Diplomacy Operations in Macedonia." *Armed Forces and Society* 23, no. 3 (spring 1997): 415–450.

Miller, Laura L., and Charles Moskos. "Humanitarians or Warriors? Race, Gender, and Combat Status in Operation Restore Hope." *Armed Forces and Society* 21, no. 4 (summer 1995): 615–637.

Mingst, Karen A. "Developing States as Peacekeepers: A Comparative Perspective." Presented at the International Studies Association Annual Meetings, Toronto, March 18–22, 1997.

———. "Why Co-operate? The New Peacekeepers—Japan and Germany." Presented at the International Studies Association Annual Meetings, Minneapolis, MN, March 1998.

Moeun Chhean Nariddh. "German Doctors Prepare to Pack Up." *Phnom Penh Post,* September 24–October 7, 1993, p. 9.

Molot, Maureen Appel. "Where Do We, Should We, or Can We Sit? A Review of the Canadian Foreign Policy Literature." *International Journal of Canadian Studies* 1–2 (spring–fall 1990): 77–96.

Moon, Katharine H. S. *Sex Among Allies: Military Prostitution in U.S.-Korea Relations.* New York: Columbia University Press, 1997.

Morgan, David H. J. "Theater of War: Combat, the Military, and Masculinities." In Harry Brod and Michael Kaufman (eds.), *Theorizing Masculinities.* London: Sage, 1994.

Morrison, Alex, and Dale Anderson. "Peacekeeping and the Coming Anarchy." Pearson Roundtable Series: Report no. 1. Cornwallis Park, NS: Canadian Peacekeeping Press, 1996.

Morrison, Alex, Douglas Fraser, and James D. Kiras (eds.). *Peacekeeping with Muscle: The Use of Force in International Conflict Resolution.* Cornwallis, NS: Canadian Peacekeeping Press, 1997.

Morrison, Alex, and Suzanne M. Plain. "Canada: The Seasoned Veteran." Presented at the International Studies Association Annual Meetings, Washington, DC, March 28–April 1, 1994.

Moser, Caroline O. N., and Fiona C. Clark (eds.). *Victims, Perpetrators, or Actors? Gender, Armed Conflict, and Political Violence.* London: Zed Books, 2001.

Moser-Puangsuwan, Yeshua. "U.N. Peacekeeping in Cambodia: Whose Needs Were Met?" *Pacifica Review* 7, no. 2 (1995): 103–127.

Moskos, Charles. *Peace Soldiers*. Chicago: University of Chicago Press, 1976.

Muir, Kate. *Arms and the Woman*. London: Sinclair-Stevenson, 1992.

Munro, David. "Cambodia: A Secret War Continues." *CovertAction* 40 (spring 1992): 52–57.

Munthit, Ker. "Akashi: Election 'Free and Fair.'" *Phnom Penh Post*, June 6–12, 1993, p. 3.

Murphy, Craig N. "Six Masculine Roles in International Relations and Their Interconnection: A Personal Investigation." In Marysia Zalewski and Jane Parpart (eds.), *The "Man" Question in International Relations*. Boulder: Westview, 1998, pp. 93–108.

Murphy, Ray. "Contributors to Peacekeeping, Seasoned and Hesitant—The Case of Ireland." Presented at the International Studies Association Annual Meetings, Washington, DC, March 28–April 1, 1994.

Mysliwiec, Eva. *Punishing the Poor: The International Isolation of Kampuchea*. Oxford: Oxfam, 1988.

NGO Working Group on Women, Peace, and Security. "Recommendations and Concerns Based on the Afghan Women Leaders Summit in Brussels on 4th and 5th December 2001." Available at www.international-alert.org/women/state2.htm.

Neack, Laura. "Peacekeeping's New Dark Age." Presented at the International Studies Association Annual Meetings, Toronto, March 18–22, 1997.

———. "UN Peace-keeping: In the Interest of Community or Self?" *Journal of Peace Research* 32, no. 2 (1995): 181–196.

Nettie, Andrew. "Cambodia: UN Mission Cited as Sex Slavery Spreads." *Sunday Age* (Melbourne), June 25, 1995.

Neufeld, Mark. "Hegemony and Foreign Policy Analysis: The Case of Canada as Middle Power." *Studies in Political Economy* 48 (autumn 1995): 7–29.

———. *The Restructuring of International Relations Theory*. Cambridge: Cambridge University Press, 1995.

Neufeld, Mark, and Sandra Whitworth. "Image(in)ing Canadian Foreign Policy." In Wallace Clement (ed.), *Building on the New Canadian Political Economy*. Montreal: McGill-Queen's University Press, 1996, pp. 197–214.

"1956: Suez and the End of Empire." *Guardian Unlimited Politics: Special Reports.* March 14, 2001. Available at http://politics.guardian.co.uk/politicspast/story/ 0,9061,451936,00.html.

Nishimura, Mutsuyoshi. "A Japanese Perspective on Peacekeeping—Japan's International Activities: The Road Behind; The Road Ahead." In Alex Morrison, Ken Eyre, and Roger Chiasson (eds.), *Facing the Future: Proceedings of the 1996 Canada-Japan Seminar on Modern Peacekeeping*. Cornwallis, NS: Canadian Peacekeeping Press, 1997, pp. 71–75.

Niva, Steve. "Tough and Tender: New World Order Masculinity and the Gulf War." In Marysia Zalewski and Jane Parpart (eds.), *The "Man" Question in International Relations*. Boulder: Westview Press, 1998, pp. 109–128.

Norden, Deborah L. "Keeping the Peace, Outside and In: Argentina's UN Missions." *International Peacekeeping* 2, no. 3 (autumn 1995): 330–349.

Novaco, Raymond W., and Claude M. Chemtob. "Anger and Combat-Related Posttraumatic Stress Disorder." *Journal of Traumatic Stress* 15, no. 2 (April 2002): 123–132.

Nyers, Peter. "Emergency or Emerging Identities? Refugees and Transformations in World Order." *Millennium: Journal of International Studies* 28, no. 1 (1999): 1–26.

Off, Carol. *The Lion, the Fox, and the Eagle: A Story of Generals and Justice in Rwanda and Yugoslavia.* Toronto: Random House Canada, 2000.

Olsson, Louise. "Do Peacekeeping Operations Affect Gender Relations in Host States? Developing a Theoretical Framework for Analyzing Peacekeeping Operations and Gender Relations." Presented at the International Studies Association Annual General Meetings, Portland, OR, February 26–March 1, 2003.

Olsson, Louise, and Torunn L. Tryggestad (eds.). *Women and International Peacekeeping.* London: Frank Cass, 2001.

Ong, Aihwa. "Mother's Milk in War and Diaspora." *Cultural Survival Quarterly* (spring 1995): 61–64.

"An Open Letter to Yasushi Akashi." *Phnom Penh Post,* October 11, 1992, p. 2.

Orford, Anne. "Feminism, Imperialism and the Mission of International Law." *Nordic Journal of International Law* 71, no. 2 (2002): 275–296.

———. "Muscular Humanitarianism: Reading the Narratives of the New Interventionism." *European Journal of International Law* 10, no. 4 (1999): 679–711.

———. *Reading Humanitarian Intervention: Human Rights and the Use of Force in International Law.* Cambridge: Cambridge University Press, 2003.

Overing, Joanna. "The Role of Myth: An Anthropological Perspective; or, 'The Reality of the Really Made-Up.'" In Geoffrey Hosking and George Schöpflin (eds.), *Myths and Nationhood.* New York: Routledge, 1997.

Owada, Hisashi. "A Japanese Perspective on Peacekeeping." In Daniel Warner (ed.), *New Dimensions of Peacekeeping.* Dordrecht: Martinus Nijhoff, 1995, pp. 103–116.

Paris, Roland. "Broadening the Study of Peace Operations." *International Studies Review* 2, no. 3 (December 2000): 27–44.

———. "International Peacebuilding and the '*Mission Civilatrice.*'" *Review of International Studies* 28 (2002): 637–656.

———. "Peacebuilding and the Limits of Liberal Internationalism." *International Security* 22, no. 2 (fall 1997): 54–89.

Peach, Katrina. "HIV Threatens to Claim UNTAC's Highest Casualties." *Phnom Penh Post,* October 22–November 4, 1993, p. 4.

Pilger, John. "Black Farce in Cambodia: The Appeasement of the Khmer Rouge Continues." *New Statesman and Society,* December 11, 1992, pp. 10–11.

———. "Peace in Our Time? The UN is Normalising the Unthinkable in Cambodia." *New Statesman and Society,* November 27, 1992, pp. 10–11.

———. "Return to Year Zero," *New Internationalist* 242 (April 1993): 4–7.

———. "The West's Lethal Illusion in Cambodia." *New Statesman and Society,* July 9, 1993, pp. 14–15.

———. "The West's War in Cambodia." *New Statesman and Society,* May 28, 1993, pp. 14–15.

Pollack, William. *Real Boys: Rescuing Our Sons from the Myths of Boyhood.* New York: Random House, 1998.

Pollitt, Katha. "Father Knows Best." *Foreign Affairs,* January–February 1999, pp. 122–125.

Postlewaite, Susan. "Sound and Light for Angkor." *Phnom Penh Post,* November 17–30, 1995.

Power, Samantha. *"A Problem from Hell": America and the Age of Genocide.* New York: Basic Books, 2002.

Pringle, James. "Peacekeepers' Odd Ways Keep Khmers Guessing." *Phnom Penh Post,* July 10, 1992, p. 5.

"The Problem of Prostitution." *Phnom Penh Post,* February 12–25, 1993, p. 6.

Project Ploughshares. *Report to Donors.* Waterloo, ON, February 1996.

Prouse, Robert. "The Dark Side That Emerged in Somalia Is Inside All Canadians." *Ottawa Citizen,* July 15, 2000, pp. A4–A6.

———. "'Everyone Is Itching to Get a Kill, Even If It Is an Innocent.'" *Ottawa Citizen,* July 16, 2000, pp. A4–A5.

Pugliese, David. "Airborne Again." *Ottawa Citizen,* April 15, 1996, p. A1.

———. "Almost 20% of '85 Airborne Unit Had Police Record, Report Found." *Ottawa Citizen,* October 4, 1995, p. A4.

———. "Ex-Airborne Member Charged with Murder in 1991 Beating Death." *Ottawa Citizen,* March 2, 1996, p. A3.

———. "Military Brass Let Racist Skinheads Go to Somalia." *Ottawa Citizen,* October 13, 1995, p. A1.

———. "Somalia: What Went So Wrong?" *Ottawa Citizen,* October 1, 1995, p. A6.

Pyle, Kenneth B. *The Japanese Question: Power and Purpose in a New Era.* Washington, DC: American Enterprise Institute Press, 1992.

"Racist Soldier with Criminal Past Allowed to Rejoin the Army, Inquiry Hears." *Ottawa Citizen,* November 3, 1995, p. A5.

Randall, Stephen J. "Peacekeeping in the Post–Cold War Era: The United Nations and the 1993 Cambodian Elections." *Behind the Headlines,* spring 1994, pp. 1–16.

Ratner, Steven R. *The New UN Peacekeeping: Building Peace in Lands of Conflict After the Cold War.* New York: St. Martin's, 1995.

Razack, Sherene H. *Dark Threats and White Knights: The Somalia Affair, Peacekeeping, and the New Imperialism.* Toronto: University of Toronto Press, forthcoming.

———. "From the 'Clean Snows of Petawawa': The Violence of Canadian Peacekeepers in Somalia." *Cultural Anthropology* 15, no. 1 (2000): 127–163.

Reardon, Betty A. *Feminism and the War System.* New York: Teachers College Press, 1985.

Rehn, Elisabeth, and Ellen Johnson Sirleaf. *Women, War, Peace: The Independent Experts' Assessment on the Impact of Armed Conflict on Women and Women's Role in Peace-building.* New York: UN Development Fund for Women, 2002.

Renner, Michael G. "A Force for Peace." *World Watch,* July–August 1992, pp. 26–33.

"Report from the National Women's Summit." Phnom Penh, March 5–8, 1993.

Reuters Library Report, November 18, 1992.

Robinson, Court. "Rupture and Return: Repatriation, Displacement, and Reintegration in Battambang Province Cambodia." Occasional Paper Series no. 7. Indochinese Refugee Information Center, Institute of Asian Studies, Chulalongkorn University, Bangkok, November 1994.

Rolle, Renate. *The World of the Scythians.* Berkeley: University of California Press, 1989.

Roper, John, Masashi Nishihara, Olara A. Otunnu, and Enid C. B. Schoettle. *Keeping the Peace in the Post–Cold War Era: Strengthening Multilateral Peacekeeping.* Report to the Trilateral Commission, no. 43. New York, 1993.

Rubinstein, Robert A. "Cultural Aspects of Peacekeeping: Notes on the Substance of Symbols." *Millennium: Journal of International Studies* 22, no. 3 (1993): 547–562.

Russell, Diana E. H. "The Nuclear Mentality: An Outgrowth of the Masculine Mentality." *Atlantis* 12, no. 1 (1987): 10–17.

Said, Edward. *Orientalism.* New York: Vintage, 1978.

Sanderson, Lieutenant General J. M. "UNTAC: Lessons Learnt. The Military Component View." *Pacifica Review* 7, no. 2 (1995): 69–85.

Saul, John Ralston. *Reflections of a Siamese Twin: Canada at the End of the Twentieth Century.* Toronto: Penguin, 1997.

Schmitt, Eric. "Military Struggling to Stem an Increase in Family Violence." *New York Times,* May 23, 1994.

Schnabel, Albrecht. "An Agenda for Peace or An Agenda for Power? Russian and German Stakes in International Peacekeeping." Presented at the Annual Meeting of the Northeastern Political Science Association, Providence, RI, November 10–12, 1994.

Schöpflin, George. "The Functions of Myth and a Taxonomy of Myths." In Geoffrey Hosking and George Schöpflin (eds.), *Myths and Nationhood.* New York: Routledge, 1997.

Secretariat of State for Women's Affairs, Kingdom of Cambodia. *Cambodia's Country Report: Women in Development.* Phnom Penh, July 1994.

Segal, David R., Jesse J. Harris, Joseph M. Rothberg, and David H. Marlowe. "Paratroopers as Peacekeepers." *Armed Forces and Society* 10, no. 1 (summer 1984): 487–506.

Segal, David R., Mady Wechsler Segal, and Dana P. Eyre. "The Social Construction of Peacekeeping in America." *Sociological Forum* 7, no. 1 (1992): 121–136.

Segal, Lynne. *Is the Future Female? Troubled Thoughts on Contemporary Feminism.* London: Virago, 1987.

———. *Slow Motion: Changing Masculinities, Changing Men.* London: Virago, 1990.

Selochan, Viberto, and Carlyle A. Thayer. *Bringing Democracy to Cambodia.* Canberra: Australian Defence Studies Center, 1996.

Sens, Allen G. *Somalia and the Changing Nature of Peacekeeping: The Implications for Canada.* Prepared for the Commission of Inquiry into the Deployment of Canadian Forces to Somalia. Ottawa: Government Services Canada, 1997.

Sens, Allen, and Peter Stoett. *Global Politics: Origins, Currents, Directions.* Toronto: ITP Nelson, 1998.

Shapiro, Michael. *Language and Political Understanding: The Politics of Discursive Practices.* New Haven: Yale University Press, 1981.

Sharoni, Simona. *Gender and the Israeli-Palestinian Conflict: The Politics of Women's Resistance.* Syracuse: Syracuse University Press, 1995.

Shawcross, William. *Deliver Us from Evil: Peacekeepers, Warlords, and a World of Endless Conflict.* New York: Simon and Schuster, 2000.

Shilts, Randy. *Conduct Unbecoming: Gays and Lesbians in the U.S. Military.* New York: Fawcett Columbine, 1994.

Showalter, Elaine. "Male Hysteria: W. H. R. Rivers and the Lessons of Shell Shock." In *The Female Malady: Women, Madness, and English Culture, 1830–1980.* New York: Penguin, 1985, pp. 167–194.

Simons, Marlise. "Professional Women from Afghanistan Meet to Press for Full Rights in Their Country." *New York Times,* December 8, 2001, p. B3.

Smith, Steve. "Power and Truth: A Reply to William Wallace." *Review of International Studies* 23 (1997): 507–516.

Sokolsky, Joel J. "Great Ideals and Uneasy Compromises: The United States Approach to Peacekeeping." *International Journal* 50, no. 2 (spring 1995): 266–293.

"Soldier Confirms Airborne Held Massacre Party." *Ottawa Citizen,* November 9, 1995, p. A3.

Solomon, Zahava, Nathaniel Laor, and Alexander C. McFarlane. "Acute Posttraumatic Reactions in Soldiers and Civilians." In Bessel A. van der Kolk, Alexander

C. McFarlane, and Lars Weisaeth (eds.), *Traumatic Stress: The Effects of Over-whelming Experience on Mind, Body, and Society.* New York: Guilford Press, 1996, pp. 102–114.

Spivak, Gayatri Chakravorty. *A Critique of Postcolonial Reason: Toward a History of the Vanishing Present.* Cambridge, MA: Harvard University Press, 1999.

Stairs, Denis. "Of Medium Powers and Middling Roles." In Ken Booth (ed.), *State-craft and Security: The Cold War and Beyond.* Cambridge: Cambridge University Press, 1998, pp. 270–286.

Stiehm, Judith Hicks. *Arms and the Enlisted Woman.* Philadelphia: Temple University Press, 1989.

———. "Peacekeeping and Peace Research: Men's and Women's Work." *Women and Politics* 18, no. 1 (1997): 27–51.

———. "Women, Peacekeeping and Peacemaking: Gender Balance and Main-streaming." In Louise Olsson and Turunn L. Tryggestad (eds.), *Women and International Peacekeeping.* London: Frank Cass, 2001, pp. 39–48.

Stouffer, S. A., et al. *The American Soldier,* vol. 2: *Combat and Its After-Math.* Princeton: Princeton University Press, 1949.

Strother, Thomas, Lieutenant Commander, U.S. Navy (Retired). "The Recruiting Problem We *Don't* Talk About." *U.S. Naval Institute Proceedings* 125, no. 5 (May 1999): 192.

Swain, Jon. "UN Losing Battle for Cambodia in the Brothels of Phnom Penh." *Sunday Times* (London), December 27, 1992.

Tagliabue, John. "Photos of Troops Abusing Somalis in '93 Shock Italians." *New York Times,* June 14, 1997, p. 4.

Takahara, Takao. "Japan." In Trevor Findlay (ed.), *Challenges for the New Peace-keepers.* Oxford: Oxford University Press, 1996, pp. 52–66.

Tamamoto, Masaru. "The Ideology of Nothingness: A Meditation on Japanese National Identity." *World Policy Journal* 11, no. 1 (spring 1994): 89–99.

Thayer, Nate. "Sihanouk Slams Political Violence." *Phnom Penh Post,* January 15–28, 1993, p. 1.

———. "Unsettled Land: UN's Delayed Arrival Starts to Undermine Peace Settlement." *Far Eastern Economic Review,* February 27, 1992, pp. 22–26

———. "UNTAC Fails to Stem Political Violence." *Phnom Penh Post,* February 12–25, 1993, p. 3.

———. "Wretched of the Earth." *Far Eastern Economic Review,* April 15, 1995, p. 21.

Thayer, Nate, and Rodney Tasker. "Voice of the People." *Far Eastern Economic Review,* June 3, 1993, p. 10.

Thompson, Allan. "Peacekeepers Accused of Role in Child Sex Ring." *Toronto Star,* March 11, 2002, p. A8.

Tiger, Lionel. *Men in Groups.* 2d ed. New York: Marion Boyars, 1984.

Tiger, Lionel, and Robin Fox. *The Imperial Animal.* Toronto: McClelland and Stewart, 1971.

Transformation Moment: A Canadian Vision of Common Security. Report of the Citizens' Inquiry into Peace and Security. Waterloo, ON, March 1992.

Trinh, T. Minh-ha. *Woman, Native, Other: Writing Postcoloniality and Feminism.* Bloomington: Indiana University Press, 1989.

True, Jacqui, and Michael Mintrom. "Transnational Networks and Policy Diffusion: The Case of Gender Mainstreaming." *International Studies Quarterly* 45 (2001): 27–57.

Turshen, Meredith, and Clotilde Twagiramariya (eds.). *What Women Do in Wartime: Gender and Conflict in Africa.* London: Zed Books, 1998.

"Unclear." *The Economist,* February 29, 1992, pp. 37–38.
UNICEF. "Cambodia: The Situation of Children and Women." Phnom Penh, 1990.
———. "The Trafficking and Prostitution of Children in Cambodia: A Situation Report." Phnom Penh, 1995.
United Nations. "Beijing Declaration and the Platform for Action." New York: UN Publications, 1996.
———. "Charter of the United Nations and Statute of the International Court of Justice." New York, 1945.
———. "From Beijing to Beijing +5, Report of the Secretary-General, Review and Appraisal of the Implementation of the Beijing Platform for Action." New York, 2001.
———. "Report of the Panel on United Nations Peace Operations." August 21, 2000, A/55/305–S/2000/809.
UN Department for Disarmament Affairs in Collaboration with the Office of the Special Adviser on Gender Issues and the Advancement of Women. "Gender Perspectives on Disarmament: Briefing Notes." New York: United Nations, March 2001.
UN Department of Peacekeeping Operations and the Joint UN Programme on HIV/AIDS. "Protect Yourself, and Those You Care About, Against HIV/AIDS." New York: United Nations, April 1998. Available at www.un.org/Depts/dpko/training/training_material/training_material_home.htm.
UN Department of Peacekeeping Operations Lessons Learned Unit. "Mainstreaming a Gender Perspective in Multidimensional Peace Operations." July 2000. Available at www.un.org/Depts/dpko/lessons/Gender%20Mainstreaming.pdf.
———. "Windhoek Declaration and the Namibia Plan of Action on Mainstreaming a Gender Perspective in Multi-Dimensional Peace Support Operations." Windhoek, Namibia, May 31, 2000. Available at www.unifem.undp.org/unseccouncil/windhoek.html.
UN Division for the Advancement of Women. "Women 2000: The Role of Women in United Nations Peacekeeping." December 1995, no. 1/1995. Available at: gopher://gopher.undp.org:70/00/secretar/dpcsd/daw/w2000/1995–1.en.
———. "Women 2000: Sexual Violence and Armed Conflict: United Nations Response." April 1998. Available at www.un.org/womenwatch/daw/public/cover.htm.
UN Economic and Social Council. "Economic and Social Council Resolution 1996/310: Mainstreaming a Gender Perspective into All Policies and Programmes of the UN System." Substantive Session for June 30–July 30, 1997.
———. "Integration of the Human Rights of Women and the Gender Perspective Violence Against Women: Report of the Special Rapporteur on Violence Against Women, Its Causes and Consequences, Ms Radhika Coomaraswamy, Submitted in Accordance with Commission on Human Rights Resolution 2000/45." January 23, 2001, E/CN.4/2001/73.
UN General Assembly. "Report of the Secretary-General on Resource Requirements for Implementation of the Report of the Panel on United Nations Peace Operations." October 27, 2000, A/55/507.
UN Mission in the Democratic Republic of Congo (MONUC). "Activities Report from the Office of Gender Affairs (OGA) of the United Nations Organization Mission in the Democratic Republic of the Congo (MONUC)." Kinshasa, January 10, 2003. Available at www.monuc.org/gender/.
UN Office of the Special Adviser on Gender Issues and Advancement of Women. "Gender Mainstreaming: An Overview." New York: United Nations, 2001.

UN Report of the Secretary-General. "An Agenda for Peace: Preventive Diplomacy, Peacemaking and Peace-keeping." January 31, 1992, A/47/277–S24/11.

———. "The Causes of Conflict and the Promotion of Durable Peace and Sustainable Development in Africa." April 13, 1998, A/52/871–S/1998/318.

———. "Improvement of the Status of Women in the Secretariat." 1985, A/C.5/40/30.

———. "Investigation into Sexual Exploitation of Refugees by Aid Workers in West Africa." October 11, 2002, A/57/465.

———. "On the Protection of Civilians in Armed Conflict." September 8, 1999, S/1999/957.

———. "Prevention of Armed Conflict." June 7, 2001, A/55/985–S/2001/574.

———. "Supplement to an Agenda for Peace: Position Paper of the Secretary-General on the Occasion of the Fiftieth Anniversary of the United Nations." January 3, 1995, A/50/60–S/1995/1,

———. "Women, Peace, and Security." October 16, 2002, S/2002/1154.

United Nations Secretary-General Study. *Women, Peace, and Security*. New York: United Nations, 2002. Available at www.un.org/womenwatch/daw/public/index.html#wps.

UN Security Council. "Speakers Emphasize Need for Gender Perspective in Peacekeeping Mandates, as Security Council Resumes Debate on Women, Peace and Security." Press release. October 29, 2002, SC/7552.

———. "Women, Peace and Security." Resolution 1325. Adopted October 31, 2000. Available at http://ods-dds-ny.un.org/doc/UNDOC/GEN/N00/720/18/PDF/N0072018.pdf?OpenElement.

"UNTAC Clears the Market." *Phnom Penh Post,* October 11, 1992, p. 9. Reprinted from *Nokorbal Pracheachun,* October 6, 1992.

"UNTAC Personnel Need to Learn How to Drive." *Phnom Penh Post,* December 18–31, 1992, p. 2. Reprinted from *Nokorbal Pracheachun,* November 2, 1992.

Urquhart, Brian. *A Life in Peace and War.* New York: Harper and Row, 1987.

"U.S. Soldier Discharged for Refusing to Serve UN." *Ottawa Citizen,* January 25, 1996, p. A8.

Utting, Peter. "Introduction: Linking Peace and Rehabilitation in Cambodia." In Peter Utting (ed.), *Between Hope and Insecurity: The Social Consequences of the Cambodian Peace Process.* Geneva: UN Research Institute for Social Development, 1994, pp. 1–38.

van Creveld, Martin. "The Great Illusion: Women in the Military." *Millennium: Journal of International Studies* 29, no. 2 (2000): 429–442.

Vetten, Lisa. "War and the Making of Men and Women." Centre for the Study of Violence and Reconciliation, South Africa. Available at www.csvr.org.za/articles/artwarl.htm. Reprinted in the *Sunday Independent* (South Africa), August 16, 1998.

Walter, Natasha. "Afghan Women Will Still Be Ignored." *The Independent,* November 15, 2001. Available at http://argument.independent.co.uk/regular columnists/natasha walter/story.

Weber, Cynthia. *Simulating Sovereignty: Intervention, the State, and Symbolic Exchange.* Cambridge: Cambridge University Press, 1995.

Wedgwood, Ruth. "The Evolution of United Nations Peacekeeping," *Cornell International Law Journal* 28 (1995): 631–643.

Weiss, Thomas G. *Military-Civilian Interactions: Intervening in Humanitarian Crises.* Lanham, MD: Rowman and Littlefield, 1999.

———. "Overcoming the Somalia Syndrome—'Operation Rekindle Hope?'" *Global Governance* 1 (1995): 171–187.

Wenek, Major R. W. J. "The Assessment of Psychological Fitness: Some Options for the Canadian Forces." Technical Note 1/84. Ottawa: Directorate of Personnel Selection, Research on Second Careers, July 1984.

Westhrop, John. "UNTAC Reels from Claims Rash." *Phnom Penh Post,* November 5–18, 1993, p. 7.

"What the United Nations Learnt in Cambodia." *The Economist,* June 19, 1993, p. 36.

Whitworth, Sandra. "11 September and the Aftermath." *Studies in Political Economy* 67 (spring 2002): 33–38.

———. *Feminism and International Relations: Towards a Political Economy of Gender in Interstate and Non-Governmental Institutions.* Basingstoke, UK: Macmillan, 1994.

———. "Gender, Race and the Politics of Peacekeeping." In Edward Moxon-Browne (ed.), *A Future for Peacekeeping?* Basingstoke, UK: Macmillan, 1998, pp. 176–191.

———. "Militarized Masculinities and the Politics of Peacekeeping: The Canadian Case." In Ken Booth (ed.), *Critical Security Studies and World Politics.* Boulder: Lynne Rienner, forthcoming 2005.

———. "The Ugly Unasked Questions about Somalia." *Globe and Mail,* February 14, 1997, p. A27.

———. "Where Is the Politics in Peacekeeping?" *International Journal* 50, no. 2 (spring 1995): 427–435.

———. "Women, and Gender, in the Foreign Policy Review Process." In M. A. Cameron and Maureen Appel Molot (eds.), *Canada Among Nations 1995: Democracy and Foreign Policy.* Ottawa: Carleton University Press, 1995, pp. 83–98.

Winslow, Donna. *The Canadian Airborne Regiment in Somalia: A Socio-Cultural Inquiry.* Prepared for the Commission of Inquiry into the Deployment of Canadian Forces to Somalia. Ottawa: Government Services Canada, 1997.

———. "Misplaced Loyalties: The Role of Military Culture in the Breakdown of Discipline in Peace Operations." *Canadian Review of Sociology and Anthropology* 35, no. 3 (1998): 345–366.

———. "Rites of Passage and Group Bonding in the Canadian Airborne." *Armed Forces and Society* 25, no. 3 (spring 1999): 429–457.

Women's Caucus for Gender Justice. "Gender and Frontline Perspectives on Peacekeeping and the Brahimi Report; Report of the Panel Discussion on the Absence of a Gender Perspective in Peacekeeping and in the Brahimi Report." New York, February–March, 2001. Available at www.iccwomen.org.

Women's Commission for Refugee Women and Children. "Cambodia Can't Wait: Report and Recommendations of the Women's Commission for Refugee Women and Children." New York, February 8–20, 1993.

"Women's Participation Not Negotiable." Editorial. *Minnesota Women's Press, Inc.,* December 5, 2001. Available at www.womenspress.com/newspaper/2001/17–19edi.html.

Worthington, Peter, and Kyle Brown. *Scapegoat: How the Army Betrayed Kyle Brown.* Toronto: McClelland Bantam, 1997.

Yuval-Davis, Nira. *Gender and Nation.* London: Sage, 1997.

Zalewski, Marysia, and Jane Parpart (eds.). *The "Man" Question in International Relations.* Boulder: Westview, 1998.

Zarkov, Dubravka. "*Srebrenica Trauma:* Masculinity, Military and National Self-image in Dutch Daily Newspapers." In Cynthia Cockburn and Dubravka

Zarkov (eds.), *The Postwar Moment: Militaries, Masculinities, and International Peacekeeping.* London: Lawrence and Wishart, 2002, pp. 183–203.

Zimmerman, Cathy, Sar Samen, and Men Savorn. *Plates in a Basket Will Rattle: Domestic Violence in Cambodia.* Phnom Penh: Asia Foundation, 1994.

INDEX

ABOUT THE BOOK

In this important, controversial, and at times troubling book, Sandra Whitworth looks behind the rhetoric to investigate from a feminist perspective some of the realities of military intervention under the UN flag.

Whitworth contends that there is a fundamental contradiction between portrayals of peacekeeping as altruistic and benign and the militarized masculinity that underpins the group identity of soldiers. Examining evidence from Cambodia and Somalia, she argues that sexual and other crimes can be seen as expressions of a violent "hypermasculinity" that is congruent with militarized identities, but entirely incongruent with missions aimed at maintaining peace. She also asserts that recent efforts within the UN to address gender issues in peacekeeping operations have failed because they fail to challenge traditional understandings of militaries, conflict, and women.

This unsettling critique of UN operations, which also investigates the interplay between gender and racial stereotyping in peacekeeping, has the power to change conventional perceptions, with considerable policy implications.

Sandra Whitworth is professor of political science and women's studies and director of the Graduate Program in Political Science at York University.